KU-481-493

HOLY CROSS
THE UNTOLD STORY

ANNE CADWALLADER

THE BREHON PRESS
BELFAST

First published 2004 by The Brehon Press Ltd
1A Bryson Street, Belfast BT5 4ES,
Northern Ireland

© 2004 Anne Cadwallader

All rights reserved. No part of this publication may be reproduced or
utilised in any form or by any means digital, electronic or mechanical
including photography, filming, video recording, photocopying, or by
any information storage and retrieval system or shall not, by way of
trade or otherwise, be lent, resold or otherwise circulated in any form
of binding or cover other than that in which it is published without
prior permission in writing from the publisher.

ISBN: 0 9544867 2 2

Front cover photograph: Brendan Murphy, *Irish News*
Back cover photograph: Thomas McMullan, *North Belfast News*
Design: December Publications
Printed in the Republic of Ireland by Betaprint

CONTENTS

For Gerard

ACKNOWLEDGEMENTS

One dark night in 1981, less than a month after I had arrived in Belfast, a BBC producer sent me into Ardoyne to find the little girl who had been shot in her mother's womb even before she was born. He reckoned it was the child's sixth birthday and my task was to interview the "miracle baby". The producer imparted a few well-chosen words of warning about how someone with a British accent poring over a map in Ardoyne could be misconstrued.

The family had moved on from the address he gave me but the woman of the house invited me in for tea and scones with blackcurrant jam, served on the best china. The same thing happened at the next forwarding address. More tea, more scones. Could these be the savages I had been warned about? The people who would cheerfully rip the head off an English stranger for breakfast before a spot of torture for elevenses?

I finally tracked the family down, did my interview and returned back to the BBC three hours later, tea and buns swirling around inside me. A full-scale alert was by then under way. From then on, while acknowledging the tragic and sometimes savage events that have taken place there, Ardoyne has always had a special place in my heart. I hope this book will contribute towards a better understanding of the lives and tribulations of this troubled part of Belfast.

My thanks, first and foremost, to all those who were interviewed. To the parents in Ardoyne who endured so much and their children whose innocence and courage should force us to realise how much we all let them down. Also to the loyalists and people of Glenbryn, all of us on differing journeys, who overcame their initial suspicions and gave generously of their time.

Then thanks above all to Tom Holland, who interviewed many of the parents, sensitively and meticulously, listening to their harrowing stories and asking many difficult questions. The power of their words, at least in part, bears testimony to his extraordinary dedication. Then to Louanne Martin, who interviewed the children with gentleness and tact, a difficult job done excellently and who encouraged when most needed. And to Helen McLarnon, whose transcriptions turned stumbling exchanges into comprehensible conversations and whose modesty is unjustified. To David McKittrick for reading and generously commenting on the book; to Martina Purdy for ambushing, cajoling and threatening me into writing it; to T L Thousand (Los Angeles) for storing and making suggestions, and to Fionnuala O Connor for reading the first drafts.

To Richie McCullen for giving me leeway in the final weeks; to Kerry Graye and Noel Fogarty, also of Independent Network News (Dublin) for being great listeners; to Roy Greenslade for reading the Media chapter. To Seamus Kelters, Sue McKay, Chris Thornton, Barry McCaffrey, Leslie Van Slyke and Danny Morrison for encouragement, and to Ray O'Hanlon, *Irish Echo* (New York).

To photographers and friends: Kelvin Boyes, Thomas McMullan (*North Belfast News*), Brendan Murphy, Ann McManus and Hugh Russell (the *Irish News*). To my publishers at the Brehon Press for their advice and support. To David Kennedy, Gail McCreevy, Lynn Hutchinson, Father John McManus, Brian Parker and Geraldine O'Hare for help with interviewees. To my friends Roisin Gibbons, John Friel (Donegal), Stephen McCabe (New York), Liam Shannon, Margaret Henry (Tennessee), Gerry and Anne Caldwell, Ann and Barney McEvoy, Mary Savage and Jude White.

To those interviewed for this book who, for one reason or another, cannot be named. They know who they are and they have my thanks. And last but not least to my long-suffering family, Jane Cadwallader, Ana, Georgie and Tessie Lezcano (Madrid), who put up with my bad temper; and to Rab and Terry McCallum, and Sean and Maureen O'Hare.

Any errors are, needless to say, all my own.

Anne Cadwallader
July 2004

Photographs in the picture section are reproduced by kind permission of the following: Kelvin Boyes, pages 1-2, top pictures on pages 4 and 6, bottom picture on page 5, and page 8; Thomas McMullan, North Belfast News, page 3, top pictures on pages 5 and 7, and bottom picture on page 6; and Brendan Murphy, Irish News, bottom pictures on pages 4 and 7.

INTERVIEWEES AND CONTRIBUTORS

Brian Barrington, Special Adviser to SDLP leader Mark Durkan

Maggie Beirne, Committee on the Administration of Justice

Anne Bill, Glenbryn resident, community worker and CRUA member

Ronnie Black, Glenbryn resident, CRUA member

Lynda Bowes, Parent of two including Amanda

Amanda Bowes, (9) Holy Cross pupil

"Stephen Brown", anthropology researcher and community worker in Protestant area of west Belfast

Frank Bunting, Northern Ireland Secretary, Irish National Teachers Organisation

Elaine Burns, Ardoyne resident, parent and member of the Ardoyne Association

Kathleen Carragher, Editor, Radio News, BBC Northern Ireland

Colette Cassidy, Parent of Caitlin (11) Holy Cross pupil

Sean and Tanya Carmichael, Parents of three including Emma (8) and Emer (4) Holy Cross pupils

Fred Cobain, Ulster Unionist Party assembly man for North Belfast

Michael Cosby, Glenbryn resident and member of CRUA

Jim Crawford, Parent of four including Roisin

Roisin Crawford, (9) Holy Cross pupil

"Denise", Glenbryn resident

Professor Brice Dickson, Chief Commissioner, Northern Ireland Human Rights Commission

Father Gary Donegan, Passionist priest, Holy Cross Monastery

Frances Doherty, Parent of Shannon (7) and Ciara (9) both Holy Cross pupils

Mark Durkan, leader, SDLP

Donal Flanagan, Director, Catholic Council for Maintained Education

Philomena Flood, former Ardoyne resident and mother of three including Eirinn (7), Holy Cross pupil

Tina Gallagher, Parent of two including Roisin and Tara (4) Holy Cross pupils

Roisin Gallagher, (8) Holy Cross pupil

"Grainne", Holy Cross teacher

Rev Harold Good, former President, Methodist Church in Ireland

Rev Norman Hamilton, Presbyterian Minister, Ballysillan

Judy Haughey, Parent of three including Cora (11) and Lucilla (10) Holy Cross pupils

Rev Stewart Heaney, former Ballysillan resident and Church of Ireland Minister

Billy Hutchinson, former PUP assembly member for North Belfast

Lisa Irvine, Parent of Shannon (9), Holy Cross pupil

Neil Jarman, Acting Director of the Institute for Conflict Research, author of "Responses to Interface Violence in North Belfast" (for OFM/DFM) and "From Outrage to Apathy: The Disputes over Parades, 1995- 2003"

Amanda Johnston, Hesketh resident, Lollipop lady, CRUA member

Gerry Kelly, Sinn Fein Assembly member for North Belfast

Roisin Kennedy, Parent of Niamh, Holy Cross pupil

Niamh Kennedy, (9) Holy Cross pupil

Terry Laverty, Principal, Holy Cross Boys school

Mickey Liggett, Ardoyne resident, Ardoyne Focus Group member

Paul Liggett, Ardoyne resident and local historian

David and Maura Lindsay, Parents of Amy and Kirsty (12)

Amy Lindsay, (9) Holy Cross pupil

Patricia McAuley, Aunt to two Holy Cross pupils

Gerard and Sharon McCabe, Parents of five including Gemma (8)

Stuart McCartney, Glenbryn resident, community worker, CRUA member

Jim McClean, former Glenbryn resident

Inez McCormack, former Human Rights Commissioner for Northern Ireland

Chris and Rita McDonald, Parents of three including Nicole (10)

Kieran and Geraldine McGrandles, Parents of four including Danielle, Holy Cross pupil

Danielle McGrandles, (10) Holy Cross pupil

Jeanette McKernan, Parent of two including Chloe (6) Holy Cross pupil

David McNarry, Special Adviser to David Trimble, leader UUP

Alan McQuillan, former Assistant Chief Constable, RUC/PSNI

Paul Mageean, Committee on the Administration of Justice

Brendan Mailey, Spokesman Right to Education group and parent

Martha or "Miss E", Parent of one Holy Cross pupil

"Mary", Parent

Chief Superintendent Roger Maxwell, former Divisional Commander, North Belfast Command, RUC/PSNI

Pat and Martin Monaghan, Parents of three including Rebekah, Holy Cross pupil

Rebekah Monaghan, (8) Holy Cross pupil

Martin Morgan, SDLP councillor, North Belfast, former Lord Mayor of Belfast

Liz Murphy, Parent of six including Niamh (7) Holy Cross pupil

Nuala O'Loan, Police Ombudsman for Northern Ireland

Official, Department of Foreign Affairs, Dublin

Bishop Alan Parker, Church of Ireland Bishop of Connor

Jim Potts, Glenbryn resident, community worker, CRUA member

Sharon Quail, Parent of Shaunalee (8)

Dr Nichola Rooney, Consultant Clinical Psychologist, Royal Victoria Hospital for Sick Children

"Sean", Ardoyne resident and taxi driver

Rev Bill Shaw, Presbyterian Minister and director of The Saltshaker Trust

Dr Peter Shirlow, anthropologist, University of Ulster, a Protestant from South Belfast

"Sinead", anonymous former Holy Cross schoolgirl

Anne Tanney, principal, Holy Cross Girls' School

Monsignor Tom Toner, joint chair, North Belfast Community Action Project

Karen Trew, senior lecturer, Department of Psychology, Queens University

Father Aidan Troy, Holy Cross parish priest and chairman of Board of Governors

NOTE – ALL CHILDREN'S AGES AS OF SEPTEMBER 3, 2001

GLOSSARY

Agreement – Good Friday Agreement peace accord of April 1998 adopted by the UUP, SDLP, Sinn Fein and both the British and Irish governments

Ardoyne Focus Group – community development organisation

Assembly – set up at Stormont after the 1998 Agreement

Black Taxis – informal community transport network

Catholic community – mainly Irish nationalists or republicans who want a united Ireland

CCMS – Catholic Council for Maintained Schools: body governing Catholic schools in the North

Civil Rights Movement – agitation for equality in housing, employment and one man/one vote at end of 1960s

CRUA – Concerned Residents of Upper Ardoyne: residents' group set up in mainly Protestant Glenbryn after June 19 incident sparked loyalist protest; various spokesmen including **Jim Potts**

Drumcree – shorthand for the annual stand-off in Portadown, County Armagh between members of the loyalist Orange Order and nationalist residents over the route of an Orange march through a Catholic area

DUP – Democratic Unionist Party: leader **Ian Paisley**; local representatives in Glenbryn are **Nigel Dodds** and **Nelson McCausland**

Executive – power-sharing administration at Stormont set up by the Agreement

INLA – Irish National Liberation Army, splinter group of the IRA with politically linked Irish Republican Socialist Party

IRA – Irish Republican Army

Loyalist Commission – group including senior UDA and UVF figures, Protestant clergy and unionist politicians

Mobile phone network – system by which agreed representatives on each side of the peaceline mediate to substantiate first reports of violence and act to prevent escalation. Patchy but effective when it works

OFM/DFM – Office of the First Minister and Deputy First Minister in the power-sharing Executive. Both must act jointly under the terms of the Good Friday Agreement

Protestant community – mainly unionists and loyalists who want to retain the constitutional link with Britain

PSNI – Police Service of Northern Ireland from November 5, 2001

PUP – Progressive Unionist Party: seen as the political wing of the UVF (Ulster Volunteer Force, the oldest loyalist paramilitary grouping)

RTE – Right to Education: group set up by parents of Holy Cross children in mainly-Catholic Ardoyne after June 19 incident, spokesman **Brendan Mailey**

RUC – Royal Ulster Constabulary until November 5, 2001

SDLP – Social Democratic and Labour Party: moderate nationalist party. Deputy leader **Seamus Mallon** and current leader **Mark Durkan** were deputy First Ministers during Holy Cross dispute

Sinn Fein – regarded as the political wing of the IRA; leader Gerry Adams

Taig/Fenian – derogatory terms used by some loyalists to describe Catholics

Twelfth – July 12 annual parades in celebration of 1690 defeat of Catholic King James by Protestant King William of Orange, after whom the **Orange Order** is named. **Eleventh Night** on July 11 is an associated event when bonfires burn throughout loyalist areas. Thousands of parades in the "marching season" pass off peacefully. A handful are contentious as they pass through Catholic areas carrying loyalist paramilitary flags and insignia

UDA – Ulster Defence Association: the largest loyalist paramilitary group, sometimes claiming attacks using the cover name **Red Hand Defenders**, and whose youth wing is called the **Ulster Young Militants**

UUP – Ulster Unionist Party: leader **David Trimble**, First Minister for most of the Holy Cross protest, replaced by **Sir Reg Empey** on his resignation in protest at lack of progress on IRA decommissioning

NOTE
Many nationalists/Catholics object to the term "protesters" to describe those who took action at Holy Cross school, preferring the term "attackers". While respecting their point of view, and without prejudice either way, I have used the term "protesters" as this is the way they want themselves to be described and for purposes of clarity.

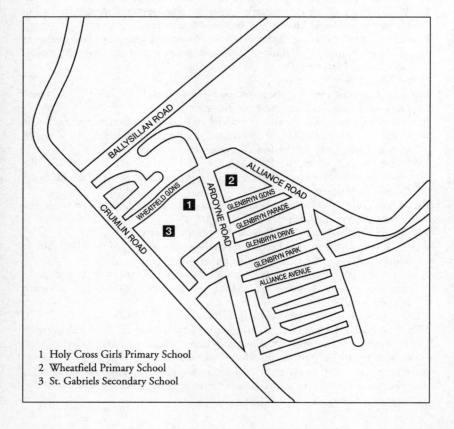

1 Holy Cross Girls Primary School
2 Wheatfield Primary School
3 St. Gabriels Secondary School

Prologue

BACKDROP TO HOLY CROSS

Ardoyne is like a big family. We have disagreements, differences of opinion, political allegiances, but if something happens like it did to our children, the community stands together. Liz Murphy, Holy Cross parent

It was after the ceasefires that things got worse. People got more and more frightened and I stopped going to the shops. There were riots on the interface and you no longer felt accepted.
Anne Bill, community worker in Protestant Glenbryn

If you stand at the children's playground in North Belfast, high up on the Oldpark Road, Ardoyne stretches out beneath you, a tightly packed enclave of tiny houses with long, narrow gardens.

Holy Cross Church across the valley looks, physically and metaphorically, like a mother hen with her chicks gathered around her. Beyond the church's twin spires, the Belfast hills reach to the sky. It is a peaceful setting. From the same spot, however, you can also see the jagged "peace-lines" encircling Ardoyne, impermeable 20 foot-high metal barriers severing the area from the surrounding Protestant housing estates. If your eye follows a straight line leading right from Holy Cross Monastery, you can also see the square block of concrete and glass that is Holy Cross Girls' primary school, just outside the main bulk of Catholic Ardoyne.

More than anywhere else in the North, apart from perhaps Derry's walls, you are seeing history writ into brick, stone and metal – outward signs of the political tensions that have riven this turbulent community for centuries. Going down into the streets of Ardoyne, teeming with small children, there are murals, social clubs, republican memorials, a

Sinn Fein advice centre and projects to create much-needed work. Every yard of pavement has a story to tell, if only you could hear it. Gardens where gunfights ended in death and imprisonment. Streets where children learned how to make petrol bombs. Pavements where British soldiers and IRA men bled to death. In the last 35 years of the conflict, 99 local Catholics have died, a disproportionately large number of its 7,000 inhabitants. Ardoyne's republicans have also inflicted much on their Protestant neighbours; the mutual hostility with the nearby staunchly loyalist Shankill Road is legendary.

The Holy Cross protest was not an aberration, divorced from history or human nature. It was the result – some would say the inevitable result – of the pressures exerted on two communities who live so close, yet so far apart, in North Belfast. Unlike the largely Catholic west of the city, or the Protestant east, or the middle-class south, North Belfast is not a homogenous community. Catholic and Protestant live close by each other in divided streets. The concept that any land is, in itself, either Catholic or Protestant is fiercely disputed by the growing Catholic population and equally fiercely defended by the diminishing Protestant one.

It is impossible to understand the tensions that led to the Holy Cross protest without some explanation of the conflict over housing in North Belfast where Protestant communities are steadily moving away into the growing satellite towns of Counties Antrim and Down. There are widely varying explanations for this seemingly unstoppable phenomenon that has led to Belfast becoming a city with a Catholic majority and Sinn Fein becoming the largest single party on its city council. Protestants, their political representatives and the main loyalist paramilitary groups, claim republican intimidation is, at least, a factor – a claim hotly denied by Catholics and their politicians, as well as the available academic and statistical evidence.

Ardoyne itself has, without doubt, a reputation for being an uncompromisingly tough, clannish, tight-knit republican community – but history made it so. There was a village called Ardoyne, probably "Eoin's Height" from the Gaelic, dating back to the 1600s or even earlier. A forge is recorded in the annals of the Chichesters, a Protestant planter family, dating back to 1601. In the 1820s, the availability of land and water persuaded the Andrews family, liberal mill-owners from Comber in north Down, to set up a damask factory and, alongside, homes and an integrated school for their workers.

What is now known as "Old Ardoyne", close to Holy Cross Church, was built near the village in the 1860s. Again, two or three textile mills came first and then associated workers' terraces. About seventy years later, just before the outbreak of World War II, the third phase of Ardoyne was built, called then and now "Glenard" by locals. These are the distinctive long parallel streets running down from the Crumlin Road. At about the same time, the 1935 "York Street riots" took place. Thirteen people were killed while about 500 Catholic families fled from their homes further south, near the Belfast docks. Some of the refugees squatted in the new houses being built in the Glenard part of Ardoyne, originally intended for Protestant mill-workers, and their descendants live there still.

Although what is now called Ardoyne was, until the late 1960s, mostly Catholic, Protestants still numbered around 15% of its population, concentrated in the Cranbrook/Farringdon Gardens/Velsheda Park area. Conversely, Upper Ardoyne, or Glenbryn, built slightly later than Glenard, was mainly Protestant with a sprinkling of Catholics. There were "Eleventh Night" Orange bonfires in Ardoyne's Velsheda Park and Cranbrook Gardens until the late 1960s and the area even had its own Orange flute band, mainly drawn from the "Upper Ardoyne"/Glenbryn area. In the 1950s and 1960s, Protestant families moved into Glenbryn from the Shankill Road, seeking larger homes with gardens.

Into this unstable community burst the 1960s agitation for civil rights, leading to the cataclysmic events of 1969, when loyalist mobs attacked Catholic Hooker and Brookfield streets, burning most homes to the ground. Nationalists, already suspicious of the over 90% Protestant Royal Ulster Constabulary (RUC), felt they provided no protection from the mobs. Quite the reverse. Survivors of those days in Ardoyne, such as local historian Paul Liggett, describe how they saw police encouraging the invading loyalists.

Although Catholics now see the civil rights movement as the beginning of a long battle for equality, the University of Ulster's Dr Peter

Shirlow, a geographer who has made a close study of demographic changes in North Belfast, says Protestants saw it as a direct threat to their hegemony. Protestant determination to preserve what it saw as its "boundaries" was not necessarily sectarian supremacism, he says.

"There is a deep-rooted fear that if an inch is given, it will have a domino effect. Catholics had been relatively compliant since the 1920s. Protestants had a strong sense of living in their own state, but were still afraid of any concessions being made to the nationalist working class."

There was a Protestant nervousness also, he says, about the impending fiftieth anniversary of the Easter Rising. It all amounted to a perception that things were slipping from the relative psychological comfort of the previous 50 years. In 1969, says Shirlow, that "nervousness" expressed itself in the onslaught on Catholic homes in Ardoyne. Two years later, in August 1971, when scores of local Catholics were arrested and interned, Protestants saw the writing on the wall, packed up and left. In a "scorched earth" operation, rather than leave behind intact homes for Catholics to occupy, those leaving ripped out gas-pipes and burned the houses. Protestant woman, Sarah Worthington, moving about in the shadows, was shot dead by the British Army. The soldier mistook her for an IRA gunman.

As in many other parts of the North, you still hear heartbreaking stories in Glenbryn of people watching as their grandparents in Ardoyne piled all their furniture onto the back of horse carts and moved out. "Denise", a 39-year-old Glenbryn mother of four children, was six when she saw her grandmother moving out of Velsheda Park on the back of a coal lorry. "She was very house-proud and loved her garden," she says.

Glenbryn was also a mixed area at the time, says the Sinn Fein Assembly member for North Belfast, Gerry Kelly. "The first threats came in letters sent by the Ulster Volunteer Force (or UVF, the oldest loyalist paramilitary group) to Catholic families telling the occupants to leave."

As many of Ardoyne's Protestants moved out, so did many of Glenbryn's Catholics and a new interface was born with Protestant Glenbryn to the north and east of the peace-line, Catholic Ardoyne on the south and west. The two communities grew apart and, while a diminishing number of family ties remained, Glenbryn, cut off by the violence from its natural hinterland in Ardoyne, gradually began a process of withering that continues to this day.

During the 1970s, when violence was at its height, Ardoyne became even more isolated as many of its access routes were sealed off to defend against further attack. It became, as some of its own inhabitants describe it, a virtual open prison, bereft of employment and hope.

The "Shankill Butchers" gang's reign of fear took its toll at around the same time. Catholics returning home at night, after work or socialising in Belfast city centre, were preyed upon by UVF knifemen who tortured them before dumping their bodies. The "black taxi" community transport service that serves Ardoyne is, to this day, forced to take a circuitous route from the city centre, avoiding the Protestant areas that enclose the district. One access road was known in the early 1990s as the "Corridor of Fear" after multiple sectarian murders. A pub that opened up nearby was dubbed the "Sitting Duck". The next-door bookmaker's shop was the scene of a triple killing when UVF gunmen opened fire indiscriminately on Catholic patrons.

The latest census figures show that, of the nearly 7,000 people who now live in Ardoyne, one third are aged under 16. Overall, 10% are unemployed. Even by Belfast standards, Ardoyne stands out as particularly deprived while nearly a third of its people suffer long-term health problems. Only 3% of the population has a degree level qualification while 62% of school children are entitled to free school meals, the accepted arbiter of poverty.

Despite the peace process, the area is exceptionally deprived and still a place of fear. That fear is not confined to Ardoyne; it is also prevalent in Glenbryn with both communities deeply suspicious of each other. The "Mapping the Spaces of Fear" research team at the University of Ulster in 1998 said both shared a "climate of apprehension and the complex use of 'avoidance' strategies". The survey concluded that the years since the 1994 loyalist and republican ceasefires had not significantly altered the already dysfunctional Ardoyne/Glenbryn relationship. The number of people in both areas who work in mixed workplaces has more than halved since 1994, from 75% to 33%, while 68% of respondents in Ardoyne, and 37.5% in Glenbryn, said fear limited where they look for work. In Ardoyne, 45% of respondents, compared to 34% from Glenbryn, have been intimidated at work and, when it comes to moving about, people in Ardoyne rarely use bus services due to the perceived threat of attack while travelling through Protestant areas.

Only one in five Protestants from Glenbryn shop in Ardoyne. Most of those who do are elderly and do not own cars. "Even those Protestants who shop in Catholic areas discard their carrier bags before going home to avoid their neighbours discovering they have been in 'enemy territory'," says Shirlow, one of the report's authors.

Only 17% of men and 3.8% of women would walk anywhere dominated by the other religion at night. Respondents in Ardoyne were three times more likely to have been physically attacked outside their own community. In Glenbryn, people are twice as likely to have been physically attacked within their own community. One in ten of respondents in Ardoyne, compared to one in a hundred in Glenbryn, have experienced violence at the hands of either the police or British Army. Such glaring differences in aspiration and experience bring huge potential for conflict.

Neil Jarman, Director of the Institute for Conflict Research, says that Protestants in North Belfast have long irrationally believed in a republican "gameplan" to force them from their traditional strongholds, with a complicit British government. Their fears are hardly allayed by speeches such as that made by the former independent unionist Assembly member for North Belfast, Frazer Agnew. In the Assembly debate on Holy Cross in September 2001, he said "ethnic cleansing" of Protestants by Catholics lay behind the protest.

"They want the Prods out of upper Ardoyne, and they want those houses for their own people. This is happening throughout North Belfast," said Agnew, going on to accuse republicans of "cleverly orchestrating" an "insidious plan to ethnically cleanse the Protestant community" from the north of the city.

Jarman says the true picture of the Protestant outflow from North Belfast is far more complex and partly historical. "It was easier for upwardly-mobile working class Protestants to leave for new estates in the 60s and early 70s because there simply weren't safe areas where Catholics could move."

Catholics, he said, tended to stay where they were, resulting in the

Belfast Protestant/Catholic balance reversing. "It was because Protestants were moving out rather than Catholics moving in," Jarman says.

He cites the example of Tiger Bay, a loyalist part of inner North Belfast in apparent irreversible decline. "Older people and the less-skilled are remaining behind while everyone else votes with their feet and moves out. The houses are upgraded, but there's no evidence of any great desire to flood back."

But why did Protestants want to leave? "There is a cycle which begins with a desire for betterment, getting a house with a bit of a garden. Then the activities of loyalist paramilitaries in the old strongholds becomes another factor," says Jarman.

Many young Protestant families, he says, are not particularly anxious to bring up their children in streets bedecked with ugly loyalist graffiti extolling the virtues of the local UDA crime boss who is known to be plying the area with dope.

The UDA (Ulster Defence Association) is the newest and largest, but less disciplined and cohesive of the two main loyalist paramilitary groups (the other being the UVF). It has descended from sectarian murder into common criminality, specialising in drug-dealing.

"The paramilitaries," says Jarman, "inevitably bring the drugs problem with them and it all pushes in the same direction with nothing to drive people back to live in their old areas."

Catholics have filled in some of the spaces where Protestants have moved out, continues Jarman, so that the general demographic shift in Belfast has almost always been from orange to green.

"This feeds into the Protestant psyche, that they're drifting from majority to minority," he says, citing avenues like the Cliftonville, Cavehill and the Antrim Roads which are "going the same way the Malone Road, a wealthy thoroughfare in south Belfast, went a long time ago".

Jarman uses the route of the annual "Tour of the North" Orange parade to illustrate his thesis. It once connected North Belfast's Protestant working class communities, but they are now disjointed, resulting in Catholic demands for its re-routing. He disputes the assumption that Catholics are deliberately forcing Protestants out and says Catholic territorial "gains" have been strictly limited.

AN LEABHARLANN

5002123 7

"If you look where there's been the most intense interface violence, the lines haven't shifted much. The Shankill/Falls divide was defined in 1969 and there's been no change. Tiger Bay may have contracted, but the Catholic New Lodge hasn't expanded. There may have been a decline in Belfast's Protestant population, but it hasn't led to Catholics claiming much new territory."

The Torrens area of North Belfast, says Jarman, is an exception, an area where Protestants did feel under threat and left. Road after road of perfectly serviceable houses now lie empty there, cheek by jowl with teeming Ardoyne.

Fred Cobain, the Ulster Unionist Assembly member for North Belfast, agrees with Jarman on the cause of declining Protestant numbers. "People who are upwardly mobile and aspire to a better life just leave. The only people who don't are those who cannot afford to. Those left behind, the elderly and unskilled, are then stranded without support and help. In the Catholic community there's an ethos that, even if you leave, you come back and sit on management committees and help with regeneration and so on."

Both Jarman and Shirlow say the inevitable result of all this is that Catholic areas are becoming more overcrowded, with expanses of empty "Protestant land" lying dormant and unoccupied – a situation Jarman describes as "absolutely crazy".

One important distinction, says Shirlow, is between private housing, where Catholics have expanded, and public/state housing, where they have not. Public housing in Belfast (28,000 homes) is 98% segregated.

"The Catholic middle-class is growing and affluent. It is young and confident and has moved into Protestant areas. Protestants see that as proof positive of nationalist expansionism and are even more determined to control the social housing sector," he says.

Ardoyne's residents, packed tightly into their tiny homes, look enviously across the peace-line to nearby Protestant areas with large open spaces and spacious gardens. "That sort of anomaly is what you get," says Shirlow, "when you have immovable boundaries and shifting populations."

Former Assistant Chief Constable Alan McQuillan believes the gradual run-down of Glenbryn, as it waited for the Housing Executive's re-development plan to kick in, played a part.

"People with young families could get a better life elsewhere and were moving out. The vacant houses left behind on the interface created a problem. The loyalist community tends to interpret that as a conscious process of republicans forcing them out, as a deliberate attack on their community, whereas it can just be part of a great demographic trend."

The notion that Glenbryn is "surrounded" is dismissed by Gerry Kelly. "It's part of a huge unionist area stretching from the Crumlin Road to the Antrim Road. It's difficult to get into Ardoyne without passing through loyalist areas."

Ardoyne also has fears of encirclement, according to republican community worker Mickey Liggett. "There's no such thing as Protestant or Catholic land. If they get a wall across the road, with gates and security cameras, they'll have turned us into a gated community. They'd also have grabbed the little remaining neutral land. Glenbryn residents complain of attacks on their area – fair enough, we can talk about that and try to get it stopped, but the vast majority of attacks over the past five years are down to loyalists."

More specific to Holy Cross, Jarman traces the start of the dispute back to the summer of 1997, when Protestants were demanding the extension of the peace-line at the back of Alliance Avenue (the Ardoyne road closest to Glenbryn).

At about that time the bus depot, built in the 1930s on the ruins of the old village of Ardoyne, was itself demolished to make way for a terrace of large new homes, occupied by their proud owners in 1998. The development further irritated local Protestants. No agreement was reached over what route a proposed new peace-line would take when it abutted the Ardoyne Road and whether there would be a barrier where the Holy Cross children walk to school. This meant the entire project was put on hold.

"Things went quiet at the end of that year, but the problem was never satisfactorily resolved and it resurfaced in 2001 over largely the same issues," says Jarman, who at the time was involved in consulting local communities over new peace-lines in North Belfast.

These ineptly named dividing walls, because they are only built in areas where community relations have reached rock bottom, almost encircle Ardoyne. More than two dozen of them are now permanent features, some tastefully draped with ivy and shrubs to soften their grim purpose.

Amanda Johnston, from the Protestant Hesketh area, a lollipop lady on the Ardoyne Road, illustrates precisely the resentment widely felt in the numerically declining Protestant community of North Belfast.

"The Oldpark and Cliftonville roads were all Protestant when I was a child. Now there's not a Protestant house there. It's a gradual process, they just move in – slowly but surely," she says, personifying Shirlow and Jarman's analysis of the Protestant fear of the domino theory.

Billy Hutchinson, a former UVF man, now a Progressive Unionist Party councillor in North Belfast, does not go that far, but even he believes Holy Cross was a subterfuge for Catholic expansionism. Hutchinson says that about 18 months before the Holy Cross protest began, people whom he describes as "guardians", as opposed to parents, of its pupils "started a sort of campaign". He remembers taking a break from interviewing applicants for a job at Wheatfield School, the Protestant school opposite Holy Cross, and going for a walk to clear his head. He was accosted, he says, by a man driving a car whose passengers were two children in Holy Cross uniforms.

"The male occupants of the car recognised me and said if I didn't get out of the area they would blow my brains out. I refused to leave the area and told them they could do what they wanted. I also told them that was nice language to use in front of two small children. I am not accusing Sinn Fein as a party, but there were individuals within the nationalist community and the IRA who thought that this was an opportunity to engage in a campaign of intimidation.

"They thought it was an opportunity to intimidate people out of Glenbryn and push the peace-line back," says Hutchinson, pointing the finger specifically at members of the INLA (Irish National Liberation Army), a small republican paramilitary group with members in the Ardoyne area.

Holy Cross parent Jim Crawford, a plasterer, contests Hutchinson's account. "What parent or guardian in their right mind is going to start trouble up that Ardoyne Road during the day or at night, knowing well that their child would suffer as a consequence?"

Other loyalists complain of increasing tensions at the Ardoyne shops. Community worker Anne Bill (author of a book on the protest from a loyalist perspective, "Beyond the Red Gauntlet") says she and her children used to go there every day in the 1980s, "although you would feel that you weren't in the right place".

"As time went on," she says, "people got more and more frightened but it was after the ceasefires that things really got worse. It happened gradually and I stopped going to the shops. There were riots on the interface and you no longer felt accepted. A lot more started to happen to young people. One 16-year-old was coming through Hesketh when two fellas jumped out of a car and started beating him. They took his shoes and pushed and shoved him. The boy has been in psychiatric care since. A milk float driving through the area crashed into ten cars and windows were put in."

She says such minor incidents, relatively speaking, amounted to sectarian intimidation of the Glenbryn population.

Nationalists dispute loyalist theories of a gradual increase in attacks across the peace-line in the run-up to the start of the Holy Cross dispute. Certainly, the official police statistics for the first half of 2001 do not back up the theory of a slow ratcheting-up of intimidation.

The figures (*see Appendix One,* page 318) show the police do not attribute a single bombing to republicans in the first half of 2001. Many nationalists will dispute the figure showing only 16 loyalist bombings, remembering half a dozen on Alliance Avenue within one 24-hour period alone. The figures also show loyalists were firing weapons four times as frequently as republicans.

Shirlow says it is ironic that, of all the interfaces around Ardoyne, Alliance/Glenbryn was the least violent until late 2000. Fred Cobain agrees. "There were incidents, but nothing ghastly. A lot of elderly people, who'd spent all their lives in Glenbryn, had built up relations with the Catholic side."

Former Assistant Chief Constable Alan McQuillan and the police commander in North Belfast, Roger Maxwell, both agree that in 2001 the violence here was the worst in living memory, despite the ceasefires, and that the UDA was behind it. The Lindsays, a Catholic couple living on the main peace-line, offer strong personal evidence. "We lived there for seven years and there was never as much as a stone thrown. We had barbecues and swings in the back garden. There wasn't even a fence. Anyone could have jumped from Glenbryn right into our back garden – that is how safe it felt."

Shirlow, however, was concerned about reports of increasing tensions at the time and made his own inquiries in Ardoyne. "In 1994-5 it was fairly quiet, before the worst of the Drumcree stand-offs. Some in Glenbryn had even started using the Ardoyne shops more."

It had not lasted, Shirlow says, and people began to complain about being spat at or that shop staff had "thrown" their change at them. "It may have happened to one person or a hundred people, it doesn't really matter. So long as it happened once, it became a story."

Asking in Ardoyne about a man dragged out of a car and assaulted in Hesketh, Shirlow was told that those responsible were also causing trouble on the nationalist side of the peace-line.

"The same guys were fighting and kicking people about in Ardoyne as well," he says. "They were just a group of bad wee lads with no republican connections. There was absolutely no evidence of any IRA involvement, but that kind of incident can drive a certain spurious logic. Those responsible were anti-social elements from Ardoyne harassing people along the first couple of streets in Glenbryn. It drove the Protestant sense of vulnerability because of the general decline, fewer houses, dereliction and so on. If a group came along and told Glenbryn they had the answers, they could fix it, you had real trouble."

The Church of Ireland minister, Rev Stewart Heaney, of Emmanuel Church on the Ardoyne Road, also says Protestant families on the peace-line felt increasingly vulnerable. "There were people on both sides, who were against the peace process, making trouble. It was like a powder keg ready to go."

He also says there seemed to be new families coming into Glenbryn from the lower Shankill. He says they "seemed to be more extreme", which fits into a theory much espoused in Ardoyne, but derided in Glenbryn, that a group of loyalists, fleeing the UDA/UVF feud in the summer of 2000, had sought refuge there.

Liz Murphy, a Holy Cross parent, has strong views on this. She can remember Catholics living in Glenbryn, including her own uncle. "I remember in 1969, my mammy bringing me up there with my First Communion dress on to visit him. It was a mixed area, nobody bothered you, nobody came out saying, 'Look at her with her white dress'. Things were really comfortable. It was an area where older people lived."

But, she says, it began changing. "When all the trouble began in 2001, I couldn't understand it. Nobody was bothering them. I asked myself was it because of Drumcree? We then noticed there were younger people moving up that we hadn't seen before."

A 1970s Holy Cross pupil, who wants to remain anonymous, says, "My mum would have known people in Glenbryn for 30 years and in all that time there was never any sectarianism about the place. The decent Protestant people moved out when the UDA moved in."

Elaine Burns, mother of Leona (7) and Niamh (4), has lived in Ardoyne all her life and, while a nationalist, would be regarded locally as more in tune with the more moderate Social Democratic and Labour Party (SDLP) than Sinn Fein.

"Loyalist people can't complain they are being forced out. They are leaving by choice. Glenbryn's young people wanted to live in the suburbs. After the blockade of the school began, yes, there were people intimidated and verbally attacked at the shop fronts – but not before."

Another parent, Roisin Kennedy, says that for the eleven summers she walked her children to school, the Glenbryn kerbs had been painted for the annual Orange Twelfth commemorations, but there were no UDA or UVF flags until 2001.

"Things then became far more threatening, there were always people hanging about, young lads flying up and down on bikes."

Lisa Irvine gives a similar account of the summer of 2001. "Coming up to June 19, they started painting the kerbs and started flicking paint at the children."

In 2001, Ardoyne woman Patricia McAuley was one of the "interface workers" appointed to liase with loyalist counterparts to maintain the peace by using the mobile phone network. This works year-round through a system of agreed representatives, on both sides of the peace-lines throughout Belfast, phoning each other at the first reports of violence. The representative of the community allegedly responsible for the outbreak first checks the report and, if substantiated, does everything possible to quell trouble. The system is patchy, but when it works, is invaluable.

"For the three previous years," says McAuley, "we had been in constant contact with the interface workers from the loyalist side and it had worked well. But in 2001, they turned off the phones without explanation and wouldn't speak to us."

She says the escalation in violence began in February or March when new people, allegedly linked to the UDA, moved into Glenbryn after its bloody Shankill Road feud with the UVF. She was out trying to calm the violence most nights from then on.

"One minute it would be quiet and then we would hear the loyalist sirens, their 'wake up call' (an unofficial loyalist signal) which alerted us to trouble which invariably came within five minutes. As interface workers, you watch and you learn. We knew the first sign of trouble would be kids throwing stones. Ours would sometimes retaliate, they weren't completely innocent. When their kids ran back, grown men would come out and our kids, being silly, would run at them. The whole thing was orchestrated."

She claims that on Father's Day 2001, a fellow interface worker was badly injured by a flying slate, knocking her unconscious. Pinned in a doorway, McAuley got through to her opposite number in Glenbryn, but he put the phone down on her.

"I cracked up and wondered what could be going on. That summer things really deteriorated. I hardly saw my own home. People were sitting eating their dinners and the next minute there was a brick on the table. People had their doors kicked in at 4am."

Many other people in Ardoyne, including Holy Cross parents, also say the violence gradually escalated in the early summer of 2001. Frightening incidents began happening close to the school. Lynda Bowes, a dark-haired, vivacious secretary from Ardoyne, was collecting her child one Friday in May 2001 and saw "a wee man" standing drinking with four or five 14- and 15-year-olds.

"He was spitting at our kids who had got out of school early. There was one in particular who wore a hat and was shouting, 'You Fenian bastards' and 'whores'. I date the real problems from about then."

Maura Lindsay says her daughter Amy was spat at and called names in June 2001. "I asked her if she was sure because I'd never heard of it before. We were worried about being burnt out of our home but we had no idea they were going to begin a protest at the school."

An account of an incident just before the June 19 flashpoint comes from Ardoyne woman, Frances Doherty. Walking her child from school, the police asked her to cross the road on to the opposite footpath to allow a group of loyalists to continue putting paramilitary flags up on lampposts. Frances objected. The loyalists called her a "Fenian bastard" and told her to "get off our road". The jeep-load of police, she says, made no attempt to ask the loyalists to refrain from their insults and threats.

While Billy Hutchinson disputes the theory that displaced UDA men were behind the Holy Cross protest, he accepts there was a lot more flag waving in the area than before.

"There is no question of that, it's true and it should have been handled better. I think the increased number of flags was because of Ardoyne protesting against Orange parades. Loyalist people were sending out a message that they lived around there as well; it was about people marking out their territory more than anything else, letting Ardoyne know that they ran the area."

On the Catholic side of the peace-line, the message was seen and understood, but not accepted. Mickey Liggett says Ardoyne had its own problems and divisions. "There's this big image that we're a monolith," he says, "but that couldn't be further from the case. There are at least two blocs here, the Chucks and the Church." "Chucks" is an abbreviated form of the Sinn Fein slogan in Irish, "Tiofaidh ar la", pronounced "Chucky are la" ("our day will come" in English). "Church" refers to the Catholic establishment and by extension the SDLP.

"There is conflict even between republicans, those who support or oppose the IRA ceasefire, especially in an area like this which is constantly under siege. There were people around who said the best way to deal with this is the way we've always dealt with it," Liggett says.

He is right, but so is Liz Murphy in saying, "Ardoyne is like a big family. We have disagreements, differences of opinion, political allegiances, but if something happens like it did to our children, the community stands together."

In June 2001, that cohesion was about to be tested to the limit.

Chapter One

THE MAN AND THE LADDER

It started as an ordinary, sunny summer's day but, even by North Belfast standards, June 19, 2001 became a milestone.

As with just about every other historic event in the area, people living across the peace-line have very different accounts of how it started. Ask anyone in Glenbryn what happened on that day and they will tell you one of their own was vindictively knocked off his ladder by a nationalist attacker in a car.

In Ardoyne they will recount the horror experienced by over 100 small children and their parents for what they say was no apparent reason other than sheer sectarian hatred. No one has ever satisfactorily got to the bottom of the "man and ladder" incident which sparked it all off. Short of a miracle, no one ever will. It is one of those maddening Belfast ironies, however, that there is one point of agreement between the two principals involved, the nationalist taxi-driver and the loyalist who was allegedly "knocked off his ladder". This is that there was never actually any physical contact between the two of them. Not that you would realise that from most eyewitness accounts who swear blind they saw the car hit the ladder, knocking the man clean off it.

It all happened, or didn't happen, a week before the end of the school summer term. It was a time of intense political and street-level tension. Firstly, there was a political ticking bomb after David Trimble's decision in May to sign a post-dated letter of resignation, taking effect on July 1, unless IRA decommissioning had begun. Then, for the fourth year in a row, the loyalist Orange Order had been barred from marching down the nationalist Garvaghy Road in Portadown, County Armagh, causing resentment in the unionist community who regard marching as a cultural right.

In the parliamentary elections on June 7, 2001, Sinn Fein had won two Westminster seats and become a larger party than the SDLP, a more moderate nationalist party. In North Belfast, the party's Gerry Kelly had overtaken the SDLP candidate. A unionist had yelled, "Provo murderer" at the tense election count. In North Belfast, a loyalist councillor was threatening to picket a cemetery in protest at the annual Catholic "Blessing of the Graves" ceremony. The largest loyalist paramilitary group, the UDA, was mid-way through a sustained campaign of attacking Catholics in Belfast and elsewhere with crude, but potentially lethal, pipe bombs. Northern Ireland was, in short, a tinderbox of seething sectarian tensions just waiting to be ignited by a spark, however small.

Although the Protestants of Glenbryn, like their co-religionists throughout the North, traditionally celebrated the annual "Twelfth" of July, until 2001 they had not made a big point of putting up flags along the road leading to the school. This year, for whatever reason, was different, according to David Lindsay, father of two children, Amy (9) and Kirsty (12) at Holy Cross. "They would have put flags up but it was never in any huge quantity."

He adds, however, "That summer, every house along the road was fully decorated and the road was ablaze with colour, as if they were trying to rub it in your face."

Two days before the "man on the ladder" episode, on June 17, Sharon Quail, mother of Shaunalee (8), was chatting with a friend on the edge of Ardoyne, waiting for their daughters to walk down from Holy Cross.

"They (loyalists) had never ever put flags up or painted kerbstones during the school term. This day, there was a couple of 14- or 15-year-old fellas painting the kerbs. It was a first. A parent's car came out of Holy Cross and, as it passed the loyalists, they threw paint tins at it. The car was hit all over."

Dozens of schoolgirls witnessed the incident and ran screaming down the road. Many ended up in Colette Cassidy's garden because she lives on the interface of Alliance Avenue and Ardoyne Road. "I immediately phoned Mrs Tanney (the Holy Cross Girls' school principal) and told her that I had 50 squealing children in the garden. I had a sense something was about to explode."

She did not have to wait long. Two days later, June 19 dawned warm and sunny. The girls of Holy Cross were looking forward to their school sports day the following week while the older girls were busy rehearsing for their annual end-of-year play, "Babes in the Wood".

That lunchtime, on the nearby Oldpark Road, Michael Cosby, a solidly built, sandy-haired, 41-year-old loyalist, was enjoying a Father's Day present from his wife – a back massage to ease his aching spine.

Police Chief Superintendent, Roger Maxwell, the Commander of the North Belfast Command Unit, was at the funeral of one of his sergeants in Larne, County Antrim. "Things were quiet when I left," he says.

Anne Bill, later to become prominent on the loyalist side, was enjoying a holiday in Spain.

A few streets away, Jim McClean, a young, dark-haired loyalist from Glenbryn, was engaged in bedecking the Ardoyne Road with loyalist flags.

Amanda Johnston, a striking, 42-year-old blonde-haired lady with a fashionable stud in her top lip, was standing on the same spot she had occupied for the previous two years as a lollipop lady, helping the children of neighbouring Catholic Holy Cross and Protestant Wheatfield schools safely across the road.

But, at about nineteen minutes past two in the afternoon, an event took place that would have a huge effect on their lives. McClean and two helpers continued putting up flags, tying them to lamp-posts along the street. McClean admits being close to members of the UDA's notorious "C Company", formerly controlled by Johnny "Mad Dog" Adair. His father, Denis, was convicted in 1988 for the theft of a cache of weapons from a British Army depot and served six years in prison. Jim was enjoying his work, climbing up and down the aluminium ladder as the three-man team made their way closer and closer towards the gates of Holy Cross.

Amanda takes up the story. "At twenty-two minutes past two o'clock, I saw a white car driving towards where a few lads were putting up flags. The passenger in the car was wearing a Celtic top. There was one fella up a ladder and two standing holding the ladder. The car drove past and I saw the guys look at the car. The next minute the car reversed a bit and rammed towards the ladder."

The car, she says, then mounted the footpath. "He reversed back and went towards the ladder and the fella was actually knocked off the ladder. He (the driver) went right into the ladder and then the car drove off."

She is sure she saw the white car hit the ladder, forcing Jim McClean to jump off, although he didn't appear seriously hurt. She then says she saw the driver of the car get out with something in his hand "as if he was going to attack the guys".

"They started shouting at the car and chasing him, which they had every right to do. Other people had seen it and started chasing the car too. He (the driver) tried to do a three-point turn, but by this stage he was sort of jammed in because other people had come out and started attacking the car."

McClean's version of events shows the gulf of perception and memory between the two sides.

"There were three of us putting up flags, me and two others about 16-years-old. We noticed a car driving up towards us. I was on my way up the ladder with a flag. They were union flags and Ulster flags. They weren't paramilitary; we were putting them up for the Queen's jubilee. The whole road was getting decorated. I remember I was up the ladder with a flag in my hand at the only wooden telegraph pole on the road. The white Vectra car pulled up in front of me. There were two people in it, a man of about 38 and a younger man in a Celtic top who was pointing the finger and 'slabbering' (Belfast slang for complaining)." The wee lads with Jim started slabbering back. "The car sped up towards the school and dropped off the fella with the Celtic football top. He ran into the school."

Jim says the car came "flying down" towards him and tried to knock down one of the other lads. The driver "threw the handbrake on" and mounted the pavement towards the telegraph pole, but then veered away from him and the pole, "or he would have wrecked the car on it". Instinctively, Jim says, he jumped down two or three rungs off the ladder. He was now standing behind the pole. The driver, he says, was confronting him "with a stick in his hand" before getting back into his car and driving away. By this time, says Jim, parents began coming from everywhere in "a matter of seconds".

"There was about 30 of them, with baseball bats and iron bars. There was fellas running at me with screwdrivers. I seemed to be surrounded," he says, but he somehow managed to run away to his own car down a side street. His hands were shaking so much, he could barely open the door, but he got in.

"Then," he says, "two men grabbed the ladders used to put up the flags and began running towards me, towards the back of the car". Jim says he was by then struggling to turn his ignition key. "I was nervous and shaking. One of them had a knife trying to get into the passenger's door. The other had a screwdriver trying to open the driver's door."

He says his ladders were then smashed through his rear window "like a battering ram" and he was hit on the back of the head. He somehow managed to race away with the ladders still sticking out of his rear window. Asked if he believes the whole incident was planned, Jim says, on the whole, he does not.

"But there was tools in their cars, crowbars in their boots, pickaxe handles, brush poles, crutches, anything you could get your hands on in their boots. Maybe they could say they were afraid of an attack happening one day or something but for 30 years those kids walked up to the school and nothing happened."

Amanda, however, is certain the whole event was pre-planned. She says it all happened too quickly to have been spontaneous and claims there were men at the school that day that she did not recognise as parents.

"Out of the blue, all of these extra cars appeared from inside and outside the school grounds, men, hurley bats and baseball bats. They came flying out to attack the fellas from this community. Our's were more trying to get at the guy in the car."

She denies that what happened next was a free for all, although she says "there was a few punches thrown".

Both these eyewitness accounts are at odds with the version of events given by the driver of the white Vectra car, who has chosen to remain anonymous for reasons that will become clear. The driver (we will call him "Sean") is a nationalist aged 34 who was born in Ardoyne but whose family were burned out in the 1969 riots. Sean, a taxi-driver, says he had a daily fare collecting a child from Holy Cross, usually accompanied by her mother.

"That day she couldn't come with me, so her son, aged about 12, came with me to pick up the daughter, then aged about six. The son was wearing a Celtic top. We turned right on to the Ardoyne Road and I noticed people putting up paramilitary flags with one guy up a ladder holding a brush-pole with a flag on it. He jumped off the ladder, he was only two or three rungs up, and began shouting at us about the Celtic top. My window was half wound-down so I could hear him. He was shouting 'Fenian bastards'.

"The next thing he hit one of my quarter-lights with the brush pole and then hit the boot with it. It must have been hard because I saw the dent later. Fixing the window cost me £85. I drove towards the school but was worried about the boy's safety and did a U-turn to get out of the area. I then realised his little sister would panic if I didn't turn up, so I took a diversion to come to the school from the other direction. All I wanted to do was avoid the man who had been shouting at me, but when I arrived at the school gates I was surrounded by a crowd of parents and other taxis and loyalists who started attacking us. They were coming out of everywhere. That is what happened and I would swear all of this is true on the Bible."

"Sean" is, of course, aware that this incident was subsequently described by the Protestant community in Glenbryn as the straw that broke the camel's back. Asked if he has any feelings of regret about his key role in what became the Holy Cross saga, he says that the people of Ardoyne know him and accept he did nothing wrong.

"I couldn't live here if they didn't trust me. What happened that day could have happened to anyone. It's unbelievable that I have been blamed for it all. The police have told me four times that I'm on a Red Hand Defenders (a loyalist paramilitary grouping) death list and that my name has been found in UDA files. I've had to move home and I've lost a lot of money because I can't work in loyalist areas."

While it is difficult, if not impossible, to ascertain what really did happen on June 19, there is probably more than a grain of truth in what one Holy Cross parent, builder Chris McDonald, later said about it.

"If you have a group of loyalists putting flags up right beside a Catholic school just as parents are arriving to collect their kids, it's only provoking trouble. We 'pulled' (Belfast slang for confronted) the police about it but they said that they couldn't stop them. It was always the same people who were doing it, putting up light blue UDA flags at the exact time the kids were getting out of school."

Colette Cassidy, mother of Holy Cross pupil, Caitlin (11), also says the June 19 incident was "an extension of the other incidents".

"It wasn't just a one-off – I knew that it was a case of things building up for weeks."

Amanda Johnston says that when she realised how serious the rioting was, she closed the Holy Cross gates. She then quickly opened them again so stranded mothers outside, who had already picked up their daughters, could take shelter in the relative safety of the school grounds. Her thoughts then turned to her own daughter.

"My head was spinning. I knew Nicky would be coming home from school. As I walked home, a woman accused me of leaving my post. But I had got the girls safely into school first. It was getting nasty and I was scared and I had done my duty by the children."

The violence began during a Board of Governors meeting at Holy Cross. It was parish priest Father Kenneth Brady's last stint as chairman and Anne Tanney had arranged for tea and sandwiches to be served at the farewell meeting. Amongst those present was the principal of nearby Holy Cross boys' school, Terry Laverty, who had noticed the men putting up flags as he drove up to the girls' school. The governors' meeting began, blissfully unaware of the rioting outside. Anne Tanney was suddenly called from the room. The meeting continued as the violence got worse outside. Then she returned, looking for Father Brady. The rest of the Board sat waiting for news. When it came, it was bad. The police had ordered the evacuation of the school.

"I remember a couple of times during the meeting I could hear kids crying. Looking back, I wonder why we all didn't jump up and leave immediately," says Laverty, adding that on his way home, it struck him he had almost been expecting something "because of the attitude of the three boys I had passed in the car".

Outside, matters were deteriorating fast. Amongst others, Jim Potts, who became the main spokesman for the Glenbryn protesters, explains what was going through his mind and that of the other loyalists on the road.

"We believed nationalists had planned the attack on the men putting up the flags to entice this community into a fight. For the last 30 years, we had allowed the nationalist community to come and collect their children freely, but some of them were gathering information on people who lived in this community. A lot of young (Catholic) lads from St Gabriel's were starting to use Hesketh as a thoroughfare. We were getting complaints that cars were being scored, fences destroyed, the lads were being abusive. Residents enjoying their front gardens were getting spat upon and abused."

Michael Cosby was also on the scene that afternoon, fresh from his back massage. He accepts the initial "ladder incident" was minor but accuses nationalists of deliberately provoking the trouble.

"It wasn't done by accident, the nationalists came equipped with baseball bats in their cars."

Ronnie Black, another loyalist on the scene says, "I can't remember how the idea came to block the road. People just gathered on the road and it was blocked. There were so many people, the police couldn't move us back."

On the road, more and more parents were gathering to find out what was going on and where their children were. Colette Cassidy was one of the first on the scene, claiming she witnessed loyalists breaking up kerbstones. She drove up to collect Caitlin as soon as she realised what was going on.

"I ended up taking a load of kids out with me. We tried our best to settle them, but you knew it wouldn't leave a child's mind easily. Caitlin was terrible, she was in hysterics. There were a lot of terribly shaken and confused children but Caitlin was just completely out of it."

Liz Murphy, mother of Niamh (7), was another parent on the scene early, finding herself at the heart of the trouble beside the school gates. She remembers the children being "all huddled together with only one teacher" in the roadway. Stones started hailing down and the children began scattering; then a Protestant woman, who lived next to the school, opened her door and remonstrated with the loyalists, shouting at them to stop. Two fathers, remembers Liz, were trying to keep things calm and push the girls back into the school grounds away from the hail of stones and bricks. The school principal, Anne Tanney, came out to try to calm things down. Liz remembers trying to persuade Mrs Tanney not to go anywhere near the protesters for her own personal safety, but – with commendable courage – off she went to speak to them, to little effect.

Humour can survive even in the midst of violence. Liz tells of how another parent, Phyllis Doherty, walked right up the Ardoyne Road even as the stones and bricks were raining down.

"I think it was a case of the loyalists not knowing if she was one of us or one of them, she just walked right up the middle of the road on her own, unscathed."

As they were wondering how to get the children home safely, someone remembered there was a back gate. "There's a wire mesh fence, so you couldn't drive through it, but there is a small single gate where you could walk through," Liz recalls.

Liz's husband, John, an electrician, wanted to use his car to ram the wire fence so cars could drive through to pick up the children, but Anne Tanney would have none of it. "Sheer panic set in. The children were in hysterics. The fear in those children's faces would have broke your heart," says Liz.

A small group of about four parents then lined the children up and walked them through the back exit. Another parent drove a mini-bus into St Gabriel's and piled in about 20 pupils. The bus began driving down the Crumlin Road. "Loyalists on the road realised who they were and began stoning it," says Liz.

She, along with other parents and teachers, began walking the remainder of the children through the back of Holy Cross, up a hill, across a football pitch and through the gate towards St Gabriel's and the Crumlin Road.

"They cried the whole way. We were shaking too. Then somebody shouted the loyalists were running around and onto the Crumlin Road to try and get at us that way. You should have seen us rushing those wee children."

The adults started walking the children down the wide Crumlin Road with the loyalists behind them, baying abuse.

"They had run around the school," Liz recalls, "knowing we were bringing the children out that way, to try and get us that way. You should have seen the speed we walked with those poor kids. I remember one or two of the loyalists making a run down the road after us. The cops never did a thing."

The children's faces were by now red and tear-stained as they made their way with their equally terrified teachers towards where their parents were anxiously waiting at the Ardoyne shops.

"Niamh was in tears and shaking," remembers Liz. "She was always a jolly wee kind of person but that day she sobbed her heart out. She held my hand so tight. She didn't have a clue what was happening and just kept asking what she had done wrong."

Another parent, Tanya Carmichael, mother of Emer and Emma (4 and 8 respectively) was amongst the group escorting children out through the back door and through the grounds of St Gabriel's. She says she pretended there was a fire drill to explain their hasty exit.

"As what had really happened filtered through, the older ones panicked. They knew they were being attacked and they were frightened. It was awful. There were kids running about screaming and crying. There were children literally wetting themselves."

One reason loyalists gave later to justify their accusation that nationalists had orchestrated the riot was the speed at which the cavalcade of black taxis arrived to ferry the children down the Crumlin Road to their waiting parents. There is, however, a simple explanation. Tanya Carmichael's husband, Sean, is the co-ordinator of Ardoyne's black taxi-drivers. She saw what was happening and decided to alert them and ask for help.

"The taxis are radio-controlled, so I flagged one down and told him to radio through quick and tell them the girls' school is being attacked."

Sean picks up the story. "One of the drivers radioed through. I asked all of the taxi men to go to either the Ardoyne Road or Crumlin Road. They all rushed up. By that time the kids had all been evacuated into St Gabriel's. At Mercy Primary school (on the Crumlin Road, opposite St Gabriel's) they were also frightened in case a crowd from Glenbryn broke through there. So the same taxi-drivers evacuated Mercy Primary."

Tanya says, "The loyalists were behaving just like a pack of wild animals. I couldn't believe it. They were saying, 'You Fenian scum, you'll never walk our road again' and 'We'll burn your school down' and what they were going to do to ourselves and our children. The venom and anger and hatred in their faces was unbelievable. Our people were angry also because we didn't know where our kids were. We were telling the cops that we had to get our kids out, but they just pushed us back." The loyalists were not locals, they had come from everywhere. I had never seen that many people in Glenbryn in my life. The police were very aggressive towards us and were constantly pushing us back. The loyalists were shouting the whole time, 'This is our road and you will not be back', and 'Provo bastards', 'No more Provie Fenian bastards are using our road'."

While some parents and the teachers were taking the children out of the back of Holy Cross via the Crumlin Road, there was total panic at the opposite side of the school, on the Ardoyne Road, where parents had gathered not knowing what was happening to their children.

Brendan Mailey, who became the main spokesman for the nationalist "Right to Education" group ("RTE" set up by the parents as a response to the crisis) says, "There were rumours going around that the school itself had been attacked, that loyalists had surrounded it and were still trying to get inside. There was all sorts of panic and hand-to-hand fighting. RUC and British Army jeeps arrived to put up a line between the parents and the loyalists. We were faced with a line of about two to three hundred loyalists shouting, 'That is the end of it, you are not getting up here no more'. Then we got word that the teachers had brought the kids out."

Chris McDonald, father of Holy Cross girl Nicole (10), says by then "the cops were really crapping themselves" because they were caught in between two crowds who "were wanting to murder each other".

Elaine Burns, a motherly woman who has worked for many years with the Ardoyne Association, describes how she tried desperately to get through police lines to find her daughter, Leona (7).

"As far as we were concerned she was trapped in the school but the police pushed us back with their riot shields. We were distracted, I was shaking and heartsore. There was a mob of loyalists and bottles and bricks flying about; panic, confusion, fear. People were crying and asking others if they had seen their children. Mothers were screaming and fathers were like bulls trying to get through while the loyalists were shouting they were going to attack the school and burn it down and that we were scumbags. Then word got round that the teachers were bringing them out the back to the Ardoyne shops."

That started a stampede as parents turned around and began running away from Holy Cross towards the shops. Chris McDonald says, "Everybody started to run; it was like a marathon race, down past the new houses, onto the Crumlin Road. All the people from Glenbryn rushed in the opposite direction, trying to get out further up the Crumlin Road."

Chris's wife, Rita, an IT co-ordinator, takes up the story. "There was no one left for the loyalists to fight on the Ardoyne Road so they ran towards the Crumlin to stop the parents getting up the other way. It was chaos."

At this stage hundreds of Ardoyne nationalists had gathered on the Crumlin Road. The police appeared to lose control. British soldiers continued to arrive in large armoured vehicles. People who were only out shopping became involved. Nobody knew what was happening.

"People started to take their frustrations out however they could," says Rita McDonald. "Loyalists were hitting Alliance Avenue and nationalists were hitting back at the houses in Glenbryn and cars were getting wrecked. The police hadn't a clue what they were doing. Carloads of loyalists started arriving. It got to the stage that both sides just wanted to kill each other and get at each other whatever way they could."

Miraculously, no one was killed or even badly hurt. That night fierce rioting raged until the early hours. Chief Superintendent Roger Maxwell, who had returned from the funeral in Larne to find "the place had gone to hell", says it was one of the worst nights of his career.

"We had sustained rioting right throughout that night. The police were out-numbered but we had to sort it. There were three blast bombs thrown, acid bombs, paint bombs. Things were really tense right throughout the night."

Meanwhile, parents and the wider community in Ardoyne met at the community centre to decide their next move.

"There was shouting and yelling," says Sean Carmichael. "I don't think anyone would have supported proposals to cause harm to anyone else. It was just the thought of young children being abused."

There were concerns raised that if parents did not walk the direct route to Holy Cross the following day, there could be a domino effect with at least four other Catholic schools targeted in the same way.

"It might not have ended in North Belfast, it could have spread throughout the six counties," says Carmichael.

Father Brady told the meeting he hoped it was a "one off" and the best thing might be to take the back route for the rest of term, but others did not agree.

Sean McMichael says, "Those who were first on the scene on June 19 said they recognised a lot of known UDA faces. It was agreed we should not storm into this blind. It was time for cool heads to see what tomorrow might bring."

In their homes, parents and children discussed what had happened and what they should do the following day. Some decided then and there not to try to make it to school the following morning; others were equally determined that life must go on as normal. Amongst the couples agonising over what to do were Elaine Burns and her husband, Danny, a postman.

"We talked to Leona (their daughter) and told her that something bad had happened but that both of us were going to take her to school the next day," says Elaine.

Brendan Mailey says his daughter Rachel (8) was too young to fully understand what was happening. "I think the children were really bewildered as to what was going on at that stage. You tend to tell children lies to keep them calm. You know exactly how serious it is, but you tell the child that it's just a little problem."

Colette Cassidy says she decided not to send Caitlin back on June 20. "The child was totally hysterical, petrified. Caitlin was one of the first children to go on Diazepam. She just couldn't face walking past the mob again. There was no way I would have forced her through. It was her decision. It was her last year at Holy Cross. A week or two and she was going to be finished. She was upset, though, about not taking part in her leaving play or saying goodbye to her teachers and friends."

Colette, like other parents, offered to drive her child to school the following day, but Caitlin declined, "she was that frightened".

Liz Murphy's daughter, Niamh, kept asking that night if she would be going to school in the morning.

"I had to let Niamh know that she hadn't done anything wrong and she was entitled to go to her school. If I had said no, she would have assumed she had done something wrong and she was being punished. She seemed happy enough because she really didn't understand what was going on. It was like a jigsaw to her."

On the morning of June 20, a group of parents assembled, some without their children until they saw the lie of the land. They began walking up the road. A line of policemen and vehicles was strung across, blocking their path.

Elaine Burns says, "They didn't speak to us except to inform us that we were not permitted to take our children up the road because it wasn't safe. We said the police were there to make sure we were safe but they said they couldn't protect us and we couldn't go any further."

Sean Carmichael has a slightly more detailed memory, remembering how the police at first told parents to walk up the left-hand pavement and reassured them that armoured vehicles would protect their flank from the loyalists. This was rapidly countermanded with the police deciding no men would be allowed to walk the road, only women and children. He accuses the police of effectively acting as intermediary with the loyalists. He says that as the loyalists' demands changed, so did police tactics.

"Then they threw their jeeps across the road and said nobody was getting up. There was a stand-off for about half an hour before Mrs Tanney sent word the school wouldn't be opening. There was a lot of anger and parents were shouting at the cops who, as usual, were manhandling people and pushing them out of the way. The loyalists just stood in the background laughing at us. At no stage during the protest in June did the RUC make a neutral decision.

"At no stage did they tell the loyalists, 'Look, it's very important these children get to school. We are putting them through no matter what.' They allowed the loyalists to dictate security," says Carmichael, claiming he and other parents witnessed RUC officers facing the protesters, joking and laughing with them.

Liz Murphy says she couldn't believe what she was seeing. "I thought the police would push the loyalists back. The cops were incapable of doing their job; they were incapable of handling the loyalists. They bowed to threats, facilitated them and blockaded the road. There were stones thrown, again by the loyalists, and our ones, naturally enough, threw them back."

One woman, says Liz, had climbed a wall to get a better view of what was happening and had seen an armed loyalist running into a house. "A (police) jeep did fly down but nothing more came out of it. It was never on the news and nobody was arrested."

This was, arguably, a point where decisive police action could have halted the protest in its tracks. It had yet to build up a head of steam and swift deterrent action might have averted a more serious protest. Parents find it difficult to believe that, had the boot been on the other foot, a similarly small group of Catholics would have faced the police down so comprehensively. Even though confronted with a hostile loyalist crowd, the police eventually allowed three parents to walk up the road, accompanied by one police officer, to see if the school was going to open.

"The abuse they got was wild; they were called 'Fenian bastards', 'whores' and 'sluts'," says Liz Murphy. "We decided to bring Niamh home, although a few took their kids up through St Gabriel's. But if you had started going in through the back door, the next thing they would have blocked that, which would have had the knock-on effect of blocking another three Catholic schools. Niamh was in a bad way that morning because of the stones that were thrown at us. She was backing herself into a wall with fear. She asked me questions for the rest of the day about whether they were going to kill us all."

One of the other parents there was Geraldine McGrandles, mother of Danielle (8). "It made me angry that the police were facing us, beating us down the road, shoving us with their batons, while the loyalists were behind them, shouting abuse and throwing things at us."

Brendan Mailey says he had not known what to expect on the second day. "I thought there'd be a few loyalists on the way up to school doing a bit of verbal intimidation, but we didn't expect there to be a full blockade of the road by the RUC. The police told us the loyalists were prepared to use violence, so parents would have to go up the other way. Some of us did go up the back way then, thinking there was only a week to the end of term, but even on the Crumlin Road loyalists confronted us, shouting that we would never get up the Ardoyne Road again so we might as well get used to it. There were TV cameras following us up but once we got up to St Gabriel's, Father Kenneth wouldn't let them in. I had a bit of an argument with him but he said he didn't want St Gabriel's pulled into the controversy."

Maura Lindsay had a better idea than most of what to expect, living as her family does right on the peace-line. "The RUC faced us and our wee children dressed in full riot gear. The loyalists stood behind them jeering. They could do what the hell they wanted. As far as the RUC was concerned, it was the parents and the children who were the problem, not the hundreds of hate-filled protesters behind them."

Not wanting to stand about too long with her already upset daughter, Amy, who suffers from chronic asthma, she decided that was effectively the end of her summer term.

Unknown to parents trying to get to school, there was yet another drama being played out. Before the loyalists had gathered on the road that morning, convincing Anne Tanney to close the school for a day, several mothers had already left their children there. Lisa Irvine was one of the early arrivals with her only child, Shannon (9), in the back of her car. Another mother who had arrived early, only to find the school closed, was Lynda Bowes. When the two realised the protest was underway and that the school day had been disrupted, they rounded up all the stranded children to take them back down the road. Lynda, in the first car, says she knew she had to "get the hell out of there" when she saw how quickly a crowd had gathered and how hostile it was. Driving the children down the road through the loyalist crowd was "like a scene out of a movie".

"The children in the back of the car, many of whom didn't know me, were panicking and the crowd was really close, virtually sitting on my bonnet and glaring in the windows. I told the kids not to look at them and not to worry. I could see the crowd closing in behind me and parting again to let Lisa down. The impression I got was that this would be the last time we would be allowed on the road."

Lisa was in the second car. "I crammed as many kids in the back as I could," she says. "It was like the parting of the Red Sea as I drove towards them. Looking in my rear view mirror, all I could see were them closing in behind us. It was terrifying."

As for how the children themselves responded, some were terrified, while others didn't really understand what was going on. Tina Gallagher says she tried to minimise what had happened when she got her daughter, Roisin (7), home.

"We didn't want to say too much about it because we didn't know what would happen the next day. We told her that there must have been a football match somewhere and that Rangers were beaten and that was why there was a bit of a riot."

There is, of course, a police explanation for the events of the morning of June 20. Former Assistant Chief Constable Alan McQuillan says numbers on the nationalist side had swollen to about 200 and 50 on the loyalist. In an effort to keep both sides apart, he says, the police had baton-charged the loyalists.

"Two minutes later police received a report of armed men having been seen in the Glenbryn area. The question was then whether we were going to push the parents and children up the road, bearing in mind there may have been armed men in the area. To me there was no decision."

Chief Superintendent Roger Maxwell says there was fury on the loyalist side after the baton charge and confirms there had been reports of gunmen in Glenbryn.

"I ask you, would you have pushed the protesters off the road and told four- and five-year-olds that it was safe? Would you? I had two sons aged seven and ten. I was a parent as well. Could I have looked at myself in the mirror if I had done something to endanger the lives of the Holy Cross children?"

On the night of June 20, another meeting took place in the community centre. "There were a lot of angry parents," remembers Liz Murphy. "Some were shouting to block Protestant schools but a majority said it wasn't fair to inflict on other innocent children what was being done to ours."

Outside, the police were facing another night of intense rioting. Chief Superintendent Maxwell says it was nightmarish. "It was dreadful; there was serious disorder on both sides of the peace-line and then the gunfire began, from both sides, against the police.

"There were blast bombs, petrol bombs and paint bombs thrown at us. I asked Alan (McQuillan) for reinforcements from across Northern Ireland. Thirty-nine police officers were injured and we fired nine plastic baton rounds. We had intelligence that the loyalists had blast bombs and were intent on throwing them over the heads of my men at the Catholic crowd. It didn't happen only because of the tactics we employed, but the threat never subsided."

The following day, June 21, a few parents arrived on the Ardoyne Road, trying again to reach Holy Cross. The police were waiting, in full riot gear, face-shields down and body-shields up. There were not more than 50 or 60 protesters on the road.

Some parents turned round and walked up via the Crumlin Road and the back way, but not Tina Gallagher. "I didn't want that. I am proud of my child and I want her to be proud of herself. I didn't feel it (the back route) was safe so she didn't go to school. I got her ready and brought her up every day but we returned home when we saw the police blocking the road. It was coming up to the summer holidays anyway and the kids would be off for eight weeks."

Liz Murphy also decided to try again to reach the school. When her daughter said she was worried that the stones would hurt her parents, Liz tried to reassure her by saying that she would see the stones coming and avoid them but that if the child was too afraid, they would come home.

"Niamh said she would be all right if I held her hand. It was heartbreaking. She was trying to be so brave, to impress us, but deep down inside she was petrified. Away we went to the school and there again were the protesters."

Some of the parents were angry at Father Brady and Anne Tanney's support for the temporary use of the back route. Liz Murphy, for one, says she understood their reasoning, but there was no way she would be setting a precedent by taking the back road.

Lynda Bowes also walked her daughter, Amanda, up to police lines on June 21. "We all met up at the shops with Anne Tanney, Father Kenneth and the rest of the governors. Mrs Tanney said that, for the sake of the children, we should take them up the back. Before this, I had always had a very good relationship with her but I had to say, sorry, I have never refused you anything before, but not this time."

Lynda was shocked at the turn of events. "People cannot believe I come from Ardoyne at times, because I am so naïve. I approached a policeman and asked why they were blocking our path. He blanked me, stonily. He didn't even look at me, as if I wasn't there.

"I told Father Kenneth I wanted somebody in charge to explain why I wasn't allowed to walk my ten-year-old child to school. He went behind police lines but returned to say there was nobody high-ranking enough to speak to. How could it be right that the police decide to allow loyalists to block a road but not explain themselves?

"I thought it was a direct lie to say there was no one there authorised to speak to us. Whoever was responsible was too cowardly to face us." Lynda conveyed these views, forcefully, to the nearest police officer. "I got it all off my chest but when I looked down, our Amanda was in a mess, the tears were streaming down her face. I asked myself what the hell I had just done, frightening her? Amanda had never been so close to a policeman before, especially one dressed like that. She knew I was upset and that something was seriously wrong. I was very, very angry."

Unlike many others, Lynda decided to take the back route for the rest of term. Amanda was just starting to work towards her Eleven Plus, a qualifying exam. "The loyalists were still making her suffer by the long hike she had to make, but they weren't going to damage her school record."

What Lynda and other parents could not know was that, even at this stage, the police feared loyalists might bomb the school. Chief Superintendent Maxwell says, "For the rest of that school term, it was always my big fear that the loyalists would throw the blast bombs we knew they had locally at the children."

On the Glenbryn side of the peace-line, people were playing it by ear. According to Michael Cosby, there was no meeting within the area to get themselves organised until the end of the summer term (which was over a week after the June 19 incident). Both he and Jim Potts agree that there was never any democratic vote within Glenbryn on blocking the road nor any discussion on possible alternative ways of raising their grievances.

Cosby says, "People just went up and blocked the road. It was the obvious place to make a protest."

Anne Bill, a spokesperson for CRUA (Concerned Residents of Upper

Ardoyne, a Protestant residents' group set up to organise the protest), says the thought that the children might be affected if the road was blocked simply did not arise.

"People just felt they needed to protest and the Ardoyne Road was the natural place to be. Nobody thought it would mean the kids couldn't get to school."

In an apparent contradiction, however, she continues, "If that did happen, people were saying they didn't care about the children. Once and for all, somebody was going to have to listen to us."

Jim Potts adds, "From June onwards, I don't think the community ever let go of the idea of blocking the road. They gave CRUA a chance to resolve it over the summer but what happened later was more or less a continuation of what was done in June."

Cosby says, "Everyone was at one mind about blocking the road. There was no discussion about tactics. It was just a question of organising and making placards."

On the nationalist side, Father Brady counselled parents to play it cool and hope things calmed down over the summer before the start of the September term. Parents focused their anger on the school governors.

"We were expected to have all of the answers; we didn't," says Terry Laverty. "There was no precedent, no textbook to consult. It was a question of trying to use common sense and to see what was reasonable against the backdrop of ever-increasing threat."

Once the loyalists and police blocked the road, he says, it was a question of deciding whether to take the back road through St Gabriel's. "Obviously, the preference was not to be bullied off the road but some parents thought the back road was acceptable as an intermediate step. We couldn't exactly break through the police lines. There were only a couple of weeks to go and we thought, 'Lets go up through St Gabriel's and see what happens'."

The dog days of the summer term played themselves out in a welter of rioting, confusion and a deep foreboding about the summer that lay ahead. At Holy Cross, the end-of-year play, "Babes in the Wood", went ahead with teachers reading the parts of the missing girls. The teachers, through their union, said it was too dangerous to hold a Sports Day and it was cancelled. Another victim of the escalating tension was a farewell

party planned by the local Church of Ireland minister, Rev Stewart
Heaney, for his friend, the then Catholic parish priest, Father Kenneth
Brady.

"The party had been planned for our Church of Emmanuel on June
20. We had planned to bring children from Wheatfield and Holy Cross
along, but what happened on the nineteenth was the end of that," says
Heaney with a sigh.

Chapter Two

SUMMERTIME

It was a case of who was going to move first. It was stalemate. Every meeting during the summer, we got an inch closer to resolving it, but we just couldn't get that final missing bit of the jigsaw.

Ronnie Black, CRUA committee member

They weren't interested in how things could be sorted out. They just wanted their 'sterile zone'. Their attitude was 'We're not here to negotiate with you, we want a wall' and that was it. Mickey Liggett, Ardoyne Focus Group

There was to be no respite for either side over the long, hot summer of 2001 – one of the most violent in North Belfast's already deeply troubled past. Week followed week of pipe bombings, riots, unmitigated hostility between the two communities and failed initiatives.

The atmosphere, already poisoned, deteriorated. With hindsight, although there were sporadic efforts to resolve the conflict, much more could – and might – have been done to resolve the conflict before the autumn. Even at this early stage in the protest, everyone appears to have had a sinking feeling that the row could worsen significantly. Many in Ardoyne feared Holy Cross would be burned down before the autumn term began.

Both sides formed committees: in Glenbryn, the Concerned Residents of Upper Ardoyne (CRUA); and, in Ardoyne, the Right to Education (RTE) group. CRUA's brief was to address all the grievances in Glenbryn, while RTE had a single issue agenda, the schoolchildren's right to walk to Holy Cross. The first of many unsuccessful meetings took place within days of the June 19 confrontation. The venue was the Everton Centre, a community health centre close to the junction of the Ardoyne and Crumlin Roads.

Although he did not attend this meeting, RTE spokesman Brendan Mailey says he knew even then, in the pit of his stomach, that the loyalists were "digging in and there was going to be a struggle".

Parent Tanya Carmichael says it began in an atmosphere of menace, with loyalist bodyguards roaming the venue. "They brought up the flags issue, saying they were attacked. They talked about a car trying to run them down while they were up a ladder. They wouldn't let the issue drop. They said they wanted to celebrate the Twelfth without us trying to kill them. They said it was their area and they were good enough to let us have our school in it. They raised housing, employment, facilities for children, none of which we could do anything about. They said that we had the best of everything in Ardoyne and they had nothing. At the end of the meeting there was no resolution. They couldn't even say definitely whether there would be more protests."

In the first of many such statements, CRUA said they were not refusing the kids access to school. "They just didn't want any men going up the road with them because they couldn't be trusted not to attack their homes or people," says Tanya. "We said we couldn't let our kids go up on their own because it wasn't safe. We asked the men at the meeting, 'Look at the age of these children, they are really terrified, would you like it for your children?' Jim Potts said he wouldn't but they had no remorse. They had their hearts set on a protest."

RTE and CRUA began lobbying for support and sending out invitations to meetings. For both groups, this was a new experience. CRUA believed, wrongly, that the RTE people were streets ahead of them in terms of organisation. Despite the long history of community mobilisation in republican areas, the RTE committee were "complete novices", says parent Liz Murphy.

"We had to learn how to hold a meeting, how to take minutes, how to raise points, tackle issues, accept responsibility and accountability. We had to learn how to listen and discuss things – all this was new. Although we might have vaguely known one another, this was the first time we had all worked together. We were just ordinary parents with absolutely no experience."

That summer also, Father Kenneth Brady ceased being parish priest of Holy Cross and Father Aidan Troy, another Passionist priest who became pivotal in the dispute, took up the reins fresh from Rome. He immediately set about trying to make friends amongst the Protestants in Glenbryn.

Father Gary Donegan, a priest at Holy Cross Church, remembers presenting his new boss with a list of "about ten things that I thought were priorities in the parish if we were going to make a go of it as a new administration".

"Number one, I told him, is the resolution of the Holy Cross blockade, as it was becoming known at that stage."

Liz Murphy had a sinking feeling. "The loyalists were accusing us of attacking elderly Protestants at the Post Office, for example – but one old lady told us they had instructed her themselves to go instead to Ballysillan Post Office and complain about us. When I went to get Niamh's new uniform, she said she mightn't need it because she wouldn't be able to get to school in the autumn and I tried to reassure her. I was hoping rather than expecting things would be OK."

CRUA had its own complaints, says Ronnie Black. "We set up numerous meetings with nationalists. The problem was that when we met the Ardoyne Focus Group (mostly republican community activists), they said they couldn't discuss the school because that had to be sorted out with the RTE group. There was a 'Catch 22' because the RTE group said they could only talk about the children while Focus said they couldn't discuss anything until the problem with the children and the school was resolved. We wanted a group on their side to discuss all our problems but they couldn't do that. It was very frustrating. We were going round in circles. What they wanted was an agreement to allow the children to walk up the road before anything had been sorted out with the Focus group."

Glenbryn loyalist Stuart McCartney, a former Shankill Road man who has lived in Wheatfield on the Protestant side of the peace-line since 1997, has wider complaints about the way nationalists approached the talks.

"We made it clear, over and over again, that the protest wasn't about stopping the children going to school. If it had been, we would have blocked the school gates and other key roads – the Crumlin, the

Ballysillan, the Ardoyne and Ligoniel Roads. That would have stopped children going to all four local Catholic schools. We let them (nationalists) know at the very beginning that we are blocking the Ardoyne Road only, in protest at their riotous behaviour, their incursions into our community and their attacks on us. Yet they persisted in saying we wanted to stop the children getting to school when they knew that there was more than one way to get there."

CRUA, he says, also found it difficult to arrange meetings with community representatives in the Focus group, as opposed to RTE. "We said at one point that we didn't want to meet the RTE group unless there were also people present who could answer our complaints about the security and safety of the Glenbryn community.

"Our concerns were simple – safety, security and survival," he says, making what the Ardoyne side would consider the exaggerated claim that nationalist intimidation had "turned Glenbryn into a ghost town".

Mickey Liggett, a founder member of the Ardoyne Focus Group and who, as a teenager, had been convicted of manslaughter and IRA membership, has a different view.

"People in Glenbryn quickly realised Focus was pivotal. We had already been instrumental in setting up the mobile phone network, although that mechanism broke down after we found there was never anyone to respond from Glenbryn when we needed them."

After the first few days in June 2001, a debate began in Ardoyne over whether parents should take the alternative route or challenge the loyalists and insist on their right to take the usual route. "It was very emotional with some extreme responses, but wiser counsels prevailed," says Liggett. He will not say what those "extreme" responses entailed, but others at the meeting, who prefer to remain anonymous, say "hot heads" were even suggesting retaliatory pickets of local Protestant schools. Liggett explains, while not justifying, those who wanted to respond "extremely".

"All that stuff about peace – it isn't happening here, no matter what Gerry Adams tells you. All the talk about the Agreement and equality and sharing this place – we still live in an apartheid system."

Liggett believes passionately that North Belfast has to become shared space for both communities – both on principle and practically, because of the limited land available to accommodate the Catholic population growth.

In June 2001, however, not even a man of his experience could see what the rest of the year would hold. "I thought it was just a flash in the pan and it would calm down over the summer. But as it got closer to the beginning of term, things got worse."

The rioting around July 12 that summer in Ardoyne was some of the fiercest of the past 30 years anywhere in Northern Ireland with nationalists bitterly resenting loyalists parading past the Ardoyne shops. Dozens of police were injured and Ardoyne resembled a battlefield on many mornings. Father Donegan once landed in the middle of it. On the night of July 11, when local Protestants were whooping it up around their traditional bonfires, he sat down to watch "The Magnificent Seven" on television in the Monastery, feeling a bit like a cowboy in a western movie with Indians war-dancing around him. The next day he said 10 o'clock Mass and decided to race down to Enniskillen to see his sister who had just given birth to a daughter. The proud uncle wanted to bless his new niece. Driving to County Fermanagh, he passed close to various Orange parades – "decommissioning" his clerical collar into a coat pocket for obvious reasons. Returning to Ardoyne, he decided not to go through the Twaddell Avenue flashpoint but to take what he thought was a safer route.

"I could see flames as I got closer. I drove through Ardoyne where vehicles were blazing and was stopped at a police barricade. I told them I wanted access to the Monastery and they let me through to great applause from the rioters. I just couldn't believe the intensity of the riots – I had never had seen one up close like this."

Ulster Unionist Fred Cobain tried frantically over the summer to dissuade CRUA from staging a protest in September. "I thought it was wrong. A protest wasn't going to achieve anything; in fact it was going to play into the hands of paramilitaries. From a Protestant point of view, it was a disaster waiting to happen. If you think the thing through to its logical conclusion, once you're dealing with kids, you have no chance. I told the people in Glenbryn a protest was impossible to win. But I didn't have the ear of those making the decisions. The people were over-emotional, carried away. They weren't listening. It was a violent summer and these things feed upon themselves. Once you light a fire it is very difficult to control."

The Presbyterian minister of Ballysillan Church, serving Glenbryn, the Rev Norman Hamilton, also tried and failed to persuade the Glenbryn loyalists to drop the idea of blocking the school road.

"I told them there would be no understanding at all in the wider world of why they were doing it. They didn't listen. Whatever clout the clergy might have once had, clearly it's diminishing."

This was the unpromising context in which the Mediation Network of Northern Ireland began its work. An independent group, it had extensive experience in mediating between communities over peace-lines and contentious loyalist marching parades. It was initially invited in by CRUA (with the later co-operation of RTE) and by mid-August it had organised a series of meetings involving all the three main parties, the Ardoyne Focus Group, RTE and CRUA. Other potentially vital agencies, such as the police, Housing Executive, the power-sharing Executive and local investment bodies left the Mediation Network to its solo run, keeping only a watching brief.

The Ardoyne position was that no meaningful talks could take place while the children were "being held hostage" to potential loyalist blockades. The Glenbryn position was that the children were not being held hostage, there being an alternative route, and that the school problem could not be tackled in isolation. Mediation Network members shuttled between the two sides throughout the summer. On August 13, they met the Ardoyne side and next day met Glenbryn. There was a huge gulf between the two, but a process had at least begun. Before much progress had been made, however, the loyalist side withdrew – partly because they alleged confidential documents had been shown to outsiders and partly because the nationalist side, they claim, didn't turn up for meetings. The Ardoyne side denies this.

Brendan Mailey says the Mediation Network did their best. "Over eight weeks, they explained the problem using black boards, chalks and diagrams. They talked about our needs and the grievances of the people in Glenbryn. We had to find some middle ground. There was a meeting between RTE and CRUA up the Antrim Road, a week before the start of term in September. The CRUA representatives took us all by surprise by reading out a statement saying the Mediation Network had tricked them in some way and that they were ending the talks. They never explained how or why. The process was their opportunity to end the stalemate. They didn't want to."

Gerald McCabe, a musician and another Holy Cross parent, says, "To be totally honest, I have never felt so sorry for two guys as I did for them (the two Mediation Network workers) in my whole life. They worked like mad to get a place where both sides would meet and when it happened, CRUA walked out."

Parent Liz Murphy was at the same meeting. "We asked them what that meant for the planned protest but they wouldn't say. They asked for an adjournment. When they didn't come back, we went looking for them but they'd left without even saying goodbye. It was going nowhere. The mediators were dumbfounded. We looked at each other and asked, 'Where do we go from here?' I realised then how rough it might be in September."

At the end of this abortive process the Chief Constable, Sir Ronnie Flanagan, gave a public guarantee that the children would get to school via the Ardoyne Road safely in September. It was a watershed.

"Although he had effectively closed down the direct route for the last week of the summer term, come September, it would be a whole different ball game and the road would be open," remembers parent Elaine Burns.

The definitive pledge caused fury amongst the loyalists who said it effectively undermined their leverage.

"Dialogue became useless," says Michael Cosby. "The 'greens' (nationalists) had got what they wanted. There was no use talking any more. The girls were going to get up anyway. It was a stupid statement."

Loyalist Stuart McCartney agrees. "The community was completely on edge, mega pissed off. Their response was 'screw this, we're having a protest'. Flanagan knows the history of this area. When he said that, he was saying he didn't care if we felt insecure."

Glenbryn community worker, Anne Bill, echoes his words. "Flanagan disempowered us at one stroke. He gave power to one community over the other."

Fellow loyalist Ronnie Black says, "Even that night there was rioting because Protestants felt so frustrated. The talks mightn't have been moving too quick – but to us we were getting an inch every time we met them. Nationalists weren't bowing down – don't get me wrong – but the meetings were getting more confident. They were constructive, but there was no friendship, no shaking hands. There was an uneasiness and watchfulness but they knew us and we knew them."

Regarding their plans for September and the autumn term, he says, "We had three or four public meetings in Glenbryn in the fortnight leading up to the start of term. There was no decision, no vote, taken by the community. People just assumed the road would be blocked again like it was in June. We didn't see any other way to protest. People had to come onto the streets."

Ulster Unionist Fred Cobain is also critical of Flanagan's pledge. "It meant any chance of negotiation was gone. The protesters were left in a situation where they felt they had to go ahead, with no end in sight."

But he also criticises them for failing to come to any understanding with Flanagan and his force. "No one had asked the police what they were going to do, or to try and influence them before they decided on the protest. They didn't look at the wider picture. They were just assuming that the police wouldn't let the parents through and would block the road as they did in June."

At the end of the summer's inconclusive talks, both sides decided to make a last ditch bid to resolve the problem before the new term. A meeting was agreed at Belfast Castle, a mock-Victorian pile on the mountains overlooking the city. The two delegations included 12 from Glenbryn (the entire CRUA committee, minus Jim Potts who didn't take part as he "didn't believe it would get anywhere") and three from Ardoyne. Both sides went into the meeting with such different preconceptions about the joint agenda and the ability of the other side to deliver that its failure was inevitable.

Remarkably, as their facilitator, the Ardoyne group chose a 46-year-old Presbyterian minister, the Rev Bill Shaw, of "The 174 Trust", a Protestant cross-community regeneration group working out of an old church in the deprived Catholic New Lodge Road area of North Belfast. Shaw was brought up in the solidly loyalist Sandy Row area of south Belfast and admits to being a "young stone-thrower" in the 1970s. A fire-fighter for many years, he was called late to the ministry. Unsurprisingly, he was taken aback when asked to facilitate the Ardoyne side at the eleventh hour. A courageous, but modest man, he felt duty-bound to do anything he could to prevent the protest re-igniting.

"The Ardoyne side felt my presence as a Presbyterian minister would be seen as a sign of goodwill. I felt ill-equipped, but said to myself that I could hardly be praying for a solution and refuse to play a part when asked. Fools rush in, I suppose. I was briefed as to what the Ardoyne ones wanted to say to the other side – which was to listen and try to address their concerns. Norman Hamilton (the Presbyterian minister serving Glenbryn) phoned me and we had a laugh between us that both of us – Presbyterian ministers – would be taking part on opposite sides."

Mickey Liggett says that when the talks began "it was a shouting match".

"They wanted 'a sterile zone', they complained that our people were attacking their houses, about school traffic, about 'IRA men in cars' and sectarian abuse from parents. They complained about Irish music being played on car radios; they didn't like people wearing Celtic football shirts when they drove up to collect their daughters. They claimed people were being attacked in the shops and the Post Office and that Protestants couldn't go to the chemist. They even claimed we wanted to take over Glenbryn. We asked them for evidence that we wanted their homes, because we didn't. They wanted solid gates at the top of Alliance Avenue that the police would control and a 'no-man's land'. Our response was that we must work to sort out the underlying problems.

"That meant we needed dates when their people had been abused in the chemist's shop or the Post Office so we could follow complaints up. They couldn't give us details. We already had a mechanism to deal with that kind of problem, the mobile phone network. We had a real commitment to make it work. We promised the Glenbryn side that we would – then and there – make a firm commitment to sorting out their problems. If difficulties arose, we pledged ourselves to find ways of working through them. We couldn't possibly negotiate with them about a wall – we were there to fix the mechanism we already had. They also said they wanted to talk directly to the IRA which they said was the only agency that could resolve their concerns."

The Ardoyne group insisted they were the right people for CRUA to deal with, but the loyalist delegation was not satisfied. Focus was routinely dealing with problems in Ardoyne, quelling riots and so on, but the Glenbryn delegation was adamant that they wanted to speak directly to the IRA.

Liggett was also talking under constraints. "We were in a 'Catch 22' because we couldn't be seen by our constituency to be negotiating with people whose strings, they believed, were being pulled by the UDA. They were all collectively threatening to attack our children."

Anne Bill of CRUA said the Glenbryn side could not say there would be no protest "because our people needed to feel secure".

"They needed to feel that something had happened to give them a reason to stop the protest. I thought all three of their people were quite genuine. I even went over to Brendan Bradley (of the Focus Group) and Mickey Liggett on the way out and shook their hands. I told them it had been the most genuine meeting since June and that I hoped there was a way out."

She says the CRUA side had still hoped to get a resolution before term began and offered to hold meetings as late as Sunday night. "They said they would see what they could do and we exchanged phone numbers."

Presbyterian minister Bill Shaw shares many of Liggett's views about the Belfast Castle meeting. "It was obvious there were different factions in the Glenbryn side. Some appeared genuinely concerned to find a compromise but others seemed to me, by their body language, to be going through the motions. I told the Glenbryn side that I believed the Ardoyne folk were there to genuinely listen to their complaints. They were offering to improve the mobile phone network and monitor any trouble in the shops.

"I felt then – and have become more convinced since – that many on the Glenbryn side were not there to try to find a compromise, that they had already made their minds up to go ahead with the protest. They didn't appear to me to want to hear what the other side was saying. During one adjournment, I put it to Norman Hamilton that if the protest went ahead they would be seen around the world as Protestant bigots attacking Catholic children and that he might help them see that. He said he had tried, but they wouldn't listen.

"I suggested that a compromise might be to postpone the protest for two weeks, during which events on the road and at the shops would be monitored, and we would have another meeting to review progress. That was turned down and they came back with their compromise that the children take the other road and use the back gate. I pointed out that this was not a true compromise as the Glenbryn side would have got what they wanted, not because of a protest but because of a threat of a protest. They refused to see it that way and were adamant that they were going to go ahead."

Even given the impossibility of such an eleventh hour meeting brokering a deal, there was a huge underlying problem it could not possibly have resolved – the vexed question of whether future housing in North Belfast would be shared or segregated.

Liggett puts it this way, "There's a huge thing about territory. They wanted a wall right across Ardoyne Road to consolidate the land they have and permanently put a ring-fence around us, limiting our growth."

It emerged later that the UDA had engaged in a crude act of intimidation by leaving a potentially lethal pipe bomb on the road to Belfast Castle.

Mickey Liggett says that as the delegation was driving up the hill towards the Castle in Bill Shaw's car, he was already frightened. "I knew their side would include UDA people from Glenbryn and they might kick the crap out of me – if I was lucky. As we were driving up, we saw this thing in the road. Bill avoided his wheels hitting it. We carried on to the meeting but as we were leaving we heard via the police that it was a pipe bomb. There was a big public meeting in Ardoyne the next night. I reported back from Belfast Castle. Because of the attempt to bomb us, at secret talks that were supposed to be about making peace, I had to tell people that someone might die or get hurt the next morning."

When she heard about the device, Anne Bill says the CRUA delegation had believed it was a republican attempt to kill them. "If you look at it from our point of view, every person from CRUA was there (minus Potts), yet only three people from their group."

However genuine Anne Bill's fears, however, neither the police nor anyone else had any doubt that the bomb had been planted by the UDA. It was, if not an attempt to kill, at very least a very threatening signal.

Former Assistant Chief Constable Alan McQuillan says, "I firmly believe a faction within the group that signed up to the talks arranged for the pipe bomb to be dropped at the castle. It was intended to mess up the talks because that faction didn't want a resolution. It wasn't designed to attack anybody but it was certainly designed to send a message."

Once the protest began again on September 3, the prospect of a solution receded. As Liggett says, "We couldn't be seen going to meetings while the protest was continuing."

One politician who says he continued trying to dissuade the loyalist side from embarking on the protest was Fred Cobain. "The problem was that they didn't think it through before they started. That's why they got painted into a corner. From a publicity and practical point of view, it was a losing game for Protestants, there was just no way you could win. I explained all of that but people just weren't listening. It was going to play into the hands of paramilitaries. It was a disaster waiting to happen."

Meanwhile, during the fruitless talking, parents like Chris McDonald could only hope and pray. "You would hear the odd bit of good news and next thing that they didn't agree with the mediators or something else. Everybody was assured the school was going to open and we would be able to get the kids there safely. We were glad to hear Ronnie Flanagan's promise but also suspicious. We had heard promises before."

As the abortive talks continued, there were repeated attacks across the peace-line and elsewhere in North Belfast that nightmarish summer. Many of the attacks were ordered by John Gregg, a drum-beating, far-right wing UDA leader later killed in an internal feud.

On July 29, Gavin Brett, an 18-year-old Protestant, was murdered by the UDA in the suburb of Glengormley, three miles from Ardoyne. Loyalists in a car opened fire on a group of youths standing at the main entrance to St Enda's GAA grounds, assuming they were all Catholic. Brett's father, a paramedic who worked out of the Ardoyne ambulance depot, tried to resuscitate his dying son. The image of a parent grieving over the body of a stricken child seemed unbearably tragic. Protestant and Catholic churches held joint services. A church sexton was stabbed the night before the funeral when he tried to investigate suspicious activity near the graveyard. More than 100 colleagues of Brett's father attended the funeral in their ambulance service uniforms.

For many living in Ardoyne, the summer of 2001 was also particularly nightmarish. Families living on the Ardoyne/Glenbryn peace-line were particularly badly affected.

"We had petrol bombs thrown at the house when we were in bed and our windows were blown in by a pipe bomb next door," says Geraldine McGrandles, a softly spoken, welcoming woman. "There were bricks, stones, golf balls, everything that you could imagine thrown at us, every single night. As the summer went on, our houses were being attacked until three and four o'clock in the morning. They then began using petrol bombs. Half of the time I had to wake the kids in the middle of the night and take them to my husband's mammy.

"One petrol bomb landed where the kids' toys and bikes were stored and burnt the whole lot. I had to call for a neighbour to help put a fire out with an extinguisher. I phoned the cops and they told me off for not phoning when the petrol bomb hit, as if I shouldn't have got my kids out first. The police never came out although we waited for them until dawn. The few times they did arrive, they just said they couldn't 'catch the wee buggers' – those were their words. They said they didn't have enough men to sit in the street 24 hours. In the end I gave up phoning them. What was the point? I was taken to the hospital during one pipe bombing incident but my main injury was mental shock."

Geraldine's husband, Kieran, also has some hair-raising stories of that summer. "One night they (loyalists) started coming down the street attacking the houses, smashing the front windows. They used bricks and bottles, anything they could get their hands on. The cops told us that the loyalists were also getting attacked and were only retaliating. My wife asked them one day to compare the two sides and to see which side had their windows all boarded up. It was quite obvious which side was telling the truth."

Geraldine remembers seeing a neighbour running for her life from a gunman. The girl was only saved when the gun jammed. Normal life for Geraldine became impossible. Her washing machine was housed in a shed used as a utility room in the back garden. Her laundry, however, piled up because she was unable to reach the building through the incessant hail of bricks and bottles coming over from Glenbryn. She was hospitalised with a nervous breakdown in September, as her mother lay dying of cancer in the Belfast Hospice.

"You never had any peace whatsoever. Even when it was quiet you were still waiting on something coming in through the window. The Housing Executive put me into a hotel for a week and then I ended up in hospital for three weeks. We made the decision to move. We had to for the children's sake. My wee boy, who was seven, was so frightened he once lifted the phone to phone the police on his own. He was threatening to throw himself out the window. When we brought him to the hospital they said he was traumatised and we had to get him out (of the area). One night, a pensioner's shed was set alight with a petrol bomb. Kieran went up the street to put the fire out with a crowd of other fellas. The loyalists saw them and opened fire on them. I was standing in my garden and heard the gunfire. We thought some of them would be carried back dead. My wee boy was in total hysterics."

Chris McDonald also remembers a summer of chaos and misery. "There was gunfire, bombs, people getting shot in the face, fighting morning, noon and night. I was out once, fighting with them, in the middle of the night in my underwear. There was myself, a guy across the street and another from around the corner. It started with stones and ended with fist-fighting in our boxer shorts at five in the morning."

Another parent, Colette Cassidy, recalls, "They would tape coins to fireworks and throw them at us. Golf balls were a favourite missile. I gathered thousands. Everyone I know has a collection of golf balls with '2001' printed on them. There were also snooker balls thrown at us, they virtually rained down on you at times. They also threw broken roof slates from the derelict houses in Glenbryn."

The summer was ending. Nothing had been agreed. People were already beginning the blame game. Anne Bill believes the nationalist side deliberately blocked a resolution. "They started to see the possible benefits of a protest, that it would give them good publicity. We would be the side that looked bad."

Twinned with that awareness, however, is what seems to have been an article of faith in Glenbryn that their behaviour had no intrinsic ugliness. Instead there is the assertion, presented as a conviction, that the outcome in terms of bad publicity was not their fault. It is only a short step from this conclusion to saying blame for the hurt caused to the children lay with those parents who walked to school up the Ardoyne Road. As the loyalist side put it, for "forcing" their children through a dreadful ordeal.

Anne Bill says, "I think that they wanted the protest to continue. I think it was deliberate to avoid getting a compromise by September. They knew the schoolchildren would be in the middle of it and that their side would look good."

Progressive Unionist Party (PUP) assemblyman, Billy Hutchinson, also believes that nationalists deliberately refused to reach a solution for political purposes. "This could have been solved on the first day but the nationalist community wanted to make an issue of it. They didn't want it resolved."

There was a meeting in the Concorde Community Centre in Glenbryn the night before the new school term. Anne Bill says that, by then, a protest was inevitable and the only outstanding issues were placards and stewarding.

"We were trying to keep people calm. We just wished the school hadn't have been where it was. This was about our security and if other people wanted to say it was all about the school, then fair enough. People certainly weren't out for trouble. At the meeting that night they were saying they wanted everything to be peaceful. They wanted to keep things legal. Our assumption was that, if there was going to be a protest that Monday, the parents would automatically take their children through St Gabriel's. Nobody believed the parents would walk their children through our protest. Who would take their child by the hand and force them through a riot? It's just something that you wouldn't do."

At that last meeting, she says, the Glenbryn community believed the police would never, irrespective of what Sir Ronnie Flanagan had said, protect the parents and children through the area.

Pat Monaghan, a watchful woman who sometimes holds up her hands in a beseeching "why?" gesture, and who has lived in Ardoyne all her life, said it was the worst summer she could ever remember.

"I took myself off to the country because it was so bad, but I ended up sitting watching it all on TV and phoning the house constantly."

She eventually counted her losses and returned early. "It was the worst rioting for years. We could sense the real hatred up there in Glenbryn. There was a new crowd up there."

The ugly scene was set for the start of the new term.

Chapter Three

BACK TO SCHOOL

It was the first time I had ever seen young children frightened so witless that they had no comprehension of what was going on. There was fear and horror in their faces. They were barely able to speak.

Donal Flanagan, director, Catholic Council for Maintained Schools

People just flipped, totally lost the rag. There was shouting and yelling and fighting and pushing. Events had taken over. It was a total nightmare.

Anne Bill, committee member, CRUA

Castlereagh police command centre, East Belfast, in the early hours of September 3, 2001. Former Assistant Chief Constable Alan McQuillan and the Chief Constable, Sir Ronnie Flanagan, were watching closed circuit television pictures beaming in from the fierce rioting in North Belfast.

The two men knew the UDA was actively considering instigating a "second Drumcree" stand-off in North Belfast. Would it be possible, the two policemen wondered, to get the Holy Cross girls to school on the first day of their autumn term?

McQuillan finally said his view was that it was "absolutely critical" that the children get to school. Flanagan, who had already given his personal guarantee to the parents, agreed and promised any resources necessary.

"Do what you have to do," said Flanagan. "We will give you everything we have. Do everything you can to get them through." The two men agreed an absolute strategy. The children must get to school.

By the time daylight dawned over the road leading to Holy Cross school, the British Army was already hard at work building a barricade to protect the parents and children from the anticipated protest. At about 6.30am a siren, used by people from Glenbryn to alert them to the presence of soldiers, was sounded. They piled out of their homes to see what was going on.

September 3 was loyalist Michael Cosby's birthday, but the opening of presents and birthday cards had to wait until the afternoon. The siren woke him and he jumped out of bed. Dragging his clothes on, he stumbled downstairs, closely followed by his elder son who was hurriedly pulling on his trousers. As father and son ran onto the Ardoyne Road, the sight of troops building the steel barricade greeted them. Smiling at his own understatement, Cosby succinctly explains what they began to do next.

"We started dismantling it. The steel barricades were mounted on big heavy rubber bases. We lifted them up and threw them over a fence into Emmanuel church grounds. While we were doing so, the police beat us with batons. There was a lot of pushing and jostling. The police also used their riot shields to try to push us off the road. We were doing all we could to stop them erecting this barricade, this tunnel."

By the time Jim Potts arrived on the scene, there was already a hand-to-hand battle raging between the troops and around 70 to 80 loyalists. "People were hyped-up. I supported them fighting back, and still do to this day," he says.

The battle continued, but they knew the better-equipped police and soldiers would get the upper hand. "Army engineers were putting the fencing up and the police were protecting them. But we held them off for about three hours. Until about 9.30," says Cosby.

Another loyalist, Ronnie Black, was also up and about early. "When the sirens went off, there were cars running around all over the place, sounding their horns. Everybody came running out of their houses."

Stuart McCartney says when he got his emergency phone call to say the British Army had descended, his first thoughts were, "Oh God, they're going to try to push this through against the community's wishes. The shit is really going to hit the fan."

Community worker Anne Bill was also on the road by 7am. "I think the police had planned to build the barricade right up to the school, but they couldn't get it finished. Lads from Glenbryn had been lifting it up and throwing it out of the way."

People were angry, she says, that the British Army was being used to force the parents and children through the community.

"They didn't have the right to do it. How dare they? Despite everything that we had agreed the night before, people began to walk into the middle of the road."

The scene was set for a confrontation. Down the hill in Ardoyne, Lynda Bowes had gone to bed early. "I tossed and turned all night. I am not an overly religious person but I prayed we would, please, all get through it safe."

Jeanette McKernan says few in Ardoyne slept well that night. She woke shortly after 6am, hearing British Army helicopters overhead and the loyalist siren going off. Going for newspapers, she met a worker coming off nightshift who told her what the soldiers were doing on the Ardoyne Road. She wandered up the road a bit and saw the barricade.

"I wondered if I would have the courage to walk up. It looked like the loyalists would be able to see us, but not touch us. It might all be OK after all."

When Jeanette returned home, however, she vomited violently from fear, before waking her children, washing them, dressing them in their new uniforms and giving them breakfast. As she walked to rendezvous with other parents at the shops, she saw a woman she knew who had just inspected the barricade and had turned to return home with her daughter. The woman said McKernan "must be mad" to even think of walking up the Ardoyne Road.

Liz Murphy's Niamh (7) had gone to bed as normal the night before. "I had left out her new uniform and pencil case and she was fixing her school bag and nervously asking if we would be alright. None of us ate our breakfast that morning. We made tea and toast but I only took two sips because my stomach was doing somersaults. Niamh would normally eat a yoghurt but she just stuck it in her schoolbag."

Her husband, John, who had been listening to the radio news, quickly turned if off to avoid frightening Niamh. "As we went out the front door, we were like jelly. None of us knew what we were going up to, but we were trying to be brave."

Lynda Bowes' husband, who had left for work at about 7am, rang her from his car to say he had seen the police and soldiers building the barricade. She was reassured, thinking she would have no problem walking through a steel corridor.

Judy Haughey says her children, Cora and Lucilla (aged 11 and 10), were excited about going back to school that morning. "They couldn't wait to put on their new uniforms and their wee polished shoes and ribbons. At the same time, though, they were a bit frightened."

As the parents gathered to walk up the road in a large group, further towards the school, the protesters – many of them maddened and exhausted after three hours fighting with the police and British Army – were being pushed back. The loyalist crowd was in no mood to take it quietly. The police were also prepared for trouble.

"The police formed a line across the road, about three or four deep. It was like something out of a film," says Anne Bill. "They began beating up people and trampling pensioners to the ground. Hugh McGarry, who is blind, was standing in the middle of the road, where people had told him to stand, thinking he was legal. The next thing he was trailed into a police vehicle and taken away."

At the bottom of the Ardoyne Road, the group of parents and children had formed up on the other side of a solid metal blockade, made up of armour-plated sheets folding out of two British Army "Saracen" personnel carriers. The parents could not see up the road to establish what was awaiting them once they passed through. They were nervous, frightened and clutched their children, trying not to frighten them further.

Sharon McCabe, a cook, was amongst the crowd. "Word filtered down that the loyalists only wanted mothers and children to walk up. By then we could hear the protesters screaming. Our men were asking if the police were for real? They wouldn't dream of letting their wives and children walk up alone."

There was a stand-off for about 20 minutes with the parents and children milling around outside the army barricade. Father Troy tried to calm people down and asked that mothers only should accompany children to school that morning. The problem of fathers could be dealt with later.

Roisin Kennedy remembers the moment she had to decide whether to go on her own with Niamh, or take the back route with her father. "I told Daddy I was going up on my own but he said he wouldn't leave me. A policeman blocked him and said it was only one parent per child, so we decided to go home. Niamh, though, said she wanted to go to school so I started to walk. Usually it takes five minutes, but that day it felt like an absolute eternity."

Tanya Carmichael says they had specific reassurances from the police. "They told us they had totally screened the protesters off and that it would be peaceful. We would all be completely safe. I assumed the police would use the same kind of 30-foot high screens they erect on the Twelfth of July when the Orangemen pass the Ardoyne shops and that every street would be screened off. The police guaranteed they would protect us."

Lisa Irvine had also expected the familiar 30-foot screens. "I thought they'd be the massive screens they put up around us when loyalist parades pass by."

Like other parents, the first she saw of the barricade was after she crossed the Rubicon by walking through the British Army screens, onto the Ardoyne Road. "By the time we saw the little bit of plastic screen holding them back, it was too late to turn and run away."

As the parents began walking up the road, they suddenly realised the protection provided was woefully inadequate against the protesters gathered in the roadway and gardens on either side. The "barricade" amounted to waist high wire mesh fencing, topped off with a layer of thin clear plastic sheeting to about the height of the average adult. The entire structure was opaque so both sides could see and hear each other. First verbal abuse and then rocks, bricks and bottles began raining down on their heads.

Lisa Irvine said that, when the dam broke, she was utterly taken aback by "the hatred, sheer viciousness aimed at women and children".

"Their spit was running down the children's faces. It was disgusting. My child's coat was covered with spit. They were fighting to get at us, screaming, 'Scum! Scum! Scum!' and throwing bottles and bricks."

Pat Monaghan says the moment she began walking up the road it was "as if a big, black hole had opened".

"The RUC closed in behind us and the fathers were distracted when we disappeared from view. As we were being herded through, we realised that we were in a sort of tunnel, but it was only one-sided. There was no protection on the left-hand side whatsoever, bar two young soldiers. The loyalists were standing in the gardens and there's a slope running down to the footpath, so they were above us. They were leaning down and smacking people across the head. They were grabbing kids and mothers by the hair. They were using their fists and the backs of their hands and rolled up newspapers. One of the protesters was hitting a mother on the head with a magazine, it was the first time I'd ever seen a porn magazine. The small plastic barricade was on our right-hand side, but before we reached the second street, it ended and the crowd started to attack the children from both sides."

Liz Murphy says as soon as she saw the half-metal/half-plastic barricade she knew it wasn't enough. "At first, it was calm but tense, but as you reached the end, it was like a balloon bursting. They shouted every possible vile thing they could. The hatred was oozing out of them. They could even touch us by stretching through the police lines."

More than insults were hurled at Philomena Flood as she walked up with Eirinn (7). She alleges a political representative shouted that she was a "Provie bastard". Another loyalist shouted threats that she would "have a bullet in your head by tonight".

One parent says the scene at the end of the screen was "like the gates of hell opening".

"There were men, women and children screaming and spitting. We had to decide in a split second whether to go on or turn and run back. They were hurling abuse. They were trying to physically hit people. They were hanging over garden fences and walls, shouting, 'Paedophiles' at the priests."

Roisin Kennedy remembers, "A plastic tunnel thing and then, at the corner where the church is, it suddenly ended. A protester in a blue shirt shouted, 'You Fenian whore, take your brat back'. Niamh was in convulsions. The next thing, I saw an open bedroom window and a couple of children from Girls' Model (a local Protestant school) with their blazers on, throwing cups, saucers and lemonade bottles at us. I had my arms wrapped around Niamh holding her. I was crying too. A woman ran across at me shouting 'You in the denim skirt. You're a Fenian bastard. Get you and your stinking whore of a child off this road'."

As the violence began, fathers left behind at the British Army blockade suddenly realised what was happening. They burst through and began running towards the women and children. Half of Ardoyne was on the road by now. In the melee, uncles and friends also ran up the road.

"I remember pushing an RUC man out of my way," says Martin Monaghan. "Other fathers climbed over the top of the British Army Saracens and ran up the road to get to the school."

To confuse matters even further, some women and children had decided to try to run back down the road, away from the school. Martin Monaghan says he saw police officers lifting batons.

"I saw people being beaten with batons, pushed, shoved and hit. I think everything just collapsed in around the RUC. They hadn't prepared for this, they hadn't done their homework. All their years of training in riot control surely should have informed them those people shouldn't have been allowed on to the road at all. If it had been done properly, the way they treat us on the Twelfth of July, this wouldn't have happened."

Pat Monaghan says that as the men caught up with the women and children, the violent abuse worsened. "Our men could hear their wives and children screaming. We were running and falling, getting hit and spat at. The protesters were even calling the children 'whores' and shouting that they would burn the school to the ground. The RUC stood facing us like statues and never tried to stop them. The only time I saw any of the protesters being dealt with was when a young soldier hit one of them with his baton. They made no attempt to beat the ones attacking us."

Martin says the scenes he witnessed that morning were unprecedented, even for people who have lived through the Troubles. "The loyalists are capable of anything. They have no mercy."

At the school gates, there was pandemonium with mobile phones ringing, mothers screaming and children crying. There were cars and taxis arriving at St Gabriel's to get people out through the back entrance.

Sharon and Gerald McCabe, accompanying Gemma, had a particularly difficult time. "The screaming," says Sharon, "was barbaric, the filthy language and the insults. I could feel Gemma's nails sinking into the palm of my hand."

What finally got to Sharon was when an elderly man screamed in her face, "Get your bastard spawn off my road." She had her hands over Gemma's ears while her husband leant over them against the missiles raining down. Then a mother walking just behind the McCabes fainted. "She literally hit the ground," says Sharon. "She couldn't take it any more. Her child was screaming and Gerald lifted both of them and ran forward."

Martin Monaghan was standing beside Lily Whelan when she was hit with a rock. "One minute she was beside me and the next blood was pouring out of her. She'd been struck on the head. It was madness. Kids were running into the school, up the hill, and being put straight into cars and taken out the back. It was a constant flow of people. There was hand-to-hand fighting at the school gates. There were bricks and bottles being thrown by loyalists trying to get in. The cops were beating fathers who'd already been beaten all the way up by protesters.

"We were getting it from all directions. There was a sound like shooting that turned out to be firecrackers. We shouted to the teachers to hit the buttons and bring the school shutters down. Then somebody said not to, in case the school went on fire and we couldn't get through the windows. The worst was the children, you can't allow someone to attack your children but it was difficult to defend yourself. Many parents moved their children to take the blows themselves."

By the time she reached the school gates, Roisin Kennedy could take no more. It came into her head that if she made it to the school, she would not get out alive. After confronting a police officer, she walked back down to the British Army barricade and Niamh was reunited with her father. "He lifted the child up in his arms and I just fell apart."

Roisin then decided to take the back road, up the Crumlin Road, to help evacuate the children that way. "Where the bravery came from, I just don't know."

On the Crumlin Road, she says, there were people grabbing children and putting them into black taxis. "The loyalists were throwing bricks over the gates. They were throwing chairs, tables with the legs broken off. Anything they could carry to throw at us."

Brendan Mailey had double trouble that morning. Not only did he have to get his daughter, Rachel (8), to school safely, he was also the main spokesman for the Right to Education committee.

"People just did not expect the hate, the rage, and the bigotry. You were standing with your six-year-old in your arms, screaming and crying that she wanted to go home, and you couldn't turn back. The horror and terror of it is very hard to explain. I was petrified, so what must a child have felt? They (loyalists) were allowed to stand within arms-reach of us. If this had happened to black kids in England, it wouldn't have lasted an hour. We were also caught in the middle. Journalists were forever asking us if we wanted the protesters beaten off the road. We didn't want that, because we've been getting beaten off roads ourselves for over thirty years."

He and other parents claim they personally witnessed two unionist politicians joining in the abuse. "Two elected representatives! Along with the rest of the UDA mob? You just shake your head in disgust. We felt totally powerless. There were lines of cops, fully armed with riot shields and batons, hundreds of them standing around, letting bigoted thugs terrorise children."

Donal Flanagan, director of the Catholic Council for Maintained Schools, witnessed parents and children arriving at Holy Cross gates that morning.

"It was a horror I hope never to see again. It is a memory that continues to haunt me. It wasn't just a protest, this was pure hatred, driven by a revulsion towards the Catholic community in general and the children in particular."

While parents were trying to come to terms with the rush of events, some community leaders on the loyalist side were also in a state of shock.

Jim Potts has the honesty to admit that his temper had "got the better" of him. "I tried hard to have dialogue over the summer. The people in Ardoyne failed us. Now here we were, in our own community, being beaten off the streets. I was so angry I didn't notice the children. It was infuriating to have nationalists come up the road, making faces, laughing, joking and winding people up. I lost my temper and began shouting. It was shown on television. It never happened again."

Another loyalist in a potential leadership position that day was Billy Hutchinson of the PUP, then Assembly member for the area.

"I had warned them it would be fatal if they didn't decide in advance how they were going to run the protest. I said there needed to be a strategy, so that everybody knew what they were doing. Otherwise they would be in trouble and anybody who wanted could use them. I still hold the RUC responsible. They were heavy-handed. They beat people into taking up positions. They didn't plan for what happened and then had to react as quickly as possible."

Stuart McCartney also has the grace to admit he was horrified at what was unleashed that day. The language disgusted him. "There's no call for it, nobody can justify it. You can use that language to the parents but not the children."

Does he accept that his community had brutalised itself? "I don't think a lot of people were deep enough to realise it. I was crying. I stood there in tears. There was absolutely fuck-all I could do about it."

That night, there was again intense rioting on the streets of North Belfast and angry pubic meetings both in Ardoyne and Glenbryn.

"In Glenbryn," Anne Bill says, "people went totally ballistic. They wanted solicitors brought in to take statements from people who had been beaten. How dare the police drive people through our area? There were a few who suggested calling it off, but most said no way should we give in, we definitely couldn't back down now."

One man who was not surprised by the events of September 3, however, was Presbyterian minister, the Rev Norman Hamilton. "I think once the talks broke down during the summer, there was a sense of dark inevitability about it. Maybe I was tuned in to the feelings of the community, maybe I could see it coming. I was distressed but I certainly wasn't surprised. I remember doing an interview for the BBC and standing in the middle of the street and weeping. I suppose it was seeing the inevitable slide into massively fractured relationships happening, irresistibly, before your eyes. Then the impact of that on individuals, on kids, on parents, on families."

In Ardoyne, says Brendan Mailey, the meeting was packed. Amongst others, Father Troy, Anne Tanney and some of the St Gabriel's staff were there. A suggestion that the children should walk up the Crumlin Road was rejected by a large majority. This being Ardoyne, there were angry demands that the IRA take defensive action, but cooler heads argued against. The prevailing mood, says Mailey, was that the community had been through over 30 years of violence and there was no way the loyalists were going to dictate their own terms. There was also concern about the knock-on effect it might have if the Holy Cross parents backed down.

Former Sinn Fein councillor, Gerard McGuigan, a member of the Holy Cross board of governors, said if people wanted to go up the Crumlin road, that was fine. If they wanted to use the Ardoyne Road, that was fine also.

"The ones who are in the wrong here," he said, "are the loyalist protesters. What you do with your child is your decision. That is your right."

The agony in Father Troy's face was clear to everyone. "He was in a terrible position. He had seen the hatred in the loyalists' faces and was genuinely concerned a child might be killed," says one parent.

Ardoyne Road next morning was ankle-deep in broken bricks and molten metal from torched cars. People living along the peace-line were, once again, deprived of much needed sleep. In homes throughout the area, mothers and fathers agonised about whether they should take their daughters to school up the Ardoyne Road, or take the longer road through "the back door". One of them was Lisa Irvine.

"For me it wasn't an issue. I believe in equal rights and what they were doing was completely wrong. I knew in my heart that we had to stand up for ourselves. We could take a longer road, through another loyalist area, making us late for work, sneaking in through a muddy field. Or we could put our heads up in the air and say that it was our right to walk to school the same way we had done for 32 years. We had already walked up the Crumlin Road to school in June. The loyalists had laughed at us, driving down in their cars, pointing and shouting insults. I said no. No, I am not going to be humiliated like this. No one was going to pigeon-hole me and tell my daughter that we are second-class citizens. I am proud of Shannon. It's an important lesson to stand up to bullies and not to run away."

There are differing views on what took place on the second day of the protest, September 4. Police tactics had obviously changed. The useless metal/plastic barricade was gone and it appeared that, in its place, were massive numbers of police and British Army vehicles, bumper-to-bumper, along the road. The problem arose because the vehicles were not close enough, even bumper-to-bumper. There were gaps between them through which the protesters could see and even reach the children. And the children could see the protesters.

Chief Superintendent Roger Maxwell, the officer in charge of policing North Belfast, says the gaps had a purpose. "Police officers have to be able to get from one side of their Land Rovers to the other. Say there are two on each side of the vehicle and a difficulty arises on one side, the other two have to be able to get round to deal with it. There were practical reasons for the gaps. It was certainly not the case that we deliberately allowed some space so the protesters could shout and throw things at the children."

Liz Murphy says the second day was as bad as the first. The loyalists, infuriated at being kept further back, "went mad". She says, "I remember looking up at them and you could see the word 'bastards' coming from the pits of their stomachs."

Sean Carmichael says, "The second day was more verbal abuse. They were screaming at us that we were Fenian bastards and they would burn the school and kill us."

His wife Tanya says the parents began putting the children in the middle, leaving themselves on the outside of the procession. "Children were sandwiched between their parents who tried to distract their attention from the protesters."

The third day, however, was something else again. The day of the bombing.

Chapter Four

PROTEST

I have heard people say you cannot put fear into words. They are right. You really, really can't.
Lynda Bowes, parent

Get back to your rat-holes and your paedophile priests, you Fenian scum.
Loyalist protester

By now, the sectarian violence gripping North Belfast had claimed another young victim. On September 4, Protestant teenager Thomas McDonald had been killed by a car driven by a Catholic woman about three miles away from Ardoyne. There was fury throughout loyalist North Belfast.

McDonald was killed after throwing a half-brick at the windscreen of a vehicle being driven by 33-year-old Alison McKeown, a Catholic mother of six. She was later convicted of manslaughter and sentenced to two years in jail. At her trial, where she pleaded guilty to manslaughter, the judge said he did not accept her claim that she had only intended to frighten Mr McDonald and ruled that she had intended to cause him harm in "an impulsive moment". He said, however, he believed her actions were "not the manifestation of sectarian hatred".

The following day, the parents of Holy Cross showed respect for the McDonald family's grief by delaying their walk to the school for 20 minutes so Glenbryn residents could hold a prayer meeting on the road. They then arranged their own inter-denominational prayer meeting.

On the loyalist side, the protest of September 5 began more quietly than the previous two days. The police had again changed tactics. "Each of us now had a designated policeman with a protective shield they held over our heads. He never left you," says Lynda Bowes.

But it was not only the police who had changed tactics. "There were fewer protesters around and, as we began walking through, they began a slow hand-clap which I thought was very odd," recalls Liz Murphy.

Tina Gallagher agrees. "That morning was generally very quiet. There was hardly a sound out of the loyalist protesters, but as we were walking up, they started to clap very slowly."

Sean Carmichael also remembers the slow hand-clap. "We were thinking we could live with that. Fair enough. Then all of a sudden there was a rain of bricks and people panicked."

Worse was to come. Martin Monaghan had noticed that the gaps between the police vehicles were widening, enough for protesters to slip through. "There were jeeps missing here and there. There was no solid row of RUC men with batons and shields, whereas the previous morning they had been thickly lined the whole way up. I have major questions about why, on that particular day, the RUC left gaps where the loyalists could get through."

The two most senior police officers in charge, Alan McQuillan and Roger Maxwell, say none of their men even noticed a change in loyalist tactics. The sequence of events was as follows: the children and parents walked through the British Army metal blockade; the metal "wings" closed and they were now out of sight of those waiting behind; the slow hand-clapping began. A fusillade of loyalist bricks and other missiles rained down from overhead. The policeman walking beside Lynda and Amanda Bowes reached out with his right hand.

"He grabbed me by the arm," Lynda says, "and pulled me right in beside him. He pulled his shield up over our heads and the bricks bounced off it. He was crouching me down, shouting – and then the protesters started to clap again, very slowly."

Other police officers moved in to push the brick-throwers down a side street. A few seconds later, the bomb was thrown from the cover of the protesters towards the parents and children, falling amongst the lines of police. The Rev Norman Hamilton and the Moderator of the Presbyterian Church, Dr Alastair Dunlop, were standing together on a high patch of ground in a garden overlooking the spot where the bomb exploded.

"I saw it as soon as it hit the ground," says Hamilton. "It was rolling towards the kerb.

I saw the fizz and smoke coming out of it. I turned to Dr Dunlop and said, 'That's a bomb. We've got ten seconds'. There was nothing more I could do, there were two lines of police between me and the bomb."

The Presbyterian Moderator himself says he did not have time to be frightened before the bomb exploded, although he will never forget the fear on the children's faces.

Liz Murphy first knew of the bomb when it exploded. "It was as if your insides had shattered. I ran for all I was worth. My heart was beating wildly. Niamh was crying and shouting. Everybody was running about screaming. It was like a horror movie."

Elaine Burns says, "I can remember Father Gary (Donegan) grabbing my arm and saying, 'Run to the gates of the school'. It was chaos."

Sean Carmichael says, "I felt Emma's hand gripping mine very tightly. The next minute there was a large bang, not far from us. A police dog was hit and bolted in front of us and I nearly fell over it. A memory that will always stick with me was when I turned round and saw a fella I went to school with, Chris McDonald, and his wife. They were in the middle of the road, frozen to the spot with fear, and had their arms wrapped around their child. People were shouting at them to get down. We knew how bad the loyalists were, we had lived with them for generations, but never would I have thought they would stoop so low as to throw a pipe bomb at children."

Martin Monaghan says, "Everyone started to panic, parents and children were running all over the place, some were lying on the ground covering their children and the children were screaming. Other parents tried to run back down the road to safety. There were parents and kids stuck in the middle, not knowing where to go. The RUC just scattered."

Lisa Irvine describes how the police told her to get down. "You were afraid to look behind you in case there were people lying dead. I grabbed my child and ran like hell."

Roisin Kennedy was with a Channel 4 cameraman when the bombers struck. "He had asked if he could walk with me and I said it was no problem. For some reason it was unusually quiet. It was dead eerie. Then all of a sudden, the Channel 4 man shouted, 'Duck!' He had seen stones flying over. Niamh and I hit the ground. The next thing was the bang. Even now I can still hear that bang. I froze on the spot but the cameraman grabbed my arm. I wrapped my arms around Niamh's neck and ran. If that guy hadn't grabbed my arm when he did, I think I would have collapsed. He was still holding his camera and running backwards, pulling me by the arm and shouting, 'Just keep running'."

The three of them made it to the school grounds. Roisin says the cameraman still keeps in contact.

Tina Gallagher claims she saw a unionist representative smiling in the immediate aftermath of the explosion and, beside herself with rage, threw herself at a police vehicle to try and get at him.

"I wanted to kill him. He just stood and smirked at us. The unmerciful screams of the kids were truly horrific. My eldest daughter, Roisin, felt the rush of air coming from the explosion and was almost knocked off her feet."

September 5 was David and Maura Lindsay's daughter's tenth birthday. Maura says, "We were all gathered like a load of cattle at the top of Alliance Avenue, standing waiting to get through. All of a sudden there was a real slow and steady clap. Then bricks came flying towards us and we ducked down and put our hands over the kids' heads. Father Troy was just in front of us telling people to protect themselves. Then the bomb went off. David scooped Amy up in his arms and run. Women were screaming, children were screaming, cops were screaming. I turned to see if there was anyone I could help and a big policeman ran into me and screamed into my face, 'Fucking run, and keep moving'. When we got to the school the teachers were crying and hugging everybody. I was vomiting, violently sick. Anne Tanney came running down, very upset. The sight of women and kids coming up that hill was something I will never forget. Even the men were crying because of the state of their kids. There were kids who were absolutely screaming and their parents were using all their strength to try to calm them down. Everybody was hugging each other. We thought they could stoop no lower until that day."

Her husband, David, said it was the lowest point. "Getting verbal abuse is one thing but to actually have a bomb thrown at you ... They said the bomb wasn't aimed at the parents and kids, that it was designed for the cops. I don't believe them."

Lynda Bowes says her daughter, Amanda, had been quite phlegmatic until the bombing. "Now she was hysterical. I told myself they could fuck their road, we wouldn't be walking up it again. They could have it, if they were prepared to do that to keep it."

Maura Lindsay saw the same unionist representative that Tina Gallagher saw, appearing to be smiling after the bombing. "He stood in a doorway and the smirk on his face was unbelievable. I am convinced that the crowd of protesters knew that there was going to be an attack. It was the way they behaved. It was different from the other days, it was as if they had known and were just waiting for it to happen."

Up in Stormont, Fred Cobain heard the news of the bombing coming through. "It was horrendous, but you have to expect that sort of thing when a crowd gathers and tensions are high. If you throw a bomb then you are prepared to kill, that is how high the stakes are. The dynamics of the crowd take over if nobody thinks straight in those circumstances."

Elaine Burns praises the teachers. "They took the children into their classrooms quickly so they couldn't see how upset we all were. They clapped their hands and had smiley faces and told them to be quick and get to class."

Back home in Ardoyne, Pat Monaghan, who was not feeling well, was watching television and saw the explosion, knowing her husband and child were there. "You could see the blast on the TV, then you heard the actual explosion. I grabbed my coat and ran."

From where the British Army barricade was sealing the road, people stood and watched and waited to hear if anyone had been hurt or killed. Miraculously, no one was killed but two policemen were injured, one seriously, while a police dog was also hurt by flying shrapnel.

The loyalists tell a different story. People like Amanda Johnston simply do not accept the bomb was intended to hurt or frighten the children. "It was nowhere near those girls. It was aimed at the policemen because they had pushed children and prams over. People had had enough."

Jim Potts denies claims that the protesters had any idea the bomb was going to be thrown. "I was standing quite close to the explosion. I was absolutely taken by surprise along with everyone else. I think the only people who knew it was going to happen were those who planned it. My first thought was shock, but asking questions afterwards we were told and assured that it wasn't directed at the children. It was directed at the RUC because of the brutal way they were treating the Protestant people.

The RUC were targeting men from the lower Shankill who had come to help. They recognised them as being dangerous. They deliberately targeted people who came into this community to support us. Those who threw the bomb said they felt frustrated because the protest wasn't working. My own personal response was that I was comfortable with the explanation they gave me."

But couldn't it have killed a parent or a kid? "I don't accept that. It wasn't close enough," says Potts.

But hadn't Billy Hutchinson's response been completely different, hadn't he said he was ashamed to be a loyalist that day? "What Billy said was his own immediate reaction. On reflection Billy retracted that statement. Billy wasn't allowed time to gather his own thoughts. He was immediately confronted by the media and he gave his own gut feeling."

Had the bombing "worked" in Potts' view? "It was discussed openly that the bomb had weakened the protest, that it had reverted to violence. Everyone had their own way of reacting, and I respect that, but that wasn't my reaction."

Jim Potts' equanimity over the bombing was not shared by Anne Bill, who says she was, personally, devastated by it. "When I realised that the bomb was thrown from people in our community, I stood and cried in the street. Nigel Dodds (Democratic Unionist Party, or DUP, MP for North Belfast), Mark (Coulter, another CRUA committee member) and I stood outside the house on the corner of Hesketh Park and cried. I was gutted. The thought that something could have happened to the children. That was the last thing you wanted to happen. It was just madness. How could anyone be stupid enough to do something like that when you were trying to make a case?"

Billy Hutchinson was standing beside Dodds and Nelson McCausland, a DUP councillor, in the garden of a house where raised ground gave them a vantage point. The bomb went off 50 yards away.

"My immediate reaction," says Hutchinson, "was one of disgust that it had been thrown at children. I know people say it wasn't, but it was thrown when children were coming up the road. People might argue that it was clearly thrown at the RUC, but it doesn't really matter who it was thrown at. OK, it was a dog that was injured, it wasn't a child, but it makes no difference."

Contrary to popular report, Hutchinson says he never withdrew his comment that he was "ashamed to be a loyalist" after the bombing. "I said it and I didn't take it back. I don't know why people say anything different. I left Ardoyne that day and went to see senior members of our party in the Shankill central office. Later, I said I shouldn't have walked away, but I never took back that I had been ashamed to be a loyalist. In my view the bomb should never have been thrown in a situation where there were children, Catholic or Protestant."

Michael Cosby says, "The bombing was bad, bad. People told them not to do it again. But it hadn't exploded near the children, it was well down the street."

The aftermath, he says, was very difficult in Glenbryn. Throughout the day, the police "went in and wrecked houses, beat women, beat kids, beat anything that moved". Other loyalists back this up, but the police deny it.

Ronnie Black believes the bombing was a "message" to the police. "You had people getting beat every night. I suppose the pipe bomb was the paramilitaries telling them to back off, or we'll come at you. At nights, the police softened up after the bomb. During the day, they still stood on the road as hard as ever – but at night they scaled down. They knew if they came in at night, the paramilitaries were going to come out. It was transparent. The police knew they could get away with being heavy-handed during the day, but if they were heavy at night, they would take flak from the paramilitaries."

The police themselves believe the bomb was aimed at them. "It appeared to be skittled up the road towards us. It wasn't actually thrown over our heads. I think it was meant for us, I really do," says Chief Superintendent Maxwell.

But why was the bomb thrown while the children were on the road and not when police guard was down? "That was the only time we moved forward against them at that junction," says Maxwell.

And did his men hear the slow hand-clap, did they think it was a signal? "The men on the ground can't say they noticed that, but then they were in full riot gear with helmets on and radios in their ears, so maybe that accounts for it."

Alan McQuillan adds, however, "I have no doubt there were people within that crowd who, if they could have got a bomb over, would have been quite happy to throw it at the kids."

The Rev Norman Hamilton says the bulk of the protesters wanted nothing to do with the bombing and managed to get that message across in the immediate aftermath.

"But," he continues, "within five seconds of the explosion, whatever credibility their case previously had, had evaporated. They were never able to recover that ground."

There was a hidden irony in the bombing. Jim McClean, the "man up the ladder" was on the scene and saw the whole thing from a rather closer vantage point than he would have liked.

"I was just behind it as it blew up. My wee girl, Jamie-Lee, she was four, was on the pavement. If it had landed in the middle of the road, the blast would have gone everywhere, 360 degrees. But it didn't. It rolled into the kerb. The blast went out 180 degrees instead. My mate was standing in a garden and his hat was blown off his head by the force of it. All the metal went out one side. If it hadn't, it could have killed my kid. There were people definitely trying to find out who it was, because they were angry. That's why there was no repeat. People stopped it, it only happened once. I saw the kids crying on the television, the fear on their faces. It made me feel bad, to a certain extent – but I was closer to it than they were. If I had been with them I would have been frightened for my life, but the bomb wasn't intended to be for the parents or the kids, it was for the police."

From personal observations on the day of the bombing, it seems the hail of missiles from Glenbryn was closely followed by a police move towards those responsible. The bomb followed. Had the missile-throwers not already been pushed slightly back away from the cavalcade of parents and children in the few seconds before the blast, the bomb would almost certainly have landed amongst them instead of a few feet away. It would then inevitably have caused injury or even death. This leaves open the possibility that it was intended to kill the children, not policemen.

The certainty loyalists and police have that the bomb was intended for the RUC, not the children, is matched by the parents' conviction of the opposite. Why, they ask, was it thrown as parents and children were walking up the road to school? Why not at some other time when the police would have been less alert? If the bomb was not intended to, at worst, terrify the children, why was it thrown while they were passing, as opposed to when parents were walking back down the road unaccompanied, after leaving their children at school?

Judy Haughey's views are typical. "I really don't believe for a minute it was thrown at the cops. Why wait until the kids were present? They had a mountain of opportunities to do it while the kids weren't there. They were always trying to make up excuses to justify themselves but they could never have justified throwing a bomb at young children. It was one of their final attempts to force us off the road."

Roisin Kennedy says it was "sick" to try to claim anything else than that the target was the children. "It seemed to me they had it timed exactly right. The slow hand-clap was a sign for the bombers that we were on our way up the road. Once the clapping stopped, they threw the bomb. It was timed perfectly. If they had thrown it any higher, it would have landed in the crowd and caused devastation."

As Liz Murphy made her way back on September 5, she says an elderly woman shouted at her from Glenbryn, "It's a pity their fucking legs weren't blown off."

In Ardoyne that night, parents had to decide what explanation to give their children. Elaine Burns decided to keep the truth from her two daughters.

"I decided to say the noise was only fireworks to celebrate Niamh's first day at school. Later, though, it came on the news. Normally I tried to stop them watching the news, but this night they saw it and challenged me. I said the television had it wrong, it was a big firework, and they seemed to accept it and went off to play."

It made some parents more determined than ever to see the protest through but others felt they had had enough. Judy Haughey said she was alternately "angry, frightened, emotional, dazed and confused".

"But most of all I would say angry. I began calling those people everything. I really did hate them. I also felt very sad and very let down. We were being treated like nobodies. I felt really hurt, most people did. It got to the point of thinking that the effort wasn't worth it and that I would not bring my kids up again because their lives are more important than their education. What could I do? Move out of this district altogether? Or do I stick with it, with the people of this community, and fight for our rights? It is a terrible way to live – but when against the wall, you have to make hard decisions."

One couple who were not on the road during the bombing the McKernans. Some sixth sense appears to have warned them. Jeanette McKernan was talking to friends on the evening of September 4, just after Thomas McDonald's death. One told her a BBC reporter had informed him that the UDA was bent on revenge, that the gloves were off. Jeanette and her husband decided then and there that they would keep their children off school the next day. "That is what we did. That was the day of the bombing," says Jeanette.

The bombing was the most deadly physical attack. There were other forms used later that have also left psychological scars. If the protesters had no intention of frightening the children, they went a strange way about it. Tina Gallagher says one tactic to instil fear was the use of masks.

"They took to wearing false faces of devils and ghouls. There were some funny ones but, taken in context, they weren't funny. You could say a clown mask is funny, but in that context it was also scary. They had Freddie Krueger and vampire masks that frightened the kids. They also zipped their coats right up with hoods or scarves over their faces."

Another, and most unpleasant, tactic was the throwing of balloons full of urine. Loyalists deny it ever happened, saying parents are either mistaken or lying, while insisting that only water balloons were thrown. Liz Murphy, however, is just one who claims they did contain urine.

"The balloon broke at my feet. I had grey trousers on and it went all over me. I thought, frig that, they hit me with a water balloon. As I started to walk on I asked John what the strange smell was. Danny Burns had previously been hit with a urine balloon and he told me it smelt the same. I never felt so sick and degraded. I went home and lay in a bath for ages. I felt filthy. There's no question that it was urine because John told me he smelt it too, a horrible, disgusting smell."

Sharon McCabe says that sometimes the urine was thrown in small plastic bags. "I was in the middle of one of the urine attacks. It didn't seem to be in a balloon but in a bag, like one of those bags you see goldfish in as prizes at fairs. It hit in front of me, splashed up my legs and hit someone else full force. People started screaming because it was a yellow colour and we thought it was petrol. I remember the person who was hit saying everything was OK because it wasn't petrol, only urine. Although it was sick, at least we knew someone couldn't throw a lighter at us and set us on fire."

Lisa Irvine also remembers that, when the first urine balloons came over, she thought it was petrol and that they were all going to be incinerated. "It was splashing all around our feet. They had been throwing fireworks and we thought we were all going to go up in flames."

Roisin Kennedy, who was also hit with a urine balloon, says the spit was just as bad. "One day Hilda Booth was walking in front of me and she got full spittle in her face. My stomach was just heaving. Hilda just wiped it off and walked on."

Maura Lindsay also says the throwing of urine was a routine occurrence. "The smell was like raw ammonia. I don't know exactly how much was thrown but you would have thought there were bucket-loads. That is how strong the smell was. The protesters would all laugh and think it was totally hilarious."

Frances Doherty thinks the urine attacks were a response to how the parents were persevering. "The more abuse the protesters were giving the parents, the stronger we were getting. The more insults the kids took every morning, the more they threw at us. Once the balloons burst open on impact, it was quite obvious they contained urine, the smell would have knocked you out. I put my hand to my face and nearly threw up when I smelt it."

Even children, she says, were hit with urine. "One day, a girl walking beside me was hit with a urine balloon. It hit her right on the face. She was saturated, she was screaming."

Martin Monaghan says when urine was thrown the first time, one of the parents shouted out, "They have thrown acid." A protester shouted back at her, "No we wouldn't waste that on you. It's fucking piss."

Even amidst such horror, Belfast humour wins out. Martin tells of a friend who always seemed to get hit with whatever was going, particularly tins of Coke. The parents used to ask him to go first up the road as a decoy, so everyone else could see what was in the protesters' arsenal that day.

Judy Haughey says the protesters threw virtually anything they could get their hands on. "Every day there were full cans of coke thrown at us, cups of hot tea and scalding water."

Another unpleasant ordeal was listening to the language used by the protesters. Amongst the phrases regularly heard were the following: "Your kids are all Fenian sluts", "Your kids are fucking stinking" and "Your kids have all got nits."

It was worrying for the parents that the UDA in Glenbryn could identify them individually. "One day they didn't know who you were," says one parent, "the next they knew your name and where you lived. It wasn't just Joe Soap of Glenbryn who knew our names, the people doing the shouting were well-known paramilitaries."

Cruelly, the protesters would pick out the physical characteristics of individual parents and children to shout insults at them. This was intended, obviously, to humiliate but had the added sting of telling parents that their names were known to the protesters, and by extension, the UDA.

One child was called "Dumbo" because of her ears. Meanwhile, John Murphy, whose wife Liz admits "carries some weight" was taunted with "Here comes Mr fucking Blobby, ugly bastard."

"He got this regularly," recalls Liz. "There was this one girl in particular who made a beeline for John every morning shouting, 'You fat ugly bastard'. She began to mimic his walk, keeping alongside him, mocking and humiliating him."

A regular chant was "Scum! Scum! Scum!" amidst other discernible cries of "You dirty stinking whores, get off our road" and "Your men are whore masters." Protesters would target children ("You don't know who your fathers are"), mothers ("You don't know who your kid's Da is") and fathers ("That's not your kid").

On the first day of term, Maura Lindsay had turned back with Amy after it all got too much and the child had broken down in tears. As she went, an elderly female protester shouted at her, "Go on, you Fenian whore you. You didn't get your child to school today did you, you fucking bastard?"

Maura was, to say the least, taken aback. "I stopped in my tracks, I couldn't believe what I was hearing. I was in absolute shock."

Several parents report that their daughters asked them what the word "whore" meant. It put the parents in a dilemma, not wanting to destroy even more of their child's innocence, but not wanting to tell lies either. A lot of the abuse was sexually explicit, and this extended to the use of pornographic images onto which photographs of individual parents were sometimes superimposed. The colour photographs, on glossy paper (presumably torn out of *Playboy*-style magazines) showed full-frontal naked women, and sometimes men, which were glued onto wooden boards and pushed out between the police jeeps into the faces of the children and parents. The parents whose photographs were superimposed are unclear where they came from. Some suspect from police files, although there is no evidence for this.

The two Holy Cross priests, Father Troy and Father Donegan, also came in for particular attention. Placards accusing them, by name, of paedophilia were held up.

Jeanette McKernan was shocked. "They would shout things like 'They're all Father Troy's children', meaning literally 'Father Troy is a child molester' and 'Father Troy gets the kids over the desks in the classrooms'."

Lisa Irvine remembers "a large poster of a very overweight naked lady with one of the parents' names written across the top of it".

"It was thrust in our faces in full view of the children," she says.

There was also homophobic abuse. David Lindsay remembers a woman who used to repeatedly call him "pretty boy" and shout that she was "sure the priests loved you when you were a kid", along with "Did Father Troy ride you?"

Brendan Mailey remembers a protester shouting, "Your Ma is a whore", and "Father Troy is screwing your fucking Ma." He says he heard children being told to get back to their "rat holes" and their "paedophile priests".

Tina Gallagher remembers hearing "You dirty Fenian bastards, get off our fucking road", and "Your children are all sluts". She says she also heard things like "You are all riding priests and they have fathered all of your children."

Liz Murphy remembers the day she saw a protester holding up a photograph, taken from a magazine, of a naked woman with a blown-up photograph of her husband's head and shoulders superimposed. "John was angry, saying if they wanted to be that sick, they should do it when the children aren't around."

Their daughter, Niamh, saw it and asked what her daddy's face was doing on the poster? Liz tried to brush it off by saying it was a photograph taken in a hall of mirrors at a fairground. Niamh asked again about it later that night. The couple knew it was preying on her mind.

Roisin Kennedy says the protesters threw pornographic photographs out onto the road at the children. "These were real dirty X-rated pictures of naked women."

One day she had reacted particularly badly to the abuse. "I was really wrecked and Father Troy was holding my arm. I was shaking from head to toe. They shouted over to us, 'There is the father and his whore'. I cried the whole way down the road. I actually felt sick. I felt so degraded for both Father Troy and myself. I knew then the protesters were demented. The two priests were heartbroken. Then the death threats started against them."

Much of the most abusive and sexually explicit language came from the women protesters, something that mother Sharon McCabe found particularly hard to accept.

"The men were bad but sometimes you can expect bad language from a man. To hear it from a woman, being a mother myself, was just awful. I still find it hard to accept that mothers screamed those obscenities at us. The venom came from the pits of their stomachs. We just couldn't understand where all that anger and frustration came from."

She remembers female protesters throwing playing cards portraying naked women and other photos onto the road. "They were shouting things like, 'Is that you, slut?' They were pictures of obscene naked women in certain poses. They seemed to have different themes. One day it was the urine and another day pornography, and so on."

Father Gary Donegan also remembers the placards directed against him and Father Troy. "If I stood in Belfast city centre with a placard saying, 'So and so is a paedophile', I would be arrested, rightly. These people were standing openly with these things. In fact Aidan's name was printed on one of them. One guy shouted to me, 'Newtownbutler priest. PAL 4029. We are coming to get you'. They didn't know my name but they knew the village where I came from and the registration number of my car.

"One day, there were women crying. I asked them what was wrong and it became apparent they were crying over us, their priests, being insulted. They were so hurt. All I could tell them was not to worry about us. Then there were the masks. I never thought they could be so intimidating, but the sillier they were, the stranger and more sinister the effect it had on you. Then there was the mask using a photo of Johnny Adair on it, wearing a woollen cap. The man wearing it would pull it off his face every now and again and shout 'Boo' right in the children's faces. There was a song at the time, 'Who let the dogs out?' and the protesters would wear dog masks and chant it at us. They shouted out people's names. There was purple dye in some of the urine balloons. There were firecrackers thrown. I remember one going off beside a child and the total mayhem that had caused."

Philomena Flood remembers a day when a woman protester held up a pornographic picture of a naked woman and shouted at her child, Eirinn, "This is the way your mammy dresses for Father Troy."

Martin Monaghan corroborates this account. "I heard them shouting at Philly Flood's wee girl, 'Father Troy is your fucking Da' and 'Your Ma is screwing the priest'."

His wife Pat says, "They had signs up reading 'Paedophile Priests' and 'Watch your children'. Any mother walking alongside Father Troy would be accused of 'screwing the priest'." Pat was herself referred to as "Father Troy's slag."

She also remembers cut-outs from porn magazines being held up to accompanying shouts of "This is what you are, you are sluts and whores"; and "You are the priests' whores".

Chris McDonald says the photographs were not limited to women. "There were posters of naked men with Father Troy's face imprinted on them."

Father Troy confirms he personally witnessed the use of pornographic photos. "Some of them appeared laminated, they weren't just crumpled bits of paper. They were maybe A4 or a bit bigger, almost like cardboard, like mounted photographs. I definitely saw pornographic pictures. I certainly didn't examine them because I was absolutely horrified, but definitely they were there. They were large enough for me to see. That's a terribly important point because if they were vivid enough for me to see, from the road to the other side of a jeep, then they were obviously visible to the children and parents. The posters were not just waist upwards, they were full frontal.

"I certainly also know that balloons with urine were thrown and hot tea. The moment the urine balloons came down, you would have smelt them. There can be no doubt what they were. Nobody could possibly realise how awful the experience was unless they were there. Watching it on television is not enough, you can't appreciate how raw, how horrible and awful it was. It was almost sanitised by the television screen. TV can actually be a barrier. There were probably people in pubs, watching it and saying, 'Jesus, look at those poor kids walking up that road', but still there was that glass wall."

Karen Trew, a senior lecturer in psychology at Queens University, says the use of explicitly sexual language, intending to humiliate and degrade, is not unique. Both striking and working miners used such images and language during their 1970s industrial action in Britain. The use of the word "whore" in a Northern context, she says, may have religious overtones (as in the "whore of Babylon").

"It's the extension of language used in some homes into the street," she says. "Its intention is to de-personalise. People will use the worst words that come into their heads to hurt and humiliate and insult women and children."

Dr Peter Shirlow sees a political lesson in how the protesters behaved. "It is not good enough to say the protesters were blood-thirsty, psychopathic maniacs, driven by sectarianism. They have lost any form of coherent leadership and been left in a vacuum."

There is also a section of the Protestant community who simply hate Catholics. "There is a supremacist loyalist notion of Protestants as an elite and Catholics as filth. If they are scum, it doesn't matter if you are abusing their children. You are reminding yourself and others around you what they are."

He says, however, that many protesters were shocked and ashamed afterwards about what they had said and done. "It is very difficult to gauge whether people are being genuine, but people told me they had said things they never believed themselves capable of."

Eight days after the protest began, while Ardoyne was still near the top of the global media agenda, came the Twin Towers disaster in New

York. According to parent Gerald McCabe, it did not put the protesters off their stride.

"I had to go and pick up Gemma about an hour after the second plane struck and I can remember some of the protesters shouting, 'Where the fuck are your American friends now?' What kind of people were they? Thousands of people were dying. They had no respect for the victims in America."

Father Troy watched live coverage of the Twin Towers disaster from the back of a Sky Television News satellite van on the Ardoyne Road. "You would never use anyone's sufferings to prove a point, but September 11 was the best exit strategy the loyalists had and they blew it."

That evening, at about 7pm, a group from Glenbryn went to Stormont (the East Belfast seat of the devolved Assembly) for a meeting with the Northern Secretary, John Reid. On the way into the meeting, Alan McQuillan had a brief word with them.

"I sat them down and said that after what had happened earlier in the day, the entire world view on violence and terrorism is going to change and that the media's focus would change. I asked them if they would consider calling the protest off and see if political negotiations could start. Half of them hadn't heard what had happened in New York. This was five hours after the event. Even when they were told, they couldn't see how it could have any impact on them."

That same evening, as he was talking to journalists on the road, Father Troy believed the world had been changed by events in New York. It was, he said, a chance for both sides to shake hands, allow the children to walk to school, go up to Stormont and talk about it.

"I was profoundly disappointed when, the next day, they jeered over to us that the IRA wouldn't be 'getting any more dollars'."

As a kind of defence mechanism, parents began making up nicknames for some of the protesters. "Spiderman" was a particular bogeyman and recurring theme in some children's nightmares. Maura Lindsay has a particular reason for remembering "Spiderman".

"David and I were walking home with Amy, both talking away but still watchful. Suddenly, Amy started to shake from head to toe and began crying. That man, 'Spiderman', had lifted his hand like a gun and aimed it at Amy, to gesture that he was going to shoot her. He was only a couple of yards away from her.

David says, "I pointed 'Spiderman' out to the police and said he had threatened us. After pointing at Amy he did the same to me, adding 'I am going to shoot you'. I asked a cop if he'd seen it but he just walked on."

They nick-named another protester "Grey Fleece" because of the same clothing she apparently wore for weeks on end. Roisin Kennedy says, "She was 30 stone, really dirty and wore the same grey fleece the whole three months of the protest. For some reason, every time she was on the road she used to eyeball Niamh who was really terrified of her. One morning, Grey Fleece lunged towards one of the parents but missed and shoved Niamh instead. She was in hysterics. Niamh, to this day, is fearful of bumping into her. Even now she would still get wee flashbacks."

There were occasions when the parents got the better of the protesters. On one such occasion, Johnny Adair's wife, Gina, and another woman, "Heather" (whom a Sunday tabloid had named as his one-time girlfriend) were standing together shouting at the parents in unison. One of the parents was undergoing chemotherapy for cancer, resulting in damage to her teeth. "Heather" was waving a big toothbrush about, making a point about the parent's teeth, yelling at her to go and clean them. The parent involved turned round and shouted at Gina Adair that her friend should use the toothbrush herself, after "giving Johnny a blow-job". Father Gary Donegan, scandalised at this crudity, admonished the sinning parent, although those who heard the exchange said "it was a cracker". The faces of the two women protesters reportedly "dropped a mile". From then on, Heather and Gina, who continued to attend the protest, stood on different sides of the road. They were never seen standing together again.

Far more serious were the two days that sniper attacks were threatened. The first threat was against the parents; the second said children were also "legitimate targets". The police passed on the warnings to Father Troy as parents gathered for the afternoon after-school walk.

Jeanette McKernan remembers the two priests speaking to different groups of parents. "Father Gary is a real wee joker and we thought that he was going to give us a laugh but he told us instead that the BBC had been warned about a sniper on the road. He said if we decided not to go up, they would be behind us 110 per cent, but that we would also be supported if we decided to walk up as usual."

The parents discussed it amongst themselves and all decided to go ahead. Judy Haughey said the episode was "surreal". On hearing the police warning about the sniper, she wondered about turning back but agreed with the collective decision to face the threat down.

"We were only walking for about a minute when they started throwing fireworks. We thought it was shooting. That was the most terrifying experience. There was a lot of smoke. You really didn't know what was happening. The fireworks were thrown deliberately at us to coincide with the death threat. It was to make us believe that we were being shot at."

One child waiting for her mother to arrive heard the bangs and saw her clutching her chest in shock as she walked up the hill. Thinking she was shot, the child began screaming. At least one mother was so frightened that she went behind a hedge and threw up.

Tanya Carmichael asks why the police did not search the roofs of the houses on receiving news of the threat, instead of just passing on the warning. "We asked why they were not looking for this sniper; it was only a very small road."

Sean, her husband, says the police stood and watched the loyalists lighting the fireworks before throwing them. "They never once attempted to stop them," he says.

Judy Haughey says, "We knew we had to keep going and stand up for our rights. That was just the way it was. It is OK for outsiders looking in, but you would have to live in this community on a daily basis to understand that we really hadn't got a choice. People may say we had choices, but we felt forced into a situation where we really didn't. When the British Army blockade closed behind us every day, we knew that whatever happened, there was no way back."

Such was the terror, amongst the mothers in particular, that at least one routinely stuffed a towel down her underpants every morning. She was regularly becoming incontinent with fear.

David Lindsay says the protesters tried and failed to provoke parents into retaliating. This story again relates to "the man up the ladder", Jim McClean.

"McClean was walking beside me and called out, 'What the fuck are you doing walking up our road?' I replied, 'It is not your road'. He then lifted his fist to hit me. I wanted to ensure that he had hit me first. I knew the cops were watching. The next thing, two cops ran over and grabbed McClean. The loyalist crowd went mad with anger."

A police officer later privately told Lindsay they knew McClean was trying to "wind someone up enough to hit him" so that a parent would be arrested. "From then on," Lindsay says, "I took dogs' abuse, but bit my lip. It was very hard. I wouldn't give him the pleasure of having me lifted."

It was not the only incident that inflamed loyalist fury. Some protesters insist they saw Sean Kelly walking up the Ardoyne Road amongst the parents, although he had no child at the school. In October 1993 Kelly was one of two IRA men who bombed a Shankill Road shop located under the local UDA meeting rooms. The bomb exploded prematurely, killing nine Protestants and an IRA man. The author saw Kelly at least once at the British Army barricade at the top of Alliance Avenue, but never walking with the parents.

According to Sinn Fein's Gerry Kelly, there may be an innocent explanation for the protesters' claims. "There are two other people the spitting image of Sean Kelly in Ardoyne, and one of them is a parent. I was face to face in North Belfast with a UDA guy recently who was pointing to a man he believed was Sean Kelly, but it wasn't."

As the protest dragged on into October and November, the story all but vanished from the headlines. The cameras departed and only returned on significant dates or if there were any reports of violence. The parents, who could not leave, however, say the pressure was relentless as they never knew what to expect from day to day. More children began to use the direct route as the protest settled into a pattern. From as low as 80 of the 220 children at the school it increased to about half.

Judy Haughey says, "As the protest went on things seemed to be getting harder to endure. It was dragging on and on. You felt tired and deflated. There were nights when I cried until dawn. I looked at my kids and broke my heart. I was crying out of anger and disappointment."

Although, by this stage, many protesters were also fed up and wanted it over, it was not so bad, according to Anne Bill.

"If it wasn't so serious it would have been funny. After the first week it started to become like going to a restaurant to meet your mates. It ended up like a social event. We felt sorry for the kids, but it wasn't our responsibility. It was the parents' fault."

Father Donegan says, "Every single day was a torment. If it seemed too quiet, people would say it was like a western movie and something was about to happen. The silence itself was sinister. The tension never lightened up. There was one day where three of the protesters were holding guitars and wearing sombreros and shawls. You wondered about people going home at night and planning how to intimidate us. One minute there was urine being thrown, then there was spittle, then people roaring abuse – and in the middle of it all, three people with sombreros on them playing guitars. 'What on earth is going on?' you say to yourself."

Through it all, UUP councillor Fred Cobain, who had vehemently argued against the protest, watched events unfolding on television. "I felt torn in two directions. These are my supporters and my constituents and look what they were doing to themselves. It was very painful to watch, knowing they were being portrayed all over the world as monsters. It was going to be a case of 'how can you expect Catholics to live in a country with these animals?'"

Lynda Bowes says, "The saddest part about it was that it became normal. I thought that was the most frightening part of it. It became normal for our children to be abused. It was normal for Amanda to cling to my hand like she hadn't done since she was a toddler. You reached the ridiculous stage that if you kept crying you would go completely under, so I just started laughing. We began to understand that the protesters really had no strategy. Any underlying reasons they had for the protest had long gone. They didn't know anymore why they were doing it. There was absolutely no rationale to it."

Some amongst the protesters, however, were beginning to accept that it could not go on forever.

Chapter Five

ENDGAME

We were promised the earth if we called off the protest but all we got were hanging baskets. We got nothing except being turned into monsters.

Amanda Johnston, lollipop lady

It has turned me into a terribly different person. I would fight Goliath now if I thought somebody was wronging me. The only winners were the kids for being so brave.

Roisin Kennedy, Holy Cross parent

As the weeks dragged on, it was finally dawning in Glenbryn, especially amongst those who had led the protest, that it had to end. But how to extricate themselves?

The protesters felt they would be the laughing stock of loyalism if they backed down with nothing to show. Pride dictated they could only leave the field carrying a few trophies. Despite a gruelling 12 weeks, a loyalist source says that there was still strong resistance within Glenbryn to ending it. "The women were worst, which was depressing."

Dr Peter Shirlow believes there is a psychological imperative within both loyalism and republicanism on refusing to admit fault. "Admitting you did anything wrong is a huge barrier to progress in all sections of Northern Irish society."

The power-sharing Executive made a stab at trying to bring the protest to an end and, as ever with politicians, there was no shortage of good intentions, but its efforts had little effect. It appointed a senior liaison officer to shuttle between Glenbryn and Ardoyne, trying to find out what was required from the loyalist side and if the agenda was acceptable to nationalists. It also responded by setting up "an inter-departmental government committee" with the then acting First

Minister, the UUP's Sir Reg Empey, promising that improving everyone's lives in North Belfast was a priority. Both he and the Deputy First Minister, Seamus Mallon, pledged the Executive to "support local communities as they work to promote a culture of tolerance and mutual understanding" and to "look at the wider difficulties facing North Belfast, many of which have their roots in social and economic conditions".

Sir Reg said, "Whatever problems people face, and we know they are serious, they cannot be sorted out against a background of violence on our streets."

The worthy words failed to persuade the Glenbryn loyalists to end the protest.

The Executive was also under pressures of its own. On July 1, David Trimble, the UUP leader, had resigned as First Minister in protest at the slow movement towards IRA decommissioning and to stave off his own hard-liners. Devolution was suspended for a day on August 10, 2001 and again on September 21. On October 18, all the UUP ministers resigned and Trimble refused to re-nominate them until five days later. On November 2, the first attempt to get the power-sharing Executive back up and running failed. It was finally re-established on November 6, although tempers ran so high that politicians pushed and shoved each other in the Great Hall at Stormont, in what became known as "The Brawl in the Hall".

Perhaps because of the intense pressure on Trimble from his own hard-liners to withdraw from government, he was reluctant to condemn the protesters. As one nationalist behind-the-scenes adviser put it, "We had to negotiate hard to get any condemnation from Trimble. We encountered a real reluctance on his part to say too much and push too far but the amount of time spent by ministers on Holy Cross was enormous, much more than the public realised."

Meanwhile, republicans were aware the dispute was drawing to a close with the Glenbryn loyalists still determined to end it on their own terms. While not wanting further trauma inflicted on the children, they were not prepared to roll over to save Protestant blushes.

"In private talks, the Glenbryn people said they knew they were painted into a corner and were looking for help," says one senior

Ardoyne republican. "The dilemma on our side was we wanted to end the children's nightmare without giving them all they were demanding to rescue them from the bloody awful mess they had created for themselves."

Ronnie Black, a CRUA committee member, says it took far too long for the politicians to do anything more than wring their hands. "When Trimble got a whisper that we were thinking of ending the protest, he came out with this big initiative to try to make out that he was the good guy to take the credit. We knew that's what he was up to but we decided that he could take the credit if he wanted to; we would always know he didn't stop it."

Anne Bill says that, although she realised the protest had to be resolved, she could not see, right up to the very end, how it could happen. "Despite all our meetings with ministers, there were still people who didn't want to end it."

The Glenbryn residents were not the only ones frustrated by the slow pace of talks. Parent Lynda Bowes says negotiating with the loyalists was like trying to catch quicksilver with a fork. "They had a shopping list but the only consistent item on it was the wall, which was the one thing they were never going to get. Everything else kept changing. It depended who was on their committee at the time."

Elaine Burns is often regarded in Ardoyne as a moderate. Her views on how the protest ended, however, are trenchant. "I asked David Trimble and Mark Durkan (UUP and SDLP leaders) once, 'Wasn't it amazing, you could abuse children for twelve long weeks and then get money for community infrastructure, the kind of thing that we fought eighteen years to get?' I put it to them, weren't they sending out a message that evil, doing wrong, abusing children, would be rewarded?"

Jim Potts dates the beginning of the end from when David Trimble became involved which, Potts says, "was pretty late on". Trimble's office sent emissaries from Stormont to hear CRUA's case and how the protest could be ended but, says Potts, the meetings were "very frustrating". Finally, round-table discussions began, involving Trimble himself and the new Deputy First Minister, Mark Durkan.

"At the time we felt something was going to happen to really benefit the community and that our case was being heard at the highest level of government. Looking back on it, we were led up the garden path."

Most of the local unionist politicians were involved at various meetings, including Fred Cobain, Billy Hutchinson, Nelson McCausland, Nigel Dodds and Frazer Agnew.

Potts denies that any new money was put on the table for housing. "I remember Gerry Kelly saying Glenbryn was being rewarded. Totally untrue. Just propaganda. The housing issue had been addressed five years previously."

The loyalist side insists that Glenbryn was not given any further public money other than what had already been budgeted for rebuilding the area, even prior to the Holy Cross dispute. Potts says that money was not the critical factor in ending the protest.

"The end came because of the security package that was on offer, because we were losing the propaganda war and people were really getting tired of it all. While people were still prepared to carry on, they were asking themselves when was it ever going to end."

The talks to end it, however, were stormy. Stuart McCartney remembers a sparring match he had with the then Northern Ireland Secretary, John Reid.

"Reid said he didn't care if it was 90, 900 or 900,000 children, they were still going to get to that school. He was putting the rights of 124 children over the rights of 900 residents. It really annoyed me. I told him I would be going back to my community and telling them that he didn't give a damn, that we were on our own. What Reid said spoke volumes. We didn't matter as much as the children. All we wanted was a gate. A wee gate that would open each day from 7am to 5pm so the kids could get to school. We were told we couldn't have one because of emergency access. We asked about radio-controlled security gates. They weren't interested."

CRUA's biggest single objective was to get a wall across the Ardoyne Road, but there were official and understandable concerns over access for fire and ambulance emergency crews.

"We had to put up an alternative," says Potts. "The new concept was a horseshoe bend in the road and a wall, like a chicane, with a roundabout to stop groups of kids making eye contact."

The nationalist side, he says, accepted the concept of the horseshoe bend "but the wall was giving them a problem". The first proposal for the wall would have seen it built perpendicular to the Ardoyne Road but gradually, says Potts, the proposed angle of the wall altered.

"Each time we met the government representatives, the proposal changed. The nationalist side wanted the wall moved further and back. In the end, the proposed wall was at such an angle it was useless to us. Finally, it was agreed that the wall was going to go ahead, although I can't remember what angle it was at that stage."

Potts remembers a day when he turned up at Stormont to see a model of how the wall, roundabout and horseshoe bend would look. He says that, for him, it was the highpoint of the entire protest.

"There was this huge model on the table. It was agreed the work would go ahead after the end of the summer term in July 2002. That was the best deal we could get and we were happy with it."

Ronnie Black felt the same way. "Our hopes were built up. They had maps and models on the table and told us, point blank, that's what we were getting."

Parallel with the Stormont talks to end the protest, a secret channel of communication was set up involving some of the main players in Ardoyne and Glenbryn. They met three times, at night at various locations around Belfast. Both sides wanted to avoid the Stormont politicians imposing their own solution without at least some community input. The loyalist/republican meetings were intended to regain the initiative. Amongst those involved were Jim Potts, Ronnie Black and Mark Coulter for Glenbryn. On the nationalist side, participants included cross-community worker, Robert McCallum, Brendan Bradley of the Survivors of Trauma group, and Mickey Liggett of the Ardoyne Focus Group.

"The first meeting was the scariest," says Liggett. "There was a lot of mysterious police activity around the supposedly secret location and I was worried we were all going to get shot."

In the feverish atmosphere of North Belfast in the autumn of 2001, such fears were far from paranoid. At their second meeting, the group tried to set an agenda for a community forum – the idea being that once the protest was over, they could meet again and take it from there for the good of both communities.

"The first item on Ardoyne's agenda was to knock any idea of any wall on the head," says Liggett. "We wanted instead to discuss how we could live together, to share North Belfast. Could we end division and pull down walls? The Glenbryn side understood where we were coming from, but it wasn't their agenda. They wanted to talk about what they called 'community safety' and putting a new wall up. What was the point, our side asked, in setting up a community forum after the protest ended to discuss how we could improve the divisions between our two communities? We were on two diametrically opposed paths. One side wanted to share North Belfast. The other wanted a segregated future."

The Ardoyne side insisted there were already adequate mechanisms in place to resolve Glenbryn's security problems. All that was needed was a determination and commitment to work the already existing structures in a more efficient manner. That did not satisfy Glenbryn.

Liggett says, "The loyalists also wanted the Ardoyne side to drop what they called our 'propaganda' that the protest was against the children. Would we make a statement to that effect? They didn't want to be called child abusers."

That was unacceptable to Ardoyne. Then the two sides got into the nub of the problem. What did Glenbryn want in return for ending the protest?

"The CRUA side said they already had a wall in the bag," says Liggett. "A senior civil servant working for the Stormont Executive had already given guarantees, along with a gate across the Ardoyne Road, provided only that they ended the protest and agreed to join a cross-community forum. We, though, were able to tell them their promise was a load of old nonsense. The very same civil servant had promised us, providing we engaged in dialogue with them, that there would definitely never be a wall. Obviously, we concluded, the authorities were playing us off against each other. The Ardoyne side then hit on the idea of asking the civil servant to come along and give both sides a joint presentation. The Glenbryn people turned us down, fearing it would look like a new negotiation and they would lose what they'd already been promised. They weren't going to challenge or embarrass the civil servant who'd been lying to them. It seemed to us like a classic divide-and-conquer routine, with the civil servant in the middle, doing nothing in public, but acting behind everyone's back so he could manoeuvre us all where he wanted.

It was beyond me why they couldn't see this too. We told the Glenbryn people that, at the end of the day, they would get nothing and neither would we, while some civil servant would get an OBE for fixing it."

Why, though, was the Ardoyne side so opposed to the wall? The statistics showed they were suffering far more than Glenbryn from the continuing sectarian violence. Would it not have protected them as well? Liggett accepts that some families, those living at the most vulnerable points along the peace-line, would probably have welcomed further security barriers – but for the future of all the people of Ardoyne, it would have been a disaster.

"Some people along Alliance Avenue want a longer peace-line for perfectly understandable reasons – they don't want to get killed. If they persuaded the rest of us, however, they would effectively be colonising the whole area. The rest of us in Ardoyne, huge crowds of us, the place is bursting at the seams, would then be living behind yet another wall, hemming us in. There would be fields, leisure centres, housing land, where we would never get access."

A different perspective entirely is offered by David Trimble's political adviser, David McNarry, who is also a member of the Loyalist Commission, an umbrella group of loyalist paramilitaries, unionist politicians and Protestant clergy.

"Jim Potts and Ronnie Black from Glenbryn asked to meet the Loyalist Commission. They wanted advice on how to end the protest. Potts was on the point of being ousted by hard-liners. The protest was out of control, there was a danger that paramilitary elements could take over and there could be severe casualties. I arranged for a full meeting of the Commission, all the tough men, and the Glenbryn side put their cards on the table.

"At a second meeting," continues McNarry, "the Commission offered to put marshals on the streets. The Glenbryn side would obey the marshals. Then we would get the police to back off. And that's what happened. The marshals were duly put in place, the crowd was controlled and the Loyalist Commission told Potts to stop the protest, now. That's how simple it was. It was all done in a matter of days. The Commission laid down the law. In effect, it was a case of the Protestant community policing itself, realising it was getting a hammering."

The final crunch came at a meeting in the Concord Community Centre in Glenbryn in mid-November. Feelings were running high. The meeting could have gone either way. As one loyalist put it, "Everybody was out for blood."

Despite McNarry's insistence that it was all effectively over by then, Potts says it was still hard to sell the final package to the by now battle-hardened community. "Our problem was that nothing was going to happen overnight, everything had to be agreed with the nationalist side and some people still wanted to continue with the protest."

Into the melee walked Billy Hutchinson, who knew what was in the final offer from the Office of the First Minister and the Deputy First Minister (OFM/DFM). He was at a prior and unrelated engagement in London but had returned home to be at the meeting. Hutchinson told the gathered crowd in Concorde that he did not believe a single word of the final deal, but the protest, nevertheless, had to end. The only way forward was to take what was on offer and fight to get it implemented.

No one at the meeting trusted David Trimble or Mark Durkan – or the British government. A number of people stood up and made passionate speeches against suspending the protest. Hutchinson waited until they had finished, according to an eyewitness, then made a speech that turned the meeting around, demolishing the arguments of those in favour of persisting with the protest. Several women, who had been the backbone of the protest and amongst its most vehement supporters, then said they supported Hutchinson. Before any vote took place, he left, followed by the Rev Norman Hamilton and the DUP's Nigel Dodds and Nelson McCausland. The meeting voted by roughly 60 to 40 to suspend the protest.

Outside, at least one of the leading lights in Glenbryn felt Hutchinson had, unfairly, been left alone to explain the harsh realities of political life to the community. According to one eyewitness, Dodds then said that he was no good in such street-level debates but "Billy is good at that sort of thing". Hutchinson himself refuses to comment on what went on inside the meeting, other than to say he believes that, in the absence of decisive action, the protest would have lingered on indefinitely.

"The politicians would have allowed the protest to drag on for weeks.

They would rather have allowed the community to go down that cul de sac than take action to resolve it. The protest was meant to be about protecting Glenbryn. Instead it was driving our own people out and making it more vulnerable."

Stuart McCartney personifies the different moods in the two camps at the meeting. "The community was up in arms when we decided to call it off, but a lot of people were fatigued. We told them we thought the plan would work, and in any case it was all we could get."

Ronnie Black says, "The protest ended to give CRUA a chance to move forward because neither the government nor the Ardoyne people would give an inch while the protest continued."

Jim Potts denies the vote split the protesters. "The overall conclusion was that, provided the government addressed our security, let's call the protest off – at least suspend it, to allow CRUA and the public reps to continue talking."

But he now feels betrayed by the lack of follow-through on the deal and says that, with hindsight, he voted the wrong way. "Those who wanted to keep up the protest believed the politicians wouldn't deliver. The 60 per cent said to give them a try. I was on that side and obviously we were proved wrong, there's nothing else you can say."

Through it all, the violence raged through North Belfast with pipe bombings, riots, the occasional shooting and widespread intimidation and fear. On November 11, the Troubles cost yet another young man his life. Glen Hugh Branagh, from North Belfast, a 16-year-old Protestant and distant relative of actor Kenneth Branagh, blew himself up with a pipe bomb he was about to throw at a nationalist crowd in the New Lodge Road area. He was a member of the "Ulster Young Militants", the UDA's youth wing. Loyalists claimed the youth was trying to return the pipe bomb, which had been thrown at them by republicans, but this was disproved by eyewitness and forensic evidence.

The book Lost Lives recounts how a police constable saw the youth being taken away after the explosion. "As the person was receiving first aid, I saw his balaclava had been removed and his right hand was missing," he said.

The blast caused severe head injuries from which Branagh died shortly after at the Mater Hospital. On the same night, 24 police officers and several civilians were injured, including a teenage girl who was hit by a plastic bullet. The dead youth was buried the day before he turned 17. Loyalists suspended their attempts to blockade Holy Cross on the day of the funeral.

For the length of the protest, from June 1 up to November 11, police statistics for North Belfast show there were 224 petrol bombings, 58 pipe bombings and 50 incidents in which blast bombs were thrown. The *Irish Times* reported 371 police officers, eight British soldiers and 103 civilians injured over the same period.

November 26 was the first day the children walked to school with no protest since June 20. The journey passed off without incident, although the police maintained a large presence along the school route. Father Troy said that, although the protest was only suspended, not ended, people should not be too concerned. "I'm interpreting that as their phase to move out of where they've been. One good day without difficulty will be the foundation for it becoming normal."

Shortly afterwards, negotiations at Stormont began in order to implement the OFM/DFM proposals. Mickey Liggett says the first meeting the Ardoyne delegation had with Mark Durkan and David McNarry, acting on behalf of David Trimble, was "a shouting match".

"We accused Durkan of promising Glenbryn a wall, which amounted to rewarding them for abusing our children, making the politicians complicit in it all. We wanted the protesters prosecuted, not rewarded. They had already forced our kids to queue up to get through a gate first thing in the morning, having to wait until the local UDA commander got out of bed and was ready to protest. It wasn't a very pleasant meeting."

Brian Barrington, Mark Durkan's special adviser, however, says he was always very clear that the protesters should not be "rewarded".

"We were also clear that, just because there was bad behaviour by some, it didn't mean the whole community should be penalised. In the deal that was negotiated to end the dispute, we were very clear that its implementation had to be by agreement between the two communities. In other words we were mediators not arbitrators. Durkan was very concerned about the fears of the Ardoyne residents, that putting a kink in the road with a wall round it would prevent parents being able to see up the road to the school. He insisted, in model after model, that the parents' sight-lines were protected. There was no way he was going to allow sight-lines to be damaged."

Mickey Liggett agrees that there was attempt after attempt to find an agreed model. "The officials tried to be clever and proposed a wall across the road, rebuilding the road around it. That way they could tell Glenbryn they had their wall and us that they didn't."

When a roundabout was put on the agenda, the Ardoyne side proposed a small lake as an alternative. That was ruled out when the officials predicted (probably accurately) that people would get thrown into it.

"We ended up telling them that we were discussing someone else's agenda and we'd prefer it if they would go in and arrest the people responsible for the abuse and charge them," says Liggett. "The idea of a wall gradually disappeared."

Jim Potts sees all this in reverse. After the critical Glenbryn meeting that called the protest off, talks resumed to implement the agreed wall and chicane. But, he complains, too much leeway was given to dissenting voices from Ardoyne.

"They had a full week after our meeting to allow objectors to come forward. Whatever happened during that week I don't know, but the government then introduced another stalling process."

The next thing Potts heard was that the proposal had changed again. What was now on offer was a parallel wall on the Ardoyne Road "which we rejected because it didn't serve any purpose".

Potts continues: "The government then, more or less, said they had fulfilled their obligations and that was it. It was all just a long stalling process to persuade us to get the protest off the road and allow tensions to die down. They tried to blame us then for rejecting the proposals, saying they had offered us a wall and we had rejected it."

Bitter divisions were not confined to the relationship between Ardoyne and Glenbryn but were mirrored in the rivalries between the Trimble and Durkan camps at Stormont. David McNarry even accuses civil servants of being split into "green" and "orange" camps.

"The great suspicion," he says, "was that the 'green' side of the civil service always went to Durkan's office before Trimble's. They were doing deals with Durkan and then coming to see us. We were the last to hear."

After the proposed wall disappeared into a miasma of paper, there was massive disillusionment and a sense of betrayal in Glenbryn. Michael Cosby's views are typical.

"People were conned into stopping the protest. There were a lot of people who didn't want it to stop. I was undecided, but in the end I went along with Ronnie (Black), Jim (Potts) and other people who I believed would not lie to me. I believed them, we all did, but we were wrong. The whole area feels conned. All we got was ramps." Cosby agrees that Potts and the CRUA committee were not to blame, because "they were lied to themselves".

Does Potts feel he was lied to? "Absolutely. They cleverly got us into a nine-month process of meetings and all we got, in the end, were some ramps and closed-circuit television cameras, which don't even work."

Anne Bill believes the outcome of the protest had increased the sense of alienation, isolation and depression in Glenbryn. "As soon as the protest finished, the wall and gate went out the window."

She asks why any of Glenbryn proposals should have required Ardoyne's consent. "I don't understand why we had to ask our attackers if it was OK to protect ourselves. If Trimble was putting a security measure up in his own house, would be go and ask the robbers for permission?"

Ronnie Black says, "We were shafted by the government, no doubt about it. The government promised them things and never delivered. The ramps are more of a hindrance than anything and the cameras are only for the benefit of the police. We were railroaded into ending the protest. We took government at their word. We put our trust in Trimble and Durkan and they let us down – that's the only way to describe it."

Fred Cobain agrees that all the talking at Stormont was a waste of time. "I was disappointed with both Durkan and Trimble but more so Durkan. After agreeing to stuff, he ran away from it. It was an absolute disgrace."

Trimble, however, doesn't escape Cobain's lash. "He should have stuck to his guns, once it was agreed. He was the First Minister after all."

David McNarry shares Cobain and Black's anger with Mark Durkan. "Durkan collapsed. He absolutely fell over on a number of occasions, once he was got at by the Ardoyne residents. He reneged on all the promises he had given to Glenbryn. I was very disappointed. He took a sectarian line on this, a totally sectarian line."

Durkan strongly contests McNarry's view, calling it "bunkum" and pointing out the reason the protest was only "suspended" and not ended was that no one could guarantee if the OFM/DFM offer would be implemented as it was contingent on Ardoyne's consent.

"We were always very clear and very up front about that," he says, pointing to the critical letter he and Trimble jointly sent to the Glenbryn Residents' Committee on November 23, 2001, just before they met to decide whether to suspend the protest. The letter, which clarified the final offer available to Glenbryn, reads, in part, that the protest should end, with no resumption, and that in return the OFM/DFM committed itself to acting on some of the protesters' demands.

On "Community Safety", the letter makes it clear that changes to the Ardoyne/Alliance intersection will go ahead "subject to agreement" on design. Also that "possible" road alignment will take place "if agreement is reached" on the scheme.

Durkan's adviser, Brian Barrington, is also clear that the deal on offer could only be implemented by agreement between Ardoyne and Glenbryn.

"The documentation proves it. This is just not allegation and counter-allegation, it is very clear in the letter. There was no doubt, the word 'agreement' was there in the November 23 letter signed off by Trimble and Durkan. There was no dishonesty or reneging. They are only kidding themselves. They maybe built up an expectation encouraged by McNarry. It was certainly never authorised by ministers that anything would happen other than by agreement between the two communities. Without that, we would be imposing something on one community against the other's wishes, which we wouldn't do. Mark was also concerned to ensure that sight-lines were protected up to the school so that parents could be reassured as to the safety of their children. To suggest that there is something sectarian about this is completely misplaced."

The fall-out, whoever was or was not at fault, is a deep bitterness in Glenbryn. Jim McClean, the man up the ladder in the June 19 incident, now says he wishes the whole affair had never started.

"At the time, no one could stop the way you were feeling. Emotions were running high. There was claim and counterclaim. I got wrapped up in it and couldn't get out. My whole life was turned upside down. The police said both the IRA and INLA were out to kill me. They tried to shoot me three times. The police told me not to expect any death threats, they would just try and kill me. The first best thing was definitely to call the protest, but the second best thing was definitely to call it off."

McClean, unlike the others, sees some positive results from the protest. "We got a wall out of it, not across the Ardoyne Road but at the back of the houses in Alliance Avenue. We got ramps and cameras which the residents wanted. It was a good package."

Stuart McCartney disagrees. "There has been no financial benefit to the community. I would love to know where the money's been spent. We got some ramps and a lot of traumatised children."

And a lot of traumatised parents.

The Presbyterian minister in Glenbryn, Rev Norman Hamilton, agrees that most of the CRUA leadership believe they were cheated but the protest was coming to an end anyhow, and people knew it. "After three months," he says, "the numbers involved on the protest were diminishing."

Three years on, in 2004, there is still the potential for violence on the Ardoyne Road. The camera sits silently watching from the top of its tall metal spire at the junction of Ardoyne Road and Alliance Avenue. Police Land Rovers patrol day and night. An ugly calm has descended.

Nasty incidents still happen. Tina Gallagher had an unpleasant encounter there with Spiderman, long after the protest ended. She spotted him, he spotted her. They were walking towards each other and neither would move aside.

"We walked right into each other. He went to hit me so I hit him and there was murder. The peelers (police) came and the road was filled in an instant. Loyalists flooded out from everywhere."

The incident sparked a riot. It does not take very much.

Chapter Six

THE ALTERNATIVE ROUTE

We have two daughters dead. I sat at their grave for three days and asked myself, 'What do I do here?' For me it was a moral decision. It wasn't anything to do with politics, Catholics, Protestants, your ground or my ground.
                                                    Patricia Monaghan, parent

Our people believed there was no way that people would walk their children through. I know I certainly wouldn't have walked my child through, no matter how much of a point I was trying to make.
                                                            Anne Bill, loyalist

From the very start of the protest, the big question constantly put to the parents by virtually everyone who was not a Holy Cross parent themselves was, "Are you using your children? If you're not, then why not spare them from harm and abuse by taking the alternative route?"

First asked by the loyalist protesters, it was taken up by their unionist supporters, finally becoming the main public debating point. Even today some people, reminded of Holy Cross, will shake their heads sadly and wonder "what kind of parents" would walk their young daughters through a protest that was increasingly vicious and unpleasant. The question fundamentally shifted the fulcrum of the discussion over the rights and wrongs of the protest, from whether protesters had the right to block the road and direct violent abuse at children, to whether the parents were right. The argument deprived the parents of some support outside Ardoyne and put them on the back foot, forcing them on the defensive.

Although the British government never came out and openly said it supported the parents choosing to take the longer alternative route, it hung in the air as its presumed position. The parents wondered if

Muslim parents, or Jewish parents, or black parents anywhere in the world would have been condemned for walking their children to school the way they had walked for over 30 years through the front, and only, gate. The loyalists argued they had more compassion for the children than their own parents to shift responsibility for the damage onto the shoulders of the parents. If an alternative route existed, they argued, the parents should take it. That point of view was put, succinctly if not elegantly, by some protesters on the Ardoyne Road. The writer herself witnessed repeated shouts at parents, typically, "You fucking bastards. I wouldn't put a child of mine through that. You are only Fenian sluts and whores." The parents regarded this argument, however it was couched, as particularly offensive. It allowed the loyalists to claim, at least publicly, that they cared for the children's welfare, while week after week, the children's tear-stained faces trekked up the road.

Abroad, the protest was often portrayed as one in which "motherhood lost out" – that the mothers (and fathers) of Ardoyne loved their principles more than their own children. As one US writer, in private correspondence, wrote to the author, "The mothers themselves decided that the 'tactic' of not going through the back door was more important than the primary code of motherhood – that under no circumstances do you subject your own children to needless harm. Even if it means creating problems for yourself. Even if it means selling your soul. Even if it means sacrificing your life. People collectively relegated the love, protection, and responsibility of motherhood to the back burner."

The watching world judged the parents in Ardoyne harshly, asking if they were so hardened by the Troubles, so dogmatic, that they were prepared to inflict this agony on their own children. The concept of parents willingly sacrificing their beloved children on the altar of their faith is ancient and powerful. It goes back to Isaac and Abraham. The image was used by the Irish singer/songwriter, Paul Brady, in his landmark song about the Northern Troubles, "The Island".

"Up here we sacrifice our children, To feed the worn-out dreams of yesterday." Could that be said of the Holy Cross parents? Did they elevate principle over the welfare of their children, the world asked.

The alternative route argument presented outsiders with an

invitation to see Holy Cross as a battle of wills between two stubborn and equally culpable forces and the children as pawns in an adult game – used by both parents and protesters to fight a war by proxy. The protesters, and the wider world, openly queried whether the parents loved their children at all. Why were they forcing girls as young as four to endure a terrifying daily ordeal? In their defence, the people of Ardoyne, while having inflicted their share of violence during the Troubles, had also endured much suffering and had voted for peace and equal rights, which surely includes the unimpeded access to an education. Conceding the direct route would have had far-reaching implications, not only for Holy Cross, but for every Catholic school and church across the North.

The loyalists watched television, read the papers and factored the obvious reaction into their tactics, repeatedly demanding the parents take the back road. In short, those who condemned the parents, however unwittingly, became the protesters' allies. There were strong practical reasons mitigating against the alternative route. First there was no "route" or pathway, as such.

To enter Holy Cross by any way other than the usual involves a longer walk, followed by a meander through the premises of another school, across its football pitch. Walking the alternative route takes 17 minutes longer, without encumbrance of stroller or toddler. With either, it increases to 20 minutes, 40 minutes daily, three-and-a-half hours a week in all weathers – more if parents make two trips to pick up younger children leaving school early. There are insurance and safety concerns. Taking the back route forced mothers with buggies and toddlers, as well as disabled people, walking over uneven ground, staircases and grass verges. There is no asphalt path.

Donal Flanagan of the CCMS (the Catholic Council for Maintained Schools) remembers parents' meetings where there was much debate on the alternative route.

"There were some who refused to subject their children to the protest. Others asked how their children would judge them in the future if they gave up such a basic right. In other words, are we going to perpetuate this concept that Catholics always have to roll over? Or do we ask people for respect and understand our position?"

Flanagan notes, however, "Parents with very different views did not fall out between themselves, which I thought was very strong. They took decisions as individual families, based their own sets of values and the sensitivities of their children."

Did the CCMS ever ask the Board of Governors to advise the parents on which road to take? "The health and well-being of the children was our absolute priority. We advised the board to point out the options but not to tell the parents which they should choose. We respected the right of parents to make whatever decision they felt was correct, which was their absolute right. Our role is to advise and guide, not control or administer."

The role of any Board of Governors, he says, is to work with the community, to follow the will of the community. "A school that does not have the support of its local community is, in my view, not a school – it is a building."

Flanagan says he respected the decisions of both groups of parents equally – those who took the longer route and those who did not want, in their terms, to see another generation of Catholic people in Northern Ireland "learning the rollover trick".

"I was full of admiration for the way they respected each others' decision, I think it was quite extraordinary when emotions were so high. There was a respect and maturity in that community that intrigued me."

He says that as the parents walked out of the packed, sometimes angry, meetings they clearly had divergent views but they continued to talk to each other. "No group was left behind and no group walked away."

Then there were the daily practical difficulties. A teacher at Holy Cross school, "Grainne" (not her real name), tells of how she saw one mother making the longer journey.

"She was heavily pregnant, with four girls aged under five already. I will never forget that woman arriving at school, mud all over and the poor wee ones, aged two and three, also covered in muck. As teachers, we still get angry when someone talks about that alternative route. If anyone tries it on with me, I pretend I don't know what they're talking about and ask if the people screaming sectarian abuse at four-year-old children on the road should have taken an alternative route. How dare somebody who knows nothing about it suggest the parents were wrong? How can standing up for your rights be okay when you're black in the US or South Africa and wrong in Belfast?. We had kids crying because their parents were trying to take them through St Gabriel's. They felt safer amongst the main pack. They would cry in front of us, 'No, let me go down the road'. That is the truth."

Fred Cobain, the Ulster Unionist Assembly member for North Belfast, openly accuses Sinn Fein of manipulating the parents for political ends, and through them, the children.

"The people from the Catholic community didn't know whether to send their kids up the Crumlin Road or up Ardoyne Road. Sinn Fein decided that the best way to exploit the protest was to send the kids up the Ardoyne Road, come what may. From Sinn Fein's point of view, this was an opportunity they weren't going to miss.

"It was pressure from republicans that forced the parents to go through with it," he claims, while conceding, "Some of the parents are republican and this is what they wanted to do."

Gerry Kelly of Sinn Fein says the argument is ludicrous. "I wouldn't get a vote in Ardoyne today if my party, or anyone in it, had made a single move to persuade the parents one way or the other. That's just unionists judging us by themselves. I think their argument is despicable. Who knows what each individual person would do in those circumstances, and who can deny their dreadful dilemma? Ardoyne has gone through hell over the past 35 years, yet some of its ex-prisoners told me that decision was the worst problem they had ever faced."

The parents back Kelly's denial of manipulation, even those who would lean towards the SDLP and are no friends of Sinn Fein. Neither Father Troy nor Father Donegan ever heard Sinn Fein trying to persuade the parents, either individually or collectively, to use one route or the other. Father Donegan goes as far as saying that, had Sinn Fein tried to put pressure on the parents, it would have rebounded.

"The one thing you will never get away with in this area is pulling the wool over people's eyes. They have had people trying to soft-soap them and brutalise them for far too long. They would spot it a mile off."

So were the children being used? And if so, by whom? Who had their best interests at heart? The protesters? Their parents? Or those observers in the outside world who seemed to have all the answers?

Loyalist community worker, Jim Potts, says the protesters had always believed, given the conditions and police presence, "which were clearly doing the kids harm", that the parents "would see sense".

"We hoped they would give everyone a breathing space by using the alternative route so that dialogue could become serious and find a resolution. While our community was being pushed back off the streets by the police every day, there was no possibility of serious dialogue."

Could he see any merit in the Ardoyne view that the protesters were using the vulnerability of small girls as an Achilles' heel? Wasn't it a cynical ploy to get to the parents through the children?

"The parents had a choice. Why did they force their kids through it every day?" he asks.

The former Holy Cross "lollipop lady", Amanda Johnston, is of the same mind. "They should have used the alternative route, and they should be using it now as well. If the shoe was on the other foot, if it had been a Protestant school and this was a Catholic area, the school would have been burned to the ground years ago."

Stuart McCartney is genuinely surprised that the parents even tried to continue using the Ardoyne Road. "We never thought the parents would consider coming up the road. We thought they would go another way. We deliberately didn't block Wheatfield Gardens (another road to the school). We didn't block the Crumlin Road and they could also have gone up through Deerpark (a mixed area). There were at least three other routes."

All of them, however, are circuitous detours – some as long as three miles. Did he not agree there were also principles involved? "OK, someone might be convinced of their rights, especially the way people are brought up in Ardoyne. I would never agree with them, though. It was a terrible thing to do."

According to Fred Cobain, the surprise felt by McCartney and others about the parents' decision to defy the loyalists and walk the Ardoyne Road merely demonstrates their naivety.

"If you had half a brain you would have predicted it. It was an open goal for republicans, and Protestants should have seen that from the very beginning. Too many Protestants look at things from their perspective only. If you are looking at it from a republican point of view, here are kids who want to go to school, who are entitled to go to school, but who are being stopped from going to school by a loyalist mob."

His conviction was shared by DUP Assembly member, Nigel Dodds, the local MP, who asked during the September 10 Stormont debate (not entirely accurately): "Who persuaded people not to take the alternative route, as advised by the local school headmaster, the board of governors, the teachers, the *Irish News* editorial, the *News Letter* and others, to allow a cooling-off period? Why was it that that advice was ignored at the behest of IRA/Sinn Fein? What has its role been in ensuring that this problem has been exacerbated, agitated and exploited? IRA/Sinn Fein are up to their necks in ensuring that this problem continues."

Protester Ronnie Black says, "The parents might be excused for the first and second day, until the pipe bomb, which no one knew was going to be thrown. Afterwards, I wouldn't have walked my child up that road, you just couldn't have done it."

He says he can understand the principles involved since his community insists on using traditional routes for Orange parades, but that doesn't amount to the same thing as forcing children to endure the protest. Black also believes the children were pressurised by their parents. "I don't honestly believe a child would say to its mammy, 'Look, I want to walk up'. I don't believe that would have happened. I don't think a child knows right from wrong. Any child walking up there would have been scared. If a child's scared, it won't go back willingly into the same situation."

Loyalist community worker, Anne Bill, says she assumed, along with everyone else, that if there were a protest, parents would automatically take their children through St Gabriel's. "I would not put my child through it. I would have walked up the Crumlin Road and returned down the Ardoyne Road on my own if I wanted to make a point. If there's a riot on, who takes their child by the hand and walks them through? I would climb a mountain to keep my child safe. I would go to the ends of the earth to keep my child safe."

Billy Hutchinson, the PUP assemblyman, believes that peer pressure from within Ardoyne persuaded many parents to defy the protesters. "Three (Catholic) families contacted me. They didn't say people put pressure on them, but they said they felt pressurised, which is different.

They blamed the school principal and blamed Father Troy."

The same three families, he said, claimed that neither the church nor the school "gave any pastoral guidance".

Not every Protestant in North Belfast blamed the parents, however. One community worker in a staunchly loyalist area of the city, who did not want to be named, says he understood why many parents had chosen to defy the protest. "Children, even young ones, have a very strong sense of right and wrong. If they see what they believe is an injustice, they stand up against it. We should encourage that."

From talking to all sides, it does appear that individual families genuinely made up their own minds on which route to take. Bearing in mind the stubborn independence of the people of Ardoyne, any attempt to influence opinions would probably have been counter-productive.

Anne Tanney, who initially favoured the alternative route as a "cooling off" measure after the June 19 fracas, says, "We decided every family had to make a decision and every decision was right, because it was the right one for them. Nobody felt guilty or was criticised, whatever they chose. I told the children in school assembly that, whether they'd come up the road or through St Gabriel's, it was wonderful that they were at school. I said they were great girls and showed them the letters from around the world that proved so many people cared about them and loved them."

Parent Sean Carmichael had a row with Father Kenneth Brady (the parish priest and chairman of the Board of Governors before August 2001) when a camera crew wanted to measure exactly how long the alternative was.

"He physically stopped a camera crew with a meter stick who wanted to measure it up. They also wanted to film the way people had to go over mucky hills which were unsafe for the kids."

One critical factor, as far as the outside world was concerned, was the presence every day on the walk to and from school of the two priests of the parish, Father Aidan Troy and Father Gary Donegan. Their very presence lent the parents' case credibility. Asked about this, Father Troy plays down his role.

"I know people sometimes say my presence was critical. It's enormously complimentary, but I don't honestly think it's true. Suppose

I had stood up during one of those angry meetings in Ardoyne and said
that I had considered it very seriously, taken advice, and my conclusion
was that they should go up the Crumlin Road. I think the parents would
have told me to get stuffed and then gone up the road anyhow. If I had
delivered such advice, I would have become irrelevant."

The decision having been made, he says, he saw his presence on the
road as supportive of parental choice. "One of the parents summed it up
very well on the first morning when she said to me, 'You are our
insurance policy'. That's all I was."

There was huge speculation about whether the Catholic Church
hierarchy had tried to "lean" on the two priests, particularly Father Troy,
to guide the parents into using the alternative route. If he had done, the
entire dynamic of the story could have fundamentally changed. The
loyalists and their unionist supporters would have arguably gained the
high moral ground. But, says Father Troy, his arrival in Belfast was such
a baptism of fire that he might not have noticed pressure.

"I felt under absolutely no pressure at all. It might be better for me if
I could say I was. Let me put it this way, there might have been more
pressure there than I picked up, but if there were raised eyebrows, I didn't
notice them. To be quite truthful, if there had been pressure, it would
have been a terrible big waste of time."

Under repeated questioning, however, Father Troy concedes, "I have
to be faithful to the truth. Looking back now, the silence and the lack of
any explicit support, in a way, was pressure."

The man who always stood silently by his side, Father Gary
Donegan, unashamedly espouses the parents' view that the alternative
route was never feasible.

"It was a far longer walk, followed by a grassy hill, a football pitch and
a hole in a fence. Where else would you ask parents with buggies to go
through that? It meant disrupting a second school and asking mothers
with babies in buggies to walk over half-a-mile extra. They weren't just
leaving toddlers up to the school, they were returning as well, trailing
more toddlers with them."

Responding to criticism that he and Father Troy should have insisted
on using the alternative route, or at least refused to accompany the
children to school every day, he says, "I thought it was my moral

obligation to accompany them. If anything happened, God forbid, I would be there to be able to help."

Had Father Donegan noticed political or church pressure to guide parents towards the alternative route? "Not overtly. I would have been aware of the 'Dublin 4' syndrome (named after an affluent suburb of Dublin, commonly thought antagonistic to Irish, especially northern, nationalism). I knew some people believed the children were being frog-marched up and down the road. That was inaccurate. People were worried. What might happen to Our Lady of Mercy school at Ballysillan if we lost Holy Cross? Or Mercy Convent?"

Father Donegan says there was only one time that he saw a child he believed was too upset to walk up the road. "The little girl was in pieces, she literally folded up in front of me. The mother and I discussed it and we agreed she wasn't in a fit state. If I had ever seen another child in that state I would have said something."

Talking to the parents, it is abundantly clear that none of the public debate about their own "culpability" was lost on them. They agonised, night after night, about what to do for the best. There were discussions within families, sometimes with strongly-held views on both sides. Patricia Monaghan, an expressive woman who is open about her bitterness, and her husband Martin, a taxi-driver, for example, had different views on the alternative route.

"I would be very politically aware myself," says Martin. "I am not the type to be downtrodden by anyone. I don't tolerate it myself and I don't expect my children to think they are second-class citizens. I don't expect them to believe they are forbidden to walk on any part of a road or city they were born in."

But his wife says, "For me it was a wee bit different. If Rebekah (8) had preferred to go up the Crumlin Road that would have been fair enough for me. She was afraid and scared, but she knew we wouldn't let any harm come to her. She felt safe with us."

The couple had already lost two daughters due to an inherited medical condition, and this increased their personal agony over which road to take.

"I sat for three days and I couldn't make my mind up," says Patricia. "We have two daughters dead and I took myself up to the graveyard and

I sat at the grave and asked myself 'What do I do here?' For me it was a moral decision, it wasn't anything to do with politics, Catholics, Protestants, your ground or my ground. I went up and sat at my kids' grave and told myself that there was a chance that, if we went up the usual way, we could get injured. We could even lose the one wee girl that we had left. But what was I going to teach her? Was I going to teach her that because she was a Catholic, she was a second-class citizen and not as worthy as Protestants? I couldn't let my child feel worthless. It wasn't an easy decision to make for me, and it wasn't easy for Martin either. The bottom line for both of us was that if Rebekah said she didn't want to go, she was definitely not going. In that sense she was an integral part of the decision-making. Every morning, when we arrived at the top of Alliance Avenue, she was asked if she wanted to go through St Gabriel's and she said she didn't."

But even so, she still felt worried. "I asked myself constantly if this was worth putting her through? Is it me putting my child through it? Every day you had to sit and examine your conscience. You would ask yourself why? Was this the right thing? Am I doing this because the protesters say I can't, or because I don't want my child to be walked over? I didn't want her to grow up thinking there was something wrong with her, that she must go through the back door."

It was galling, to say the least, for people like Pat Monaghan, wrestling with their consciences every day, when people like Irish pop star, Ronan Keating (formerly of Boyzone), appeared to equate their predicament with that of the protesters. On June 22, 2002, six months after the protest had ended, but still recent enough for it to be raw in the minds of parents and children, Keating was interviewed in the *Irish News*, the morning paper read by most Catholics in the North.

He was quoted saying, "What really wound me up, I have to say, is all of that stuff that went on – I can't remember the name of the road – where the Catholics were bringing their kids to school through the Protestant area. For me, I'm looking at this and going, 'Well, there's two people to blame here'. Fine, these kids were being brought to school and this is being pushed in front of their faces by the Protestants. But the Catholics are bringing their children purposely when they could bring them another way, so there's two people to blame here."

The off-the-cuff comments caused huge hurt and anger in Ardoyne. Roisin Kennedy, for example, says, "Ronan couldn't even remember the name of the road, let alone know where it is, but he accused us of trailing our children up it. Father Troy cracked up and wrote a letter to the *Irish News*. People were saying if he ever showed his face about here, he would get lynched."

Much later, Keating did in fact visit the Crumlin Road, while on a charity fund-raising walk. Roisin says when he saw girls from Holy Cross in their uniforms, "he nearly collapsed".

She concludes, "It was a case of people making ill-informed comments on something they knew nothing about, jumping on the bandwagon. Ronan knew absolutely nothing about it. I just wished he could have walked the road with us, or even seen what we were going through, maybe that would have changed his mind."

Another parent, "Mary", also remembers the Keating comments with "amazement and total shock" that he viewed the parents equally to blame as the loyalist protesters. "How can you say people throwing bombs and urine at schoolchildren are as guilty as parents trying to get their children to school through the front gate? My niece is at Holy Cross. She ripped down a poster of Ronan Keating from her bedroom wall. She really did love him at that time. It just added insult to injury. She and her wee friends cried their eyes out."

The Rev Stewart Heaney showed more compassion towards the parents. "There must have been many of them worried sick about the effect it had on their children, but there was a principle at stake. It was an awful dilemma."

The accounts given by individual parents show they continually consulted their own children and never ceased to agonise over the choices they were being forced to make.

"Niamh had a right to be there. She wasn't doing anything wrong," says Liz Murphy. "I wasn't abusing anybody, the protesters were abusing her. We were prepared to use our bodies on either side of her to ensure she was safe. I told Niamh that, if at anytime she didn't want to go up the road, to tell me. I didn't trail her up by the arm. Both John (her husband) and I said to her, numerous times, that if she was too frightened, she needn't go."

The Murphys bought Niamh a portable CD player to use as she walked to school to drown out the noise of the protest.

"We had already walked the Crumlin Road in June, and the loyalists had laughed at us. They had shouted at us from their cars, pointing and hurling insults. Nobody had the right to humiliate us like that. She has learned to stand up to bullies and not to run away. I am proud of her. The choice was between walking through yet another loyalist area, through a muddy field and the back door, or holding our heads up and going our usual way."

Lynda Bowes says she would never have forced Amanda (9) through the school gates. "We both came to the conclusion that her wishes were paramount. If the child couldn't take it, we would have taken her up the back way or out of the school. She was the most important part of the decision-making. Amanda was born in 1992, so she was about three when the first ceasefire was declared. If I had walked away after the bombing, the loyalists would have won, but more importantly they would have won in her eyes. Amanda knew that she hadn't done anything wrong, neither had the school. So why would we run away? We told ourselves the loyalists could shout all they wanted. Whatever they threw at us, we could take it."

Sharon Quail took her daughter, Shaunalee (8), through St Gabriel's until she complained that it took too long. "I told her that she knew the consequences if we went up the front way but she said she didn't care as long as I was with her. At the end of the day, I had always told her she couldn't run away from trouble. No matter what it was, you mustn't run away, you have to stand up for yourself."

The resilience of some of the children was amazing. Even a child like Amy Lindsay (9), who had been so terrified on the first day of term that her parents had taken her home, eventually decided she wanted to walk the Ardoyne Road.

"We didn't know whether to hike it through the mucky field or not," says Maura Lindsay. "To be honest, I wanted to bring Amy through St Gabriel's, even through the muck, after the bombing. But Amy didn't want to, she wanted to go back down the road with all of her friends."

Jeanette McKernan says it was the same with her daughters, Chloe and Rebecca (4 and 6). "We make decisions collectively in our house.

There was not one morning when I didn't ask my kids which way they wanted to walk. I think the way Chloe saw it was that there was safety in numbers. There wasn't a chance of the protesters forcing me up the back. There were parents being attacked going up there as well, despite loyalist promises it would be safe."

There would also have been difficulties for St Gabriel's had all the Holy Cross parents had to trek through its grounds. Firstly it might have become the target of more loyalist protests. Secondly its school day would have been seriously disrupted by the constant flow of parents and buggies through the grounds.

"Their football pitch was churned up by Holy Cross teachers having to park their cars on it," says parent Tanya Carmichael.

Judy Haughey embodies all the problems, both practical and principled, that the parents had about the alternative route. She had two girls at Holy Cross Cora (11) and Lucilla (10).

"The cheek of people saying there was an alternative route! The trouble we had was desperate. If you could have seen me trying to push the buggy, holding another child by the hand. If people hadn't helped me up the steps and over the fields, I wouldn't have managed it. I never ever felt safe on the Crumlin Road either. I was worried they would attack us on the back road. Some parents already had been attacked there. So, what were we to do?"

It was hurtful, she says, to hear people saying that the parents of Ardoyne could not love their children. "In this district, we have had to fight all our lives for everything. Anthony and I talked about it until we were blue in the face. If we didn't get the kids to Holy Cross, it would end up closing. It would only be a matter of time before the loyalists would start blocking the other way. On a few mornings there were already blockades on the Crumlin Road. They didn't want Catholic children there either. Were we going to start transferring them to other schools?"

Cora Haughey has asthma and Judy occasionally had to run up to Holy Cross with her inhalers, via the Crumlin Road and St Gabriel's. She regularly passed through groups of protesters, "grown men with scarves over their heads".

She said nothing as she passed them, hoping they assumed she was a

Protestant. "If they had known I was a Catholic, I would have got such a kicking. Attacks were already starting along the back route, although it was kept hush-hush."

Who in their right mind, she asks, would choose to walk anywhere they were at risk of attack? "Do we not love our children? Of course we do. We would die for our children. It's ridiculous to claim we were only using the Ardoyne Road to make a point. Every day we were tempted to give up. But when you thought it over, you knew you had to stand up for yourself."

Some families did decide to use the back route. Ironically, one was Brendan Mailey's, the spokesman for the parents' group who regularly defended their use of the direct route in television interviews. His daughter, Rachel (8), had refused point blank to walk the direct route. Brendan, who is clearly devoted to his daughter, duly walked her to school that way, although he was still fearful of using the Crumlin Road. "It wasn't as risk-free as it appeared to outsiders," he says.

The McCabes also ended up taking Gemma (8) through the back door of St Gabriel's. On the second morning of the autumn term, the child had told them she did not want to walk up Ardoyne Road, and that was it.

"We took it on a day-to-day basis. If Gemma felt she couldn't face it, she came back down again; if she felt strong enough, she went ahead," says Sharon McCabe. "Sometimes she didn't want to go to school at all, even through the back way. It was always her decision."

After a newspaper carried a report about parents "being armed" on their way to school, Gemma's brother would tease her as she got ready for school and ask her if she had a "lethal weapon" in her schoolbag. "He would pull out her Barbie doll, just to try and lighten the mood," says Sharon.

Early on in the protest, parent Tanya Carmichael decided to take the back road, but there too she ran into protesters. "There was one loyalist girl with a baby in her arms with a big blue hat and a large pom-pom, a lovely child. What that girl shouted at us was unbelievable. We still got abuse no matter what way we walked. You were never safe whichever way you went."

The Carmichaels eventually reverted to the main road, surprised at the fortitude of their daughter, Emma (8).

It wasn't just a simple question of Sinn Fein supporters taking the direct route and more moderate SDLP supporters taking the back road. Terry Laverty, the headmaster of Holy Cross Boys' school, says he saw people whom he knew to have no political affiliation taking their children to school via the direct route.

"There was no Sinn Fein agenda or anything like that. It was just parents wanting the right to go through the front gate like they themselves had done."

Elaine Burns, who is no Sinn Fein supporter, says there was "nothing political" in the decision-making. "I love my children to bits and they weren't going to be treated like second class citizens. No one has a right to tell me any different."

Brendan Mailey, the Right to Education spokesman whose own daughter, Rachel, took the alternative route, says, "The bottom line was no child went up that road unless they agreed. I heard one or two kids the second day, saying they didn't want to go and their mothers took them away. The children had brains and were capable of making decisions. There was never one word said out of place about parents who decided to take their children up the Crumlin Road. Everybody was respectful of other people's decisions. If anyone had been critical of anyone else, they would have got into trouble. The loyalists were the problem. They were in the wrong, not any parent. We had to stay united, which we did for 99.9% of the blockade."

The Ardoyne-born novelist, Anna Burns, writing in the *Sunday Times* in 2001, memorably recalled her days walking to Holy Cross at the height of the Troubles. A rota system operated: "I was always sure Ma was dead whenever it was her turn not to be there." Sometimes on the way to school, she wrote, the children would be bought sweets. They knew this meant there was "something wrong around the corner".

"The thing I remember about the Ardoyne Road was the bloodstains there always seemed to be all over it. Nobody ever commented on them. If the rioting was too vicious on the Ardoyne Road, we'd turn back and not go to school at all. Only once do I remember the 'safe' back route being used. When we reached the Crumlin Road through this back exit, the rioting had spilt to there, too."

Some things never change.

Chapter Seven

CHILDREN

Mummy, what's a filthy Fenian bitch?   Holy Cross child

Everything has suffered, her schoolwork has slipped. The child is a nervous wreck. She is scarred for life.
                    Jim Crawford, speaking of his daughter, Roisin, aged nine

When you're going up the Shankill, And it's running down your ankle? Diarrhoea!   Ardoyne children's street song

All the public protagonists in the Holy Cross protest — politicians, clergymen, British government ministers, loyalists and police officers — professed repeatedly that it was the children who mattered most.

But from day one, it was the children who suffered most. For 12 long weeks (longer than that if you include the previous summer and far longer if you include the time that has elapsed since) they suffered the kind of fear and hurt that adults can only imagine.

The loyalist protesters, along with those who should have intervened to protect the children, put their interests at the bottom on the ladder, far below their own desires and ambitions. Defending the protesters, community worker and CRUA spokesperson, Anne Bill, says that although it concerns her that the children were hurt, "it also annoys me a wee bit" that she and her group were held responsible.

"I don't believe I am to blame at all, I didn't make those kids go up there. There is such a thing as parental responsibility. To be honest, the (British) government should have done something. They can ensure parents take responsibility under child protection law. They shouldn't have let parents drag their kids up. I wouldn't have taken a child through it."

The professed concern felt by the loyalists infuriated the parents. Their compassion, the parents pointed out, did not prevent them concentrating their activities at precisely the times that the children walked to school. Although the protesters contend they had no deliberate wish to harm children, that was the effect of their actions over the 12 weeks of the protest. After the first day, they could not possibly have been unaware that the children were inevitably going to be, at the very least, terribly frightened.

Parents also agonised over the inevitable fact that their children might be irreparably damaged by their walk to school via the Ardoyne Road. But the parents, at least, were surely acting in what they genuinely believed were the children's best interests. No one could make that claim for the loyalists.

Children are always, of course, particularly vulnerable and least able to protect themselves in civil conflict, as evidenced by global statistics. Northern Ireland is no different. Of the 3,598 people killed in the Troubles, 257 were aged 17 or under (7.5%). Twenty-three of those (0.64%) were five or under, 24 were aged 11 or under (0.67%) and 210 aged 17 or under (5.84%).

To speak of the "average" child's experience in Northern Ireland can be misleading. Children's experiences are widely diverse, with most children having little experience of the Troubles. Despite that, a relatively small number of children have suffered terribly in the Troubles and have either been killed or lived their childhood years overshadowed by life-threatening events, including the loss of family and friends. Catholic children are the most vulnerable. Of the 257 killed aged 17 or under, 74% are Catholic. Children and young people have also been combatants. Forty members of the IRA aged under 18 have been killed. The most frequent cause of death in children in the North under the age of 18 is shooting, followed by explosions. Together these account for 224, or 87%, of all deaths of children. Fourteen children have been killed by plastic bullets.

Children, then, have been far from immune from the worst effects of the Troubles. What made Holy Cross unique, however, was the sustained and conscious infliction of fear on children aged between four and eleven. Whatever cause the protesters had, cruelty towards physically disabled children was surely inexcusable.

Although parent Frances Doherty tried to shield her child, Shannon, from abuse (she was born with one arm shorter than the other), it was to no avail. "The first day we held on to her tightly. The second morning, Shannon wanted to walk with other children, instead of clinging to us all the time. But the protesters shouted at me, 'Here love, are you not fucking ashamed bringing something like that to school', 'She's a freak', and 'Look at One Arm'."

But all parents noticed changes in their children. Roisin Kennedy, mother of Niamh (9), says they were significant. "She turned into the type of child that has an answer to everything, cheeky, aggressive. I couldn't get through to her. She used to be a wee softy and would never fight, but now she says things like 'I hate you' and lashes out at her younger brother. Her whole personality has changed."

Roisin's family doctor says Niamh is taking her anger out on her brother. "He's younger, she feels she had power over him. The protesters had power over her and she is bullying him back."

Niamh told an American psychologist visiting the school that she was frightened to sleep in case "the men in masks come in the middle of the night and kill my mammy and daddy".

"Then the bed-wetting started, the first of many physical signs," says Roisin who, like many parents, also feels guilty that her other children suffered — in her case her son, Ryan. "I wasn't there for my son's first day at school. That killed me. My daddy took him to school instead. I couldn't give him my time."

Terry Laverty, the principal of Holy Cross Boys' school, believes many brothers of Holy Cross girls suffered likewise. "Rightly, the spotlight was on the girls but they also had brothers."

Worried about the knock-on effect on his pupils, Laverty organised what's called "circle time", a form of group counselling in which everyone gets a turn to speak.

"Very few of the statutory agencies were offering practical help for brothers; it was all going to the girls and Wheatfield (the nearby Protestant school). We felt a little isolated. Our boys were suffering and some of their parents were going through what I can only describe as nervous breakdowns. They were being attacked and threatened in their homes and some were made homeless. Boys were not able to play normally, they had trouble sleeping; some were wetting the bed because of fears their parents would be hurt. Some worried that the loyalists were going to come and burn the school down."

Some boys pulled through somehow. Chris and Rita McDonald's son, Gavin (11), even won an award from his school, St Malachy's. "We had to tell the school that he wasn't living at home for the last two weeks of term because ours was under constant attack. He was talking about it at school and they felt sorry for him and gave him the award because, basically, despite it all, he had still done so well," says father Chris, proudly.

Kieran McGrandles said his son Marc (7) became "very clingy" and never wanted him to leave the house. "None of them would go to bed for fear of something happening. Danielle (9) wouldn't go to the bathroom on her own. I had to stand behind the door while she went to the loo. She became very quiet, she wouldn't talk about it and if anyone else did, she left the room. That's when we decided to sell up, although we loved that wee house."

Pat Monaghan says her daughter, Rebekah (8), became increasingly withdrawn. It was only when they shared experiences with other parents that they realised other children were acting the same way. She remembers a day when Rebekah changed into her pyjamas, refused to leave the house and stuck very close. It was only later that she realised why. So long as she was in her pyjamas, the child would not be asked to leave the house and face the protesters.

Rebekah was also telling her older brother about her worries and he fed it back to his mother. "She was waking up at nights, coming into our bed and, as it dragged on, began to wet the bed. She was losing all her self-confidence."

Martin Monaghan said the bombing really hit hard. "Rebekah was starting to ask questions like 'Are they going to throw more bombs at us?' and 'Are they going to shoot us dead?'"

After witnessing threats being shouted at her father on the protest, Rebekah worried he might be shot and began discouraging him from walking her to school but, he says, he became more determined.

"She was frightened for herself, but ever more so for me. She would have appealed to me to stay behind and that she'd be OK."

The protest left the parents with another dilemma. How much should they tell their daughters? How to explain it? "I always tried to get it through Shannon's head that, no matter what people do to you, whatever their reasons may be, you should always forgive them," says Lisa Irvine.

Shannon needed counselling for three months after the protest. "She was afraid of loud noises and wouldn't sleep in her own room, she slept in my bed with me. Kids have this unfounded belief that you will always be able to protect them. They think nothing bad can happen because Mummy is going to protect them. She was physically sick from fear a couple of times during the protest; she was also very weepy and clingy. At the end of the school day, the kids would be looking out the windows, waiting for the protesters to gather, knowing they had to go through it all over again."

The school was, of course, always watchful for signs of distress, amongst which, says Anne Tanney, were "lack of concentration, constant queries about their parents, a tendency to cry easily and a general wariness".

Jim Crawford says Roisin (9) "had night terrors and sometimes couldn't sleep all night".

"She became clingy and would beg me not to leave the house, even when I had to go to work. She had to take two different kinds of medication and needed counselling for a long time. She's now at secondary school but it has set her back a year or two. She's 12 now but thinks like a 10-year-old."

Gemma McCabe (8) could not sleep and wandered around the house at night, getting into different beds.

"She always seemed to end up in bed beside her big brother for some reason," says her mother Sharon. "The counsellor said Gemma saw her big brother as security. He wasn't walking up the road. He was her big brother, he's very tall, and she felt safer with him."

Gemma went to counselling after wetting the bed and having nightmares. "She woke up screaming in her sleep again just the other night but I couldn't get sense out of her. She just says she's afraid."

Although bed-wetting was a frequent problem with the children, Jeanette McKernan says her two girls suffered more "from demons" in their sleep.

"If Rebecca had a bad dream, Chloe would also own up to one. I tried to explain they could tell me absolutely anything," she says, but even so she was shocked when she discovered the girls were too frightened to leave Ardoyne with their school uniforms on. If they were out with the girls in the family car, they would duck down on the floor in the back if they saw Union Jacks tied to lamp-posts. "Normally, I would never let a child into the car without a seat belt on, but how can you put a seat belt on a child who is cowering on the floor?"

Jeanette took her children for counselling, but believed they were making a good recovery as they rarely talked about the protest. Eventually she told the counsellor she was concerned they were wasting his time and maybe other children needed help more.

His reply was chilling. "The way he put it was, 'They don't want to talk to you in case they hurt you. When they're with me, from the minute they arrive to the minute they leave, they do nothing but talk about it'."

Her children were not talking to her about the protest because they did not want to upset her after witnessing her reaction when she had been told of a death threat from the "Red Hand Defenders" (a cover name for the UDA). The counsellor had encouraged her daughters to draw pictures of the protest, using any colours they liked. Her two girls were only drawing in black.

"When I saw the drawings, I was really depressed. I felt I was fighting a losing battle. I didn't know what to do. The counsellor said I was doing right to try to keep to a normal routine."

Many Holy Cross children never felt safe during the protest, even in their own homes, far less outside Ardoyne. Rita McDonald remembers an incident at Christmas 2001, when she had taken a group of children to the pantomime in Belfast city centre as a special treat.

"A wee girl from Holy Cross asked me if we were safe there. I remember asking her what she meant and her reply was 'Are there Protestants here?' She was only seven years old. I told her that, yes, there were, but it was a neutral place and she was OK. Nobody could touch her. The child then totally relaxed and enjoyed the rest of the pantomime. But for that to be on her mind — the child thought that any Protestant was going to hurt her."

Tanya Carmichael, like several other parents, had the idea of telling her younger daughter, Emer (4), that the whistling and jeering on the road was really people celebrating her first day at school. "To this day, she believes it."

"Emma," says Sean Carmichael, "is more vocal with her opinions now. From an early age she was able to stand up to people. She is very forceful, she won't back down and answers back."

Tanya says, "Emma is a real wee fighter, it definitely hardened her. Before, she had been bullied at another school and we had to transfer her to Holy Cross. Right from the second day there, she said she was taking her camogie stick (a wooden stick used in women's Gaelic games) with her to school and that if anybody came near her she would use it."

The Carmichaels believe they were lucky as both their girls reacted relatively well. Other families with two daughters at the school sometimes found varying reactions. Elaine and Danny Burns' daughters, Niamh (4) and Leona (7), were a case in point.

"Niamh seemed to be coping," says Elaine, "but then things went really wrong after about the first week and she began wetting the bed. Leona, who was always placid, a lovely wee, caring girl, just became quieter and quieter. The counsellors told me Niamh's anxiety levels were increasing towards night-time because she knew that after night came morning. She wouldn't go to bed on her own, or without the light on. She became angry and frustrated and bad-tempered. She would lash out and hit her sister, throwing pots and pans about. Leona was withdrawn and wouldn't defend herself. We had months of problems like that."

Another Niamh, Niamh Murphy, also experienced significant personality changes, according to her mother, Liz. "She just continually ate, whereas before she hardly ate a bite. She also talked, continuously and nervously. She never shut up."

A family friend made a joke out of it, nicknaming Niamh "Seventeen Seconds" because that was the longest she would ever stay quiet. Liz thought if that was her only problem she had got off lightly compared to other mothers dealing with bed-wetting and counselling.

"A few weeks after the protest ended, I looked at Niamh and asked myself why she was always hungry. You couldn't get her to bed. She talked and she talked, even as I put her to bed, she talked and talked and talked to the very last second. She was literally talking until her eyes closed. I even laughed about it with John because before we couldn't have had a conversation with her. Then she started refusing to leave the house, she just wanted to stay with us."

Niamh began to refuse to use the lavatory. She was too afraid to go into a room on her own. Her parents could see she needed to go, but she would not. "She would say she was too afraid to go."

This went on for about a year. Niamh now has to take metabolic tablets every day. The doctor says her condition is stress-related. "She is frightened of everything. She would let people hit her in the street. She doesn't fight back. Her personality totally changed."

Tina Gallagher's two girls, Roisin and Tara (8 and 4), were both badly affected. "After the first day back in September 2001," she says, "Roisin was absolutely wrecked. Most of the kids were. They couldn't take in what had happened. They had seen it and heard it but they couldn't believe it. They were clinging to adults and sobbing in shock. Not only at what had been shouted at them but the very loudness, it was deafening. Roisin started to have terrible nightmares. One was about the alarm clock going off and getting ready for school. Everything in the dream is normal but as soon as she puts her uniform on and goes downstairs, her daddy and I turn into crocodiles and try to eat her."

Roisin was additionally upset by counselling because she "had to recall events" so her mother thought she should stop. Both Roisin and Tara ended up on tranquillisers. Tara was only four. Roisin began to refer to the protesters as "Orangies" (a pejorative term, after the Orange Order, a loyalist marching institution), a word she had never heard before. Her parents would never use such a sectarian term in the house. The two girls also now recognise the British flag. If they are going out, they ask their parents if they're going to "a red, white and blue place or a green, white and gold place". Roisin won't wear her uniform outside Ardoyne fearing she might be attacked. "She thinks that, because she is a Holy Cross girl, somebody can go and hit her with impunity. It's still playing on her mind."

Like Rebekah Monaghan, Tara began returning from school and putting on her pyjamas straightaway. When Tina asked why, the child replied, "Because when you have your pyjamas on, you don't have to go out."

One of Judy Haughey's children, Cora (11), also became politicised by the protest. "They had never heard the word loyalist in the house, yet all of a sudden it was, 'What are the loyalists going to do next?' I tried to explain that it wasn't the ordinary Protestant people up there who were responsible, that there was good and bad everywhere and that it wasn't the good people of Glenbryn who were at fault. But it was an uphill battle. All that they knew is that the bad people are from up there, coming out of those houses — which wasn't the case anyhow as the protesters were being bussed in from everywhere. The children were frightened and scared. My wee girl said she was going to join Sinn Fein youth, and I thought to myself, here we go. Lucilla wasn't too bad but Cora was getting very bitter and angry and I didn't want that."

This was a recurrent theme with the parents: trying to stop their children becoming bitter and sectarian. Lynda Bowes says they will not know until they have grown up how successful, or otherwise, those efforts were.

"In years to come, when Amanda starts venturing into town on her own and coming into contact with Protestants, I think it will start to show if the experience made a difference. At the moment I can't really tell. Amanda asked me once if our doctor was a Catholic or a Protestant. I replied by asking if she thought it would make any difference to the medicine. I explained that the protesters were wrong but not all Protestants were like them and you couldn't judge them all the same. As you go through life, I said, you will find there will be some bad Catholics too."

Most of the parents were careful not to allow their children to watch the television news. Tanya Carmichael explains that it could have re-traumatised the children a second time.

"We didn't want her to be reminded of what had happened to her. We wanted her to settle down and come back to some kind of normality and relax, to keep the household routine as normal and regimented as normal."

Maura Lindsay's daughter, Amy (9), coped by becoming withdrawn and quiet. "She would cry for no reason and was angry all the time; she seemed to take a lot of her anger out on her older sister. If her older sister so much as looked at her sideways, Amy would scream at her. She had stopped sleeping in her own bed, she wouldn't go to the toilet on her own and she wouldn't even have a shower in the house, she had to go to my mother's house.

"Physically, her asthma was getting worse and she needed to use her inhaler more, due to nerves and rapid breathing. The child's confidence went right downhill. She is slowly coming round with adults within her own family. Adults outside the family haven't a hope in hell of getting a word out of her."

Of course, there was a completely separate group of children involved in the protest — those who stood beside their loyalist parents, shouting at the Catholic children as they walked up the road. Maura Lindsay herself talks of the old days, when Holy Cross and Wheatfield shared cross-community activities. One day her daughter said to her that she had spotted a particular girl whom she had befriended on one of the trips.

"There she was, aged about 10, standing at the side of the road, screaming, 'You Fenian bastards'. The child's mother had her by the hand and was shouting even louder again. They really are sick people. Imagine letting your child shout and curse like that, filling them with hatred. As if it was not bad enough the adults doing it, but to actually breed it into your kids, how pathetic."

Lisa Irvine had a similar experience. "I saw kids blowing whistles and shouting names, standing side by side with their parents. They were as young as 11 or 12 and there were teenagers who brought their babies along in pushchairs, as if it was a morning's outing. The babies used to hold little flags. I just couldn't get my head around that."

But not all Protestant children sided with the loyalists. The Holy Cross protest had a far greater impact on children than may have hitherto been thought. From his research work investigating sectarian attitudes amongst Protestant children in west Belfast, one student discovered they, also, had been affected. The student, who did not want to be named, said he had been surprised to find the children, aged between six and 11, voluntarily raising the issue during questioning, even though the dispute had ended nearly three years previously.

"The Protestant children very much sided with the children at Holy Cross, not with the Protestant adults involved. They used words like 'horrible', 'frightening' and 'terrible' to describe what the children had been through. They clearly disapproved of what the loyalist adults had done, although they came from the same community. It had clearly had a big impact on them — greater than that of the loyalist feud, to which they were closer, both geographically and socially."

Remarkably, seven Holy Cross girls volunteered, with the consent of their parents, to be interviewed for this book so they could express their own views and give an insight into how they responded to their ordeal. They are Roisin Crawford, Amy Lindsay, Niamh Kennedy, Roisin Gallagher, Amanda Bowes, Danielle McGrandles and Rebekah Monaghan, all ages given as of September 2001. These interviews were felt justified because the children had a right to be heard, they were willing to be interviewed and their parents agreed that it would not do them any harm.

Louanne Martin, a trainee counsellor with experience of working with young people, conducted the interviews over a period of weeks in the spring and summer of 2004. She says she found the experience immensely moving, and came away with a sense of children who were "hurt, but very courageous". During interviews, if they became upset, Louanne offered repeatedly to finish, but invariably the children were determined to have their say. It was the first time the girls had been asked for their views with a purpose to publishing them. They seemed to look forward to it, says Louanne.

"It appeared to give them a sense of value, that their views were worthy of publication. Each child reacted differently to the protest. By asking them to re-live it, we were not necessarily trapping them in the past but, I hope, helping them to move forward through the catharsis of being able to express themselves to the outside world."

Roisin Crawford (9) is a gently-spoken child with big brown eyes, a freckled face and chestnut brown hair tied in two pigtails. She was sometimes animated, but on occasion her voice disappeared to a whisper. She enjoys camogie and football. She says the June 19 rioting was "scary" and hated the protest because of people spitting at her, calling her names and pulling her hair. As it continued, she admits it sometimes made her want to avoid going to school at all.

Asked about the protesters, she says they were "bad" and that they had no reason to shout at her. She says she could clearly hear the names she was being called, although she is not allowed to repeat the words. She remembers the protesters being close and that "stones and fireworks" were thrown.

"There were men and women, over their fences, shouting names and spitting and pulling people's hair and throwing tea all round the adults. We were walking up and everyone just says 'Watch!' and then a bomb flew over. Father Troy told us all to run. I thought everyone was going to die."

Roisin says that walking between her parents made her feel safer but that she had nightmares about the protest. The nightmares involved "Billy Hutchinson coming into the house and shooting my mummy and my daddy".

Of the police, she says their riot gear was "scary" and she preferred it when they did not wear face-masks. When she grows up and has children, she says, she won't send them to Holy Cross, in case it happens again. She says Father Troy helped everyone. "If you asked him to walk beside you, he would walk beside you", which made her feel safer. Watching it on the news was "scary", but counselling was helpful. It spoilt her memories of the school, she says.

Amy Lindsay (9) is a wide-eyed, shy, slender child with dark-brown hair tied back in a pony tail. "There was an extraordinary sense of stillness about Amy," says Louanne, adding that she spoke very quietly, looking into the middle distance. Amy's mother, Maura, and her father, David, sat in on the interview. When Amy became upset, Maura rubbed her back and whispered comforting words. David looked bewildered by emotion during the interview and got his daughter a handkerchief and water when she was upset.

"Both parents' love for their daughter is palpable. Their pain at her distress is heartbreaking," says Louanne.

Amy says she enjoyed her days at Holy Cross, seeing her friends and loving the teachers and the school uniform. Her memories of June 19 are of "shouting and we weren't allowed near the window". She felt scared running out the back of the school and she did not go to school the next day.

The trouble that summer deeply worried her (the Lindsays' home was attacked, on a daily basis, by loyalists from Glenbryn throughout the summer of 2001). "You could hear them talking and sometimes you could see them on the roof," says Amy. She had dreams of people "coming into the street and throwing bombs".

On the first day of the new term, she says, she tried to ignore the shouting and "tried not to look at them", but she and her mother never made it to the school gates that day. Amy became so upset that mother and daughter returned home.

"People were crying and it was too much," she remembers. Later, she decided to try the main road again. "Because there was no back door, you had to walk round the front and into the school."

She says she could hear what the protesters were shouting and that neither she nor her friends could understand why they were doing it. The teachers "got us drinks and calmed us down". Asked what she thought of the protesters, Amy hesitates a long time before spitting out, "I hated them", and starts to cry.

Later in the interview, she remembers the loyalist nicknamed Spiderman. "He put his fingers in a shape of a gun and pointed it at his head and then pointed it at me," she says.

Of the day of the bombing, she says, "We were walking up and then bricks were coming over and then everybody started shouting to run and then the bomb went off. Everybody was losing their children and all. My mummy got pushed back and my dad lifted me. Father Gary and Father Troy would tell you jokes so you wouldn't think about it." She adds that if she has a daughter of her own, she will send her to Holy Cross, "because it is a good school".

She now feels "angry and sad" about the protest, asking, "Why would they stand there when we were only trying to get to school, shouting the stuff that they were shouting at us?" The protest, she says, has made her an angry person.

Niamh Kennedy (6) is very friendly and chatty, confident and articulate. She enjoys swimming and dancing and likes the girl band, "Girls Aloud". She wants to be a barrister when she grows up.

She loves Holy Cross. "The teachers are very friendly and the principal is very nice. They would always help you, if you were scared of anything. When the protest and all was going on everybody was helping. There was everybody's mummy and daddy there and they were all helping each other and everybody was just, like, coming together. They were making everybody think they weren't allowed to do this because it was wrong.

"In September, there was this big tunnel thing we had to go through. It was on the right hand side and all the Protestants were on the next side and they were all shouting. They were hitting everybody, it was scary and they were throwing tea cups at us, cups and knives and forks and saucers and water and all.

"I remember one day when me and my daddy was walking up with my mummy and my granda, and there was a big girl – she never changed her clothes, she always had the same pair of jeans on, and jumper – she came out of the Land Rover, she just pushed through all the police and banged into me.

"My daddy gave me a hug. I was very, very scared. She (the protester) kept looking back and going — you know — like giving you the eyes (Niamh scrunches her eyes up into narrow little creases). I was very scared.

"They were calling us — I don't like saying the word. They were calling us all different names because we were Catholics. They were blowing their whistles. There was even girls from Girls Model (a local Protestant school) and wee kids and all blowing whistles and calling us all names.

"My mummy, my friend Maura and Deirdre were walking up one day and a wee girl waved at us. Then me and Maura were coming back down and she stuck up the middle finger at us and called us a bad name. Me and Maura just walked on and she stuck her tongue out at us. She just kept on looking at us, just staring us down the road.

"A couple of my friends had to walk up the back way and it was so, so cold and my granda gave them a lift to school. It was so scary. Everybody was calling names. I just looked at the ground and at my mummy. I was crying and my mummy just held me and I never looked at them. When we were coming back down we used to sing a song, just to keep our minds off it.

"There was Protestants, like, if you went up the Crumlin Road. There would be a couple of streets, everybody used to be standing there. It was still hard to get up.

"The teachers told us to be calm. They never wanted us to look out.

They just kept our eyes on the board. I had a very nice teacher, she only got there the day of the protest. She was very, very nice. You kept on getting, like, a scary thing just going into your eyes and you started to feel, like, you started shaking. It was just when you looked at them and their faces saying, 'I don't like you, go away'. We were only trying to get to school to learn and they were stopping us. There's no point, it's only people trying to go and learn."

Father Troy, she says, "guided me and he was very, very nice", but she did not like the television coverage. "It seemed like just 'Oh, the Protestants have started a wee riot at Holy Cross Girls' school but it will stop soon'. I asked my mummy why were people like that? She said there were bad people in the world. But she and my daddy said all Protestants aren't bad. My daddy says he works with Protestants and he knows very nice Protestants.

"I couldn't get to bed at night. I used to have really bad dreams about men coming with masks on and big guns and hurting my mummy and daddy. I used to cry and all in my sleep.

"I still fear about people coming with masks," she says, although she adds the priests and her family had helped her. "I remember when everybody used to stand at the shops and wait for us, when we came through the barricade. There were loads of people there, standing clapping."

(At this point in the interview, Niamh's words come spilling out of her, in disjointed sentences.)

"You were just walking down, and the blast bomb went off and I remember mummy was going for a job interview when it went off and my mummy was holding my cheeks and I was crying. All you heard was the big, we were just outside the gates and all you heard was this big bang.

"My mummy goes, 'Oh my God' and I started crying it was so noisy and the loyalists all started cheering."

Niamh says she is still scared, "In case they come out, just hurt you, bring you into their houses and hurt you, I would be really scared and, I don't know, just looking at them would scare me.

"I remember coming through the barricade one day and, like, all the Falls (the Falls Road in Catholic west Belfast) came over and they all had packets of crisps and all for us. They had wee roses and all to give us.

"I never knew what a Protestant was and I never knew what flags or anything meant. I never even knew what bad men were or anything down the Shankill and all. I never even knew that they were bad people."

Roisin Gallagher (8) is a wide-eyed, earnest girl, softly spoken. She has long blond hair, blue eyes and freckles across her nose. She enjoys swimming, camogie, netball and basketball. She plans to be a beautician. She remembers being right beside the bomb when it went off.

"Me and my mummy's friend were walking up and they were calling us names and shouting and they were throwing cups of tea all round us. They were sitting abusing us and we didn't even do anything wrong. And there was a big bang and my mummy's friend put a big long coat over my head and we had to run and I was squealing. It was really scary. I thought they were all going to come to my house. And I started wetting my bed and all, I was really scared. When you go to the toilet, the wee-wee, they put that in a balloon. It splashed all over.

"There was Brits and peelers, and we had to walk through these big gates but they were still shouting stuff and abusing us. They were throwing stones and some of us were getting hit. I went to run and everybody else started running and then I got lost."

Asked if she ever walked round the long way, through St Gabriel's, Roisin says, "No. Because we shouldn't have to do that. Our school is up there and we should be able to walk up there."

She says she prayed for it all to stop, but it did not seem to help. Despite it all, she says, she would send her own daughters to Holy Cross, "because it is a good school. The teachers in it are good. You go out to play, 'chaseys' and all. It's good. I do maths and English and history and science and all different stuff."

She says she still "gets the shivers" if she ever sees crowds of people standing about. "When I was in bed I used to have these dreams that they were rapping on the window and that they were going to kill me. I have a back room and I keep on thinking they are coming down the entry when my mummy and daddy are asleep. Coming to get me. I sometimes still get dreams like that."

Counselling, she says, "was good".

"We talked about stuff and we used to watch tapes and draw. And then we used to get wee sweets. It was good. But I'm just all different now. There's a woman in our school that comes, if you've got any worries, she'll come and give you massages. She tells you wee stories, that you will be alright. If you bite your nails and if you worry, she does reflexology. You can get a hand massage."

Like others, Roisin particularly remembers Spiderman. "He used to always give me the creeps. Sometimes he drives past and you don't look at him and you try to think of something else."

Amanda Bowes (9) is a very articulate girl with long brown hair and laughing, mischievous eyes. She has a wicked sense of humour and her mother believes it saw her through. She plans to be a scientist when she grows up.

"Some mornings it felt that the road was getting longer but you started to get used to it after a wee while. I remember name-calling, blowing whistles and horns."

She says, "The first day (of the autumn term) was terrible, because they had a barrier but you were walking up along beside them and they spat on you. A couple of my mates got spat on a bit. You could hear them calling you names.

"Getting up in the morning was worst because you didn't know what they were going to do. When you came out, you knew that it was the end of the day and you didn't have to go back up again to them until the next day. I did want to go to school, it was just that it was scary in the mornings. Sometimes they stood quiet and the next morning they blew whistles and the next morning they would stay quiet a bit and then they blew horns the next morning. So it was unexpected.

"My mummy used to come up through St Gabriel's to pick me up but I wanted to walk down the front.

"The teachers tried to make you ignore it, take your mind of it when you got into school. You had assembly and they tried to act normal, as if nothing was going on so we didn't really think about it that much.

"Father Troy came in every morning to check up on the classes, to make sure they were alright. He came up to the assembly some mornings just to make sure the kids were alright, making sure and talking to Miss Tanney and that.

"I never used to watch the news until then and I don't watch it anymore! But I did watch to see what way they would put it. They said things that weren't exactly true sometimes. Sometimes they just fiddled it about a bit to make it suited the people who were watching it.

"There were some mornings when the cameras were staring at you. You tried not to look at them, to ignore them but sometimes they were right in your face and you just couldn't ignore them. It was sort of annoying sometimes.

"I didn't have that many nightmares about it, I just tried to ignore it as much as possible and think about something else. I was reading at night so it sort of blocked it out a bit.

"I thought they (the protesters) were doing what they thought was right, but I didn't think it was right. Just because they weren't getting what they wanted, they started picking on us and I didn't think that was right.

"Now that they've calmed down a bit, I think they've got what they wanted because they got security cameras and all. I think they shouldn't have got what they wanted just because of what they were doing.

"They should have protested somewhere else, in front of the place where the people who weren't giving them what they wanted. They shouldn't have protested where they were. They were all shouting, 'We're getting new houses' and my mummy said, 'Aye, the insane asylum'.

"I didn't want to use the school buses. They got school buses near the end. It was shown on the news about people stoning the buses. I didn't think it was safe. I didn't want to use them.

"Circle time was once a week and you felt safe there because you could tell her things, and she wouldn't tell anyone else. You had to say something you were scared about and it made you feel reassured. You knew the teachers were there in case you needed them. And it sort of helped.

"My best mate, the day the bomb was thrown, burst out in tears halfway through school. It was during lunch and I had to bring her in. Miss Tanney sat and talked to her. I was sitting in the corner waiting to see if she would be okay and we brought her back out and she was okay after that."

She, also, would send her daughters to Holy Cross. "It is a really good school, apart from what they did."

Danielle McGrandles (10) listened attentively during the interview and answered each question carefully. She likes swimming and her favourite subject is art.

"The first day back, we had to walk on the footpath with big barricades so they couldn't see us. Some man poked me with an umbrella. He was standing right beside us in his garden. My daddy had to swap sides with me.

"They (protesters) were very close. My friend's mummy had to take her back down the road. She was crying and she didn't go to school for the first couple of days because she has got very bad asthma and she took loads of asthma attacks."

She says it felt "sad" when the bomb went off. "You weren't expecting things to happen like that. The day of the pipe bomb, they were throwing stones. My daddy went to lift me as the stones were getting heavier and then that's when it went off. It was just behind us. I thought it would have hit one of my friends. Daddy didn't leave the school that day. He wanted to wait to see if anything else happened. And then, I just got too scared and he took me home.

"The principal would bring us into the assembly hall and she would just read us stories and everything to keep our mind off it. Stories about whenever she was young, the things that happened and what school was like.

"I stayed off a couple of days 'til the shouting stopped. Not stopped, quietened down. Rachel (her sister), she had to wear earplugs going to school and then she got too scared and my mummy just had to move her school.

"The first day (at the new school), she asked mummy why there was no police and no people shouting at her? It makes me angry. I thought they were bad people. My mummy told me to ignore them and my daddy had to cover my eyes 'cos they were doing (*hesitates*) just things.

"One day it got really bad and my daddy walked me down the back way 'cos things were getting worse. We were walking home and there was people throwing paint at us and hot water round us.

"My mummy and her friend were going shopping and there was people shouting at her in the car and she had to turn back. She couldn't go shopping then. My friend's mummy was walking and they threw a water balloon with urine at her.

"We had to go to counselling; we're still going now because my granny and grandad died in the same year. My granny had cancer but then my grandad got diagnosed with cancer and they said he had three months to live but he only lived for three weeks — that was all going on too.

"All my friends go to counselling. She talks to us on our own and then she talks to us all together. You couldn't believe you were going through it. You thought you were dreaming.

"We had to move house 'cos when we went home, there was trouble there as well. We're still a wee bit scared now but we're not as bad as we were. There was a loyalist man and he gave me and my daddy a death threat.

"We wouldn't go another way to school because that's the way our school route is. That's the front of our school and to go through the back gate, to go through to a wee boys' school, walk across a pitch and through and round takes too long. The front way to school is our proper way to go to school.

"Mummy asked me did I want to move school but it was my last year and I liked that school so I wouldn't move. The teachers and all were very, very kind and we got to go swimming every Friday and we got to have a party every Friday.

"It's quietened down now. My friend was crying the other day because she didn't want to leave Holy Cross. On our last day we were all crying too because we didn't want to leave. We wore white shirts and I got all the teachers to sign it.

"Father Troy was really funny and Father Gary. Father Troy used to go to my friend's house 'cos her mummy was taking it really bad and her daddy was upset. He used to buy us sweets and talk to us."

Rebekah Monaghan (7) is a happy child with a fair ponytail who enjoys painting and computers. She has two older brothers, aged 18 and 13 with whom she gets on well. Going back to school in September 2001 was "upsetting", the tunnel was "really scary" and she was "sad because they were shouting", although later she had a portable CD player and would listen to it to drown out the noise. The people were "close" and "nasty" and she could see their faces. She can remember the sound of firecrackers and believing they were shots. Some of the protesters had frightening masks on, she says.

Rebekah remembers cross-community painting trips with Wheatfield. "We used to be out in the field playing." She later saw the same children she had played with on the protest. "We're not allowed over there (Wheatfield) now," she says. It makes her sad that the lollipop lady, Amanda, and the people she went painting with went on the protest. "Every day after school she (Amanda) would walk me down the road." Rebekah adds that, now, she "didn't like her" since she took the protesters' side.

A woman that her father used to work with would call her daddy names, she says, remembering how she had once tripped "over a stone that was lying there, it was just a scrape on my knee". The police did not make her feel safe, she says.

Watching the television news coverage was not as scary as actually being there. "I remember one of the days when I was going up to school and the people were on ahead and the bomb was thrown over a couple of us." She also remembers "spit and pee-pee", and that Father Gary Donegan was "really funny". Their window-cleaner would always get hit with a can of Coke, every day, she says, and another neighbour got hit with a glass bottle. These days, she says, the girls "just get on with our normal lives" although she can remember stones smashing the windows in one classroom.

Rebekah can list off all the fire exits in the school. They have regular fire drills and she says the teachers have a "wee window" to watch the children when they are out playing in the schoolyard.

But she also thinks of the presents she got from abroad: the book from Japan, the Easter eggs from America, the pen-pals from Australia and Bishop Desmond Tutu's visit. She would not send a child of her own to Holy Cross.

So, what was done by parents, the school and the statutory authorities to protect the children and mitigate against the potential long-term psychological harm inflicted by the protest? The parents took advice wherever they could get it: from their family doctor, from each other and from an intuitive belief that telling them they were loved and maintaining the household routine as closely as possible.

The school also called in outside experts and selected the worst affected children for counselling, with specially-trained teachers using the "circle time" technique, whereby each child would express their feelings in turn. The government allocated special funds for counselling, although other schools throughout North Belfast were offered similar funding, which annoyed some at Holy Cross who felt others were benefiting from their suffering.

One of Ardoyne's family doctors is Michael Tan, who treated more than 20 children. Some were as young as four and five, and were "severely stressed-out" in a way he had never before encountered in this age group.

"The most common complaints were of children wetting the bed, having flashbacks and nightmares, afraid to leave their parent's side and refusing to go to school. The parents wanted something done immediately, to relieve their anxiety, help them sleep and calm down when they came in, crying and tearful. What I had to offer was short-term anxiety treatment in the form of minor sedatives, which I was reluctant to do. But it came to that. Some children had vivid recollection of the incidents, especially the blast bomb. There really was no other option in the short-term but to give them some sort of medicine to try to allow them a night's sleep, with the usual warning on the addiction potential.

"My worry was that we were risking a new generation of people addicted to prescription drugs. It was deeply worrying to see children under the age of ten taking addictive drugs. My fear was that in the future any sort of stressful situation may well trigger off this learned response, that the only way to cope is to 'take something for your nerves'. When you treat people for stress with sedatives it can sometimes prime the craving for other illicit drugs, but there really wasn't any other solution to quell the anxiety. It was unbelievable, incredible. There was always an unwritten law that primary schools were the last sanctuary, but that law was broken. Half the children were sleeping with their parents."

Dr Nichola Rooney is a consultant psychologist at the Royal Belfast Hospital for Sick Children. She says children can react to the same events differently because they interpret them differently. For example, some children can cope with major surgery while others collapse at the sight of a needle.

"Some of the Holy Cross children appear to have been able to make sense of the violence directed at them, allowing them to cope better than others. This might depend on the child's past experience of trauma, their personality, their IQ and even their gender. Also, children learn from adults. They see their coping strategies and model their own on them. Most behaviours are learnt. A child who is smacked will smack other children. A child who looks at adults expressing hatred, or adults asserting their rights, is likely to learn from that, good or ill."

From our interviews with the children, Dr Rooney says, there was clear evidence of what is known as emotional contagion; that is, the children have picked up on the parents' anxiety and stress. In the script of the interviews, the parents' reactions were as marked as the children's. The parents were clearly upset and the children realised this.

"Sometimes in an unfamiliar situation, children interpret an event and react to it based on how they see or sense their parents' reactions."

On the ability of a child aged under 12 to make decisions, as all those at Holy Cross were, Dr Rooney says that legally any child aged under 16 is viewed as incapable of giving informed consent – although there is recognition that some children below this age have the competence to understand issues and consent. Asking a child of 12 to understand complex issues and make choices would be very difficult for the child.

"Ultimately it is the parent who must make the decision on a child's behalf, with the child's needs and well-being being paramount. Given a choice, a child will often feel under pressure to do what they think is wanted or expected of them. Consent and compliance are very different. Young children are unable to rationalise and generalise and see things only in very concrete terms. They are egocentric, only seeing things from their own perspective, hence they will tend to blame themselves if things go wrong, believing they have been responsible in some way.

"Any four-year-old attending school for the first time is facing a new challenge. This may be the first step a child takes in learning to be independent of their parents, to learn there are other care-givers in the outside environment and to make new attachment relationships. This experience is daunting in itself and to associate such frightening scenes with school will certainly make this transition more difficult. For these children, going to school was not safe. The older a child is, the more conscious it is of being under threat. The younger child will be less likely to be able to understand what is happening and why. Older children may show more typical signs of stress such as nightmares, anxiety attacks, poorer academic performance, et cetera.

"Younger children are often more likely to regress and temporarily lose some of their developmental milestones. For example, they may begin to bed-wet again, become clingy, engage in baby-talk and so on. Such behaviour represents the child psychologically moving to a previous time in their lives when they felt safe."

In such cases, the best thing a parent can do is, firstly, to notice what is going on and then to nurture as they did when the child was a baby. On counselling, Dr Rooney says some children respond but the intervention should be tailored to the symptoms. Post-traumatic stress can be revisited through counselling and could be counterproductive if not timed right.

"The wrong therapy could be worse than nothing. Children are, however, very treatable if the therapy is tailored to the problem correctly and it is timed right. If, for example, a child of three is sexually abused, therapy might not be appropriate until the child is aged 15. Some children may respond by feeling heroic, that they had stood up for their rights. But saying, 'Well done' is not the same as saying, 'You showed them'. Some children may feel they failed because they cried and their picture was in the papers and people saw they weren't being brave. These children need to have their confidence restored and told how appropriate it is to be afraid. Bravery is about doing things that we find difficult.

"In therapy, a child has to be considered within its family/school system. Parents need to be involved/informed at all stages. Parents often worry about their children's dreams. However, dreams can be useful as they process information that the person can't deal with otherwise. The brain is trying to make sense of experience. If a child is having recurrent nightmares, one way of addressing this is to talk through the dreams with the child and begin introducing different/positive endings to the dreams."

In the Holy Cross case, she says, children were living with highly emotional experiences, especially those who returned to homes along the peace-line where violence was a daily occurrence.

"Children need routines, consistency and clear guidance and boundaries. Obviously because of the high levels of emotion around, one can see how the normal rules of the house may fall by the wayside.

Children clearly distressed tend to be afforded more freedom and less discipline. Their care-givers may not be emotionally or physically available to them. Unfortunately this can serve to increase problems for children who now begin to experience chaos at home as well as outside. Home needs to feel as safe and normal as possible."

She has words of praise for the teachers at Holy Cross. "It was good that the school understood that the teachers should behave normally and get on with their work, that they had jobs to do. A child who misbehaved should still be told that their behaviour was not acceptable."

As for the longer term, she says children need to develop "coping skills". Some may continue to experience long-term effects and be rendered vulnerable to future psychological difficulties. "Some may be able to feel a sense of mastery and achievement and feel stronger."

Dr Rooney said she responded both personally and professionally to Holy Cross. "I was horrified it went on for 12 weeks. A society can be judged on how it treats its children and I didn't want to belong to a society which could treat children that way. On a personal level, I watched as a mother, horrified that human beings could involve children in such an ordeal. On a professional level I realised the psychological damage that it was causing. I also felt concerned that professional groups remained silent.

"We have open public debates about smacking children and yet in this instance the professional bodies seemed reluctant to speak out. All adults should act at all times to protect the needs of the child."

A final word in this chapter should go to the children themselves. One parent, who wanted to remain nameless, told of how the children staged their own fight-back against their abusers.

"One day, as the whistles and horns blared out, the kids started singing. I cried my eyes out. They were singing to drown out the noise. It broke my heart. The kids made the decision to sing all by themselves. When they started singing their hearts out, you couldn't hear the loyalists. It didn't matter what they were shouting because you couldn't hear them anymore. Even Father Aidan and Father Gary joined in. I was really proud of the children for being so brave. I now believe it was the turning point; the kids were now starting to fight back, all by themselves."

Roisin Kennedy says Bruce Channel's 1962 hit, "Hey Baby", was another favourite song along Ardoyne Road.

"Even the Brits (British soldiers) were singing it; they would encourage the children to begin singing. It so angered the protesters that the kids were coping and able to ignore them. The children were a lot jollier and happier."

Chapter Eight

SCHOOL

The Holy Cross protest didn't make Anne Tanney a good principal. Anne Tanney was always a good principal. If ever there was a woman for the job, it was her. No one speaks with more quiet authority.
Donal Flanagan, Director, Catholic Council for Maintained Schools

I think it has changed me and changed all of us. It has become part of me and part of my experience. It would be nice to think that some good could come out of it, although it's very difficult to imagine what.
Anne Tanney, principal of Holy Cross

All schools are special but, long before it ever hit the headlines, Holy Cross was unique as it straddles one of the fiercest sectarian fault-lines in North Belfast, itself the hottest cauldron of the Troubles.

Accentuating the positive, it has attracted two redoubtable women as its most recent principals: Anne Tanney and Mary Hanson. Both are considered outstanding by all who know them; a third, Betty Quinn, took up the reins in September 2004.

The first impression you get at the school's main entrance is how overwhelmingly normal it appears. On the notice board, there is a pupil's painting of a nun on a skateboard and a tank of plump goldfish proudly labelled, "We are 20 years old."

More seriously, there is the school principal's "Values Board", telling the girls what they are expected to take home with them. Kindness, compassion and respect are favourites, with a significant new addition: forgiveness.

"If you fall and cut your knee and don't clean out the cut, it will seem to heal but will become infected," Anne Tanney tells her girls.

"Forgiveness is the way we clean our emotional hurts."

Those words have a special meaning for the children, staff and principal of Holy Cross. Loyalists routinely accuse the Catholic Church of deliberately locating the school in "their" territory as a kind of Vatican bridgehead, a staging post to taking over more Protestant land. The site on which it stands, however, has been owned by the Catholic Church since 1922 when Wheatfield House, which once stood there, was bought by the Passionist Order as a noviciate for young students training for the priesthood. In 1952, when numbers had grown, the noviciate moved to Crossgar, County Down. Part of the land was then used to build St Gabriel's Boys' school, which opened in 1956. That left a small site that became Holy Cross Girls' school in 1969. The Catholic Church, therefore, owned land at Glenbryn before the partition of Ireland took effect, while Holy Cross itself was established before the Troubles and long before its location became a sectarian flashpoint.

Despite the economic deprivation suffered by most of its parents, many ex-Holy Cross students have become successful women. One such success story is "Sinead" (not her real name), who was a student between 1965 and 1972 and who now works for a major information technology company.

When she first went to Holy Cross, as a four-year-old, the school was split into several sites. "We started off as four-year-olds in an old stone building beside the church and progressed to tin huts. It was fairly grim, with outside toilets, rats running about and no heating to speak of. Before the Troubles began, the new school opened. It couldn't have happened at a worse time, although it was wonderful to have indoor toilets, a canteen, a hall and a playground. They couldn't have known that the Troubles would go on so long. I remember the first time someone spat at me. I was nine or ten. Coming out of school a woman called me a 'Fenian bitch'. I didn't even know what it meant."

As in many other towns and cities across the world, schools tend to come along in twos and threes. Housing estates come first and schools, almost as an afterthought, are slotted into the land between them. It is certainly that way in North Belfast with a cluster of schools along the Crumlin Road, both Protestant and Catholic. Given its history, trouble was almost inevitable.

"There were buses going in every direction, carrying children from the schools to loyalist and nationalist parts of the city. They used to try to stagger school closing times to try to prevent conflict," says Sinead.

Her eyes light up when she remembers her old headmistress, Mary Hanson. "She was an inspiration. There might be turmoil outside, soldiers raiding and children not getting any sleep, but the school was a sanctuary. She even had sleeping bags in school in case they were needed. If someone didn't turn up for class, she would always check. The girls won many different competitions. Our parents might have come from underprivileged backgrounds, but her ethos was that every girl was special. Like everyone else, I was frightened getting to and from school but inside you felt safe. Miss Hanson was rock solid."

Sinead remembers her "getting home" routine was to scout about as she left to see if there were any Protestant girls around and, if there were not, running fast to get home quickly.

No one would pretend the intimidation was one-way. The antipathy between Ardoyne and the staunchly loyalist Shankill Road area is well-established. Many Glenbryn families moved from the Shankill in the 1950s and brought their old hostilities with them. Obviously there was, and is, intimidation in both directions across North Belfast and Ardoyne quickly gained a reputation for producing more than its share of IRA men, people with fearsome reputations. But the girls of Holy Cross had it particularly hard.

"Some Catholic families," says Sinead, "were put out, although we had no problem with our neighbours. I'd go as far as saying that without our Protestant neighbours we would never have survived. Loads of our ex-pupils went on to become successes. There are authors, scientists, bank executives – a lot moved away to make better lives for themselves outside Belfast. I wouldn't be the person I am today if it hadn't been for Holy Cross. I was privileged to go there. In the midst of the worst that the Troubles could throw at us, Miss Hanson brought out the best. How did she manage to keep the school going in that madness? Whole streets burning, a mass exodus of people. It wasn't ethnic cleansing on the scale of Bosnia, but there were many like the McAleese family."

Mary McAleese, then Leneghan, who went on to become President of Ireland, although not a pupil at Holy Cross, spent her childhood and teenage years close by. Loyalists burned out the family bar and her profoundly deaf brother was badly beaten in a sectarian attack.

A former pupil who remembers her schooldays between 1974 and 1981 as idyllic is Jeanette McKernan, now the mother of two Holy Cross girls herself. A tall, chatty, warm woman, she remembers that "running home through Glenbryn was the best bit of the day".

"I loved the school. I would never have considered sending my kids anywhere else. It was a home from home. The teachers were as loving as parents."

Maura Lindsay, whose daughter Amy is a Holy Cross girl, says her school days, at the height of the Troubles, were "brilliant", although she remembers Miss Hanson getting hit over the head while intervening to prevent trouble.

Geraldine McGrandles, whose daughter Danielle goes to the school, remembers Miss Hanson walking up and down every day to ensure the children's safety. "She was a great lady who cared for those children and supported them and their families."

Another pupil, who wishes to be known only as "Mary", attended between 1970 and 1977 saying she had some of the best days of her life there. "It was like being in another world where nothing could harm you and your mind had a wee break. The 1970s were the worst of the Troubles, with the Shankill Butchers, and at home you constantly lived in fear. You were always waiting for someone to get killed."

The people of Glenbryn "would never have given us any hassle", although the girls of the Protestant school at Everton (now closed) were a different matter.

"I remember them calling us 'whores'. We didn't know what that meant. I thought it was another word for Catholics. There was a girl in my class, I remember her crying her heart out. The teachers asked us to pray for her Daddy. Then she stayed off school for a few days. Word came through that her Daddy had been abducted by the Shankill Butchers and was found barely alive. They had put an electric drill through his head and left him for dead.

"In 1973, a girl's father was shot dead by loyalists. Her uncle took over looking after her and the Shankill Butchers cut his throat in 1975. Almost every other day you were hearing something about somebody belonging to you, a friend or someone from your district, being killed whether by the RUC, the British Army or loyalists. We were four-years-old and never knew any other way of life."

On April 20, 1977 there was heavy tension in Ardoyne. Three days previously, a young man called Trevor McKibbin had been killed by the British Army (McKibbin, an IRA man, was shot dead "on active service").

"His funeral was taking place that day," says Mary, "and we weren't our usual happy-go-lucky selves. During lunch, there was a large explosion. We ran from our classrooms to look out of the windows on the top floor. There was smoke bellowing out of Ardoyne. We were all in hysterics, screaming and crying, worried about our families. It seemed the world was coming to an end. Parents started arriving to take us home. Word filtered through people had been killed at the funeral. We imagined our families lying dead. As we left school, a crowd of loyalist women gathered outside the gates. Miss Hanson went out first, like walking into the lion's den. The women were calling us names, threatening to burn the school to the ground. We were all clinging onto each other, huddling and crying our eyes out. Mrs Hanson told us not to worry and led us through the crowd."

The crowd parted to let the children down, but then a hail of fists came down on their backs and heads. The children panicked and ran, with the teachers trying to protect them.

"The crowd was shouting that they hoped our fathers were dead and our families had been blown up. It was the loyalists who planted the bomb in Ardoyne. What did they think we were going home to?"

(The book *Lost Lives* recalls that, on April 20, 1977, the UVF planted a bomb outside McKibbin's home to go off as his remains were leaving. Scores of people were injured and two local people lost their lives: Sean McBride and Sean Campbell. The following day the IRA killed a 24-year-old Protestant, Brian Smith on the Shankill, using a car hijacked in Ardoyne.)

Mary says all her old fears came back to her when the Holy Cross protest began in 2001. "One of the children said her school uniform made her feel like a target. That was the way I had always felt at school. I used to ask God why had I been born a Catholic? I hated being a

Catholic. We must be very bad people for all this to happen to us. Why couldn't he have let me be born a Protestant?"

The school was regularly attacked. Even in the late 1960s, neighbours remember loyalists breaking in, taking out the plaster saints and smashing them on the roadway. More recently, school windows were routinely broken every summer until the school installed metal shutters. There are still repeated attempts to burn it down. The teaching staff would minimise their own fears and refuse to allow it to dominate their lives. So the history of Holy Cross was always one of endurance in the face of tragedy and of its staff battling to give the school's pupils some grounding in normality. Although obviously far from idyllic, there is something about the Irish village school in Holy Cross, perhaps because of the inter-generational allegiance it attracts from the people of Ardoyne. Lynda Bowes, for example, decided to send her daughter, Amanda, there because her mother and all her aunts (now old age pensioners) were ex-pupils and her mother still works at the school. Lynda was a pupil there herself, as were all her cousins. She says there was never a day when Amanda went to school reluctantly. "She thinks of the place as a second home. There were all sorts of extra-curricula schemes and Amanda loves the school and all the teachers to death."

The school was never untroubled, but what turned it into a sectarian cockpit in 2001? Geographer at the University of Ulster, Dr Peter Shirlow, believes it became a symbol of the "spatial vulnerability" felt in Glenbryn.

"You had Wheatfield school in apparent decline and Holy Cross thriving. A certain sectarian consciousness kicked in, saying to itself that Protestants had accommodated Holy Cross for years, while never really happy about it being there."

None of it deters parents from sending their children to Holy Cross, partly because so many had attended themselves, and partly because of its reputation as a family-orientated, friendly place.

Sharon McCabe, from Ardoyne, moved her eldest daughter, Catriona, after she failed to settle in nearby Mercy Primary. "I loved the idea of them having an Easter bonnet parade and wee plays. When I moved Caitriona over, within a week, she had made friends, loved the teachers and I liked the whole way the school was run."

When she retired from Holy Cross in June 2004, Anne Tanney had been school principal for 17 years, following nine previous years as vice principal. She had worked at the school since it moved to the new site on Ardoyne Road in 1969. Mrs Tanney, who turned 59 the month she retired, had her own share of troubles even before the Holy Cross controversy. As a newly-wed, she was forced out of her home, close to the old school beside the Monastery.

Resolutely cheerful, she makes light of the school's problems, prior to June 2001. "There might be the odd stone thrown at a child and the school was set on fire a couple of times, but we just used to get on with it. We did have a lot of windows broken in the weeks before it all started, an unusually large number of windows. Perhaps I should have realised there was trouble ahead."

When she realised there was a riot on the road on June 19, she left the school and stood between the two groups and asked them to allow the children to get home.

"A woman shouted at me that her boy had been beaten up. I told her that we didn't want her boy beaten up, we didn't want anyone beaten up, our children have never hurt anybody, we've been working with Wheatfield for years, and she backed off."

But this time things had gone too far for Mrs Tanney's diplomacy. A car nearly knocked her down and, although she tried to continue talking, the police arrived and the school was evacuated via St Gabriel's.

"The next day I came in very early and spoke to Billy Hutchinson. He said there was no way the children were going to get to school. The governors decided to close the school for the day instead of trying to push them through."

The last few days of term went by in a blur, she says, although she laughs, remembering the end of term play, "Babes in the Wood". Half the "cast" could not get to school and the teachers read the missing parts.

"We had to cancel Sports Day, which was always held at the front of the school. People were very upset about that. We always had such fun. I had meetings all summer, trying to explain to the authorities how serious the problem was, how volatile things here can be, but I still hoped that good sense would prevail. That first day, though, they ran into the school screaming and crying. I just felt sick. I ran out and talked to children and hugged them. In the classrooms everything had to be absolutely normal, no matter what. I told the teachers to smile, smile, smile but some of the children were very upset. We had flowers sent in from well-wishers and I asked the children who were most upset to come round and give flowers out to the classrooms. We made bouquets of flowers for every class. Some of them coped better than others. Some seemed alright at the time but later it became clear they weren't – whereas others were very definitely not alright from the start."

Mrs Tanney says they had to be quite imaginative about the way they dealt with problems. One ten-year-old, who was particularly traumatised, explained she didn't like sitting with her back to the window because she would not be able to see when "they" were coming.

"I told her 'they' would not be coming, but I also explained the problem to her teacher and we re-arranged the desks with some excuse about reading groups."

Sixty of 200 children needed help particularly urgently and qualified counsellors were drafted in.

"We told the parents if they were worried about their children, if they were weepy or difficult, to let us know. The teachers were wonderful, they were totally focused on the children. They knew that if they appeared frightened, the children would feel it. So, no matter what was happening, I smiled and the teachers smiled, although some days I had to grit my teeth and force myself not to cry."

On the day of the bombing, she says she heard the explosion and ran out into the driveway of the school. "I thought a child was going to be carried in dead. That was one of the worst days."

The police told an emergency meeting of the Board of Governors that they, the police, had been the bombers' target, so the school remained open.

"The children found it very difficult to concentrate. We kept everything as normal as possible but there was still tension. One afternoon a teacher said she had a surprise for her class. Normally children would like that, but this time they immediately asked what was wrong."

The Eleven Plus (selection to secondary school exam) class that year did terribly well, she says.

*Every day, the routine was the same: the children in their red uniforms
(above, Alice-Lee Campbell) contrasting with the "Robocop" riot gear
of the police officers forming the cavalcade to school*

*September 5, 2001. A police officer lies in the gutter receiving first aid after the loyalists threw a
blast bomb as the children and parents walked past. Two officers and a police dog were injured*

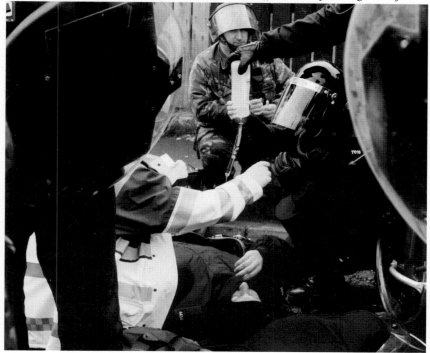

Sinn Fein assembly member Gerry Kelly: "I'm not one for crying, but was I emotionally affected? Yes, absolutely. It was heartrending."

Every morning, this was the formidable British Army barricade that parents and children like Nicola Bradley, daughter Shannon, a Holy Cross pupil, and son Sean had to cross. Once through, those left behind had no visual contact with their children as they made their way through the loyalist protest

Billy Hutchinson stands
between a crowd of
loyalists blocking the
road and Father
Kenneth Brady, and
mother and daughter,
Angie and Helen Boyle

Minnie Jean Brown-
Trickey, one of the "Little
Rock Nine", who visited
Ardoyne, against a
backdrop of Danny
Devenney's mural
drawing comparisons
with the US. She is
accompanied by Enya
McMullan (left) and
Emma Mulhearn (right)

Father Troy accompanies parents and children on the "school run". Left to right: Geraldine Tolan, Lucilla Haughey, Allison McClafferty, Cora Haughey and Judy Haughey

In an example of how the Holy Cross issue captured worldwide attention, Archbishop Desmond Tutu visited Ardoyne in a bid to help resolve the dispute. He spoke of being "very distressed, especially for the children". Anne Tanney can be seen on the right of the picture

Left to right (mothers only): Lisa Irvine, Lynda Bowes and Judy Haughey

The loyalists said they hadn't intended to frighten the children. The masks and "fancy dress" used by the protesters, however, often appeared deliberately intimidating

Left to right: DUP councillor Nelson McCausland;
North Belfast MP, Nigel Dodds (also DUP);
and the Moderator of the Presbyterian Church in 2001, Dr Alastair Dunlop

Father Troy was concerned that this image would be broadcast on the evening news.
His father was lying terminally ill in a County Wicklow hospital

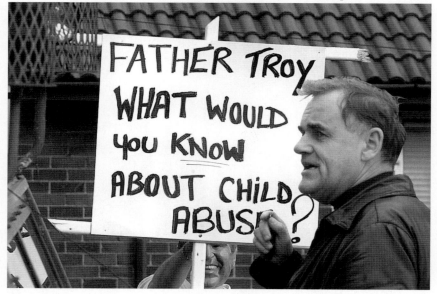

Loyalist protester, Stuart McCartney, says he became increasingly disturbed at the way the protest developed

Right to Education group spokesman, Brendan Mailey, doing his best to cover Lynda Bowes and her daughter, Amanda

As the pipe bomb exploded, there was panic. Roisin Kennedy and her daughter, Niamh, fled with others away from the blast. They were joined (from left to right in the background) by Janette Milne, Shauna Clarke, Alicia Milligan and Margaret Foster

There was no escape from the daily ordeal of facing the protesters and the police along the road to school. The anguish in Philomena Flood's face tells the story

"They just kept their heads down, working, working, working through it all. All the parents of the girls taking the exam agreed to come through St Gabriel's. We heard on the news that the loyalists weren't going to protest that day, but we didn't know whether to believe them. They were affected, their results could have been better. So we made a special case on their behalf with the education board and those who wanted to go to grammar school the following year were accepted. One girl was particularly bad. She was a very good student, but she started to cry at the end of the test and said she thought there were owls knocking at the window. I think she might have got the idea from Harry Potter. It was really quite upsetting."

Mrs Tanney says the two days when the loyalists threatened to have snipers on the roofs to kill parents and children were probably the worst. "One day, near Halloween, someone threw firecrackers on the road and the parents came screaming through the gate because they thought they were being fired at. We told them they would have to calm down before they could go into the school. We brought them tea, then we let them collect their children."

On the second "sniper day" she decided, against her own practice, to accompany the children home, believing she might attract the sniper's attention and thereby save the children. She did not know then it was an empty threat. The children who most concerned her were those who lived on the interface.

"Not only were they getting it at school, they were getting it at night when they went home. One little girl, on her way back from swimming, put two fingers up at the men standing in the road. She was such a quiet, lovely, well-behaved girl. When I asked, she explained her mother had had a mental breakdown because of the men shouting at her. I asked her why she thought they were shouting and she said because we are Catholic, but I said, 'No, it's because they're afraid of us. When they were little boys they were taught to be afraid of us and they grew up wanting to hurt us. That's why you have to try not to be afraid of them because, if you start hating them, you will grow up wanting to hurt them and that doesn't help anybody.'"

At this distance, Anne Tanney is still bewildered about what it was all about. "I began by thinking they might be motivated by fear of their territory being taken over. Now I think it started because of sectarian hatred, a terrible reflection on human nature. When the mob gets together, the lowest common denominator takes over. I find it very hard to reconcile the Christian principle of loving everybody and the questions that are still there in my mind. Father Troy says that because people perceive they've been hurt, we must accept they have been hurt. If you thought every single one of those people knew what they were doing, and had deliberately set out to hurt the children, the only response would be to hate them back."

Her favourite quotation, one she pinned over the entrance to the school, is Abraham Lincoln's: "If we were born where they were born, were taught what they were taught, we would believe what they believe."

Another member of the all-female teaching staff puts it this way. "What encouraged me was the corresponding amount of goodwill that came from all around the world and from within our own community to equal the amount of evil we saw."

Anne Tanney says it is wrong to look at the dispute as a win-lose equation. "People in Ardoyne believe the loyalists got quite a lot out of it, that they were rewarded for bad behaviour. It's not the right way of looking at it. I think we have to tell them that they hurt us badly but we do not wish them any harm, we wish them well in spite of everything and we hope to reconcile ourselves with them. We are not a threat to them and we don't want their houses or territory, we just want to live in peace together. If we can tell them that, then we will surmount the badness and survive what happened to us."

The numbers applying to attend the school are down. Long-term, she says, you cannot expect people to send their children to a school they are worried about. Asked if she thinks the school will, eventually, be forced to close and if that would mean the loyalists had won, she smiles a sad smile and says she hopes Holy Cross survives.

Donal Flanagan of the CCMS summarises many parents' views. "She is a leader as opposed to an authority. She is a very ordinary person, with exceptional talents. That is a rare gift. She never moved away from the people."

And the teachers? "They showed a courage, bravery and a commitment I have very seldom seen. The protest acted as a catalyst, bringing the profession together, which was one of the few positive things to come out of it."

"Grainne" (not her real name) has been a teacher at Holy Cross since the mid-90s. In her thirties, she loves her work but admits that the staff came close to breaking point in 2001. Anne Tanney, she says, had always made a point of fostering good relations with the pupils and staff of Wheatfield across the road. Mrs Tanney and the previous principal at Wheatfield, Mrs Enid Kennedy, would make a point of walking the road together at times of tension. Grainne says they never believed loyalists would attack Holy Cross during school hours, although even before 2001 the school had ostensibly ornamental railings inside the windows to stop petrol bombs coming through. "It was just part of life."

On June 19, 2001, she says, she was teaching on the first floor and had a perfect view of what went on. About two o'clock, cars start pulling up for parents to collect the younger ones.

"The first sign of trouble was a siren. It seemed to go on and on. It was a warm day and the windows were all open. I could hear car doors slamming and people shouting. The kids were aware of the siren but I persuaded them all to sit down. When I looked out again, there was obviously something wrong. People were running about madly. I tried to settle the kids and told them not to look out of the window and that the siren was just an ambulance. Helicopters arrived overhead. The front hall was just below me and I could hear loud noises. About five minutes later I got a message to evacuate the school through St Gabriel's. It was difficult to keep the kids calm. I told them I was a big coward and if there were anything wrong I would be running away myself. The girls are from Ardoyne, they know all about trouble and you could only pull the wool over their eyes so far."

By this time, parents were running towards the school "bringing all sorts of stories, in a total panic".

"A woman ran into the school screaming, running up the stairs and shouting that the loyalists were coming to attack the children. Our eyes began to fill with tears, we tried to calm her down, but she began screaming louder that the loyalists were coming in. My kids were stunned. It was our worst nightmare. We got their little coats on and began to take them out, walking through the front door where the riot was audible, yelling and shouting and fighting. The wee ones were crying. We took them round the side and up into St Gabriel's and over the pitch, trying to make it seem normal, saying what a lovely day it was and 'Imagine! Getting out of school early, aren't you lucky?'"

The teachers got to St Gabriel's gate on the Crumlin Road with the children nervous but calm. Then all hell broke loose. Dozens of police armoured vehicles screamed to a halt outside the school before scores of policemen got out, banging their doors and putting on their riot gear, including balaclavas, in full view of the children. The police were just following normal procedures after being called to a full-scale riot, but it caused panic.

"The children began crying and asking if the police had come to get them," says Grainne. "We had to physically cling on to the children and got them to hug each other. Somehow we managed to walk them down to the shops where it seemed like the whole of Ardoyne had gathered. There were mothers frantic with fear running towards their children to see if they were alright. I will never forget those parents' faces."

Most of the children were immediately seized the minute the cavalcade of pupils and teachers arrived but there were some children whose parents were not there. "I remember little Gemma McCabe who broke her heart crying for her mother."

Grainne was worried watching that evening's television news, but was relieved the next morning to arrive on the Ardoyne Road and find it deserted.

"As other teachers began arriving, they said there were a couple of people on the road. Then that there were a fair few people. When the last teacher came in, she was seven months pregnant, she was grey with fear because there were about 200 men on the road."

She had driven though the crowd before she realised what was going on and it was too late to turn back. No children arrived. The staff did not know what to do. Then the police advised them to close the school for the day. The next day, and for the remaining week of term, children either came to school through St Gabriel's or not at all.

"Father Donegan took a brilliant Mass on the last day. He was new to the parish and no one knew anything about him but by the end of the Mass, he had won us all over. The children's hymns were so beautiful, about God watching over them, and we were all weeping. Anne Tanney's last words to us were to go home and enjoy our holidays because there was nothing more we could do. As it got closer to September, however, I was increasingly anxious. We met Father Troy for the first time during early term training at the end of August. We were all a bit worried about him, being so new to the area, but he seemed gentle and spiritual rather than official and bureaucratic."

The teaching staff was also nervous about what might greet them on the first day of term with rumours of protests and blockades. When they told the Catholic Council for Maintained Schools of their concerns, they received generalised reassurances that failed to convince.

On the Monday morning, Grainne says, the teachers stood in their classrooms waiting for the girls, "like good little soldiers".

"We didn't have a clue what was going on down the road. I opened my windows because it was a lovely day and heard a sound I had never heard in my life before. It was pure hate, pure evil, a mob shouting and screaming. We all heard it. The teacher in the next-door classroom was putting out all her new paints and jigsaws on the desks. She said if the kids were coming through that noise, they were going to play with anything the heck they wanted. Then we saw the first of the parents coming up the hill. We opened the school doors and they fell in with their kids, screaming and crying. Anne Tanney and I looked at each other, our mouths open, aghast. Even the fathers were crying."

Some of the children were so upset they went straight home, while others and their parents stayed on. The loyalists threw loud fire-crackers into the grounds. The children thought they were being shot at. Some were brought to greater safety at the back of the building. One father refused to allow his child out of his sight, even through a classroom door. He frightened the children even more.

Grainne is still angry at loyalist claims that the children were specially spruced up for the cameras on that first day. "Our children always look beautiful. That day, they were gleaming but it was the first day of term so of course they had their new ribbons and bows."

Inside the classrooms, somehow things settled. Then, at lunch hour, the teachers wheeled a television into the staff room and watched the news. "We were horrified. We couldn't speak." It was the first time they had seen what the children had been through. There was talk of closing the school for a few days, but this was ruled out. How would they be able to open it again? The teachers' unions met political parties to try and bring it all to an end. Nothing worked. Some parents wanted the teachers to walk alongside them to demonstrate solidarity. Their union, the Irish National Teachers' Organisation (INTO) ruled this out on health and safety grounds.

One significant piece of first-hand evidence about the nature of the loyalist protest came from the principal of another school in a staunchly UDA part of Belfast. On a visit to Holy Cross, he recognised a number of known members of Johnny Adair's gang in the crowd. The principal of the Protestant school told Anne Tanney that "half of 'C' Company" was on the road. He was able to name them because he knew them personally as parents of children at his own school.

Grainne says that when she heard that, her stomach sank, for she knew then what they were up against. Adair himself was already back behind bars, but he still exerted a baleful influence over his small but dedicated group of acolytes. His mate, "Smicker" Smith was convicted for phoning in a hoax warning that a bomb was hanging on the school gates. Unfortunately for the hapless Smicker, the RUC were already on his tail, looking for an opportune time to arrest him and revoke his early-release licence. They pounced just as he left the phone box. Word came through on Smicker's journey to the nearest police station of the bomb threat. Putting two and two together, the cops sealed off the phone box, took fingerprints and Smicker was caught red-handed.

September 4, the second day of term, was easier. Anne Tanney said the teachers should take the children, as soon as they arrived, straight to their classrooms and start work as though everything was perfectly normal. She also told her staff not to watch any TV or listen to the radio in school.

"Our job was to get on with teaching, there was no point in bringing the children through it if we weren't fit to teach them because we were angry or crying. We had to have smiles on our faces, whatever was going on outside," says Grainne.

All the teachers found it difficult to maintain discipline while the school was full of parents, talking frenetically amongst themselves and watching every news bulletin.

"It was important to keep your door closed. I don't mean to sound nasty but it was very difficult to function otherwise. The children needed to focus on me and on each other, to make friends and become a class, learning stuff like 'Our rhyme for lining up' and 'This is what we do when we have a story, we sit on the mat nice and quietly'. Every minute of those first weeks, the children had to be told what was happening. If I left the room for 10 seconds they were asking where I was going and when I would be coming back. It was hard work. We had to be even more regimented, not in a harsh way, just to reassure them."

When teachers arrived home at night, they themselves needed help. "Every single teacher's family suffered terribly. We all came home and yelled at our husbands from nerves and stress. I changed, especially after September 11, because I thought that the world was going to end. I just couldn't believe that thousands of people had died in the USA and the protesters were still at it. There was no logic to anything."

The CCMS then arranged for a weekend of therapy for their deeply-traumatised staff at a hotel in Newcastle, County Down. Father John Friel, another Passionist priest, was to take a session with them. The group was sceptical about what he could contribute.

"When they started," remembers Grainne, "nobody wanted to admit how hard it was. It was difficult opening up and then our newest teacher, from the same village in County Fermanagh as Father Donegan, broke down crying and then everybody broke down. She started to talk about a child in her class who was really suffering and everybody just went to pieces. Father Friel was fantastic. He rescued it because we could have all gone to pieces. He posed questions, so gently and quietly, and he listened."

Some teachers, she says, were consumed with fury. Others were becoming bitter, sectarian and taking politics seriously for the first time in their lives, and they did not like it. Grainne began to feel angry with her colleagues who, she felt, had isolated themselves from the Troubles until now, when their noses were being rubbed in it. "You had to put yourself in their shoes because they were changing and change is always difficult."

The teachers came up with different ideas for helping the school cope, like extra help with homework, art therapy and counselling, some of which materialised and some of which did not. A yoga expert taught the kids about breathing, for example.

"With the really little ones, she told them about this 'invisible cloak' which she said would protect them. She told each child to put on their 'invisible cloak' when they got up in the mornings and that nobody could hurt them, no matter what anyone said to them, or did to them, or even how they looked at them. Children love pretend and magic. They would tell their mothers, 'I have to put my magic cloak on before I go up the Ardoyne Road and it will keep me safe'."

On one of the "sniper days", the parents arrived to pick up their daughters at the usual time but were held back in the school driveway for half an hour while the police decided what to do next.

"Mrs Tanney had never walked the road, because she felt her place was to be in school, but this day she went to the front. A couple of us wanted to join her but she said no. I lost it that day. I just broke down, but another teacher sent me inside saying I shouldn't dare to let the children see me crying. I couldn't believe that it had come to this."

As the children and parents left the school, the teachers waved and smiled, reminding them about their homework. Then they waited for the sound of gunfire, but it never came.

"That day was bad, but so was every day. The loyalists used a siren to get their people together, ready to abuse four-year-olds as they walked home. When we heard that they had jeered at a girl who had fallen over, it broke our hearts."

Another bad day was when news filtered through that loyalists had smashed up teachers' cars at Our Lady of Mercy secondary school nearby. Frank Bunting of the Irish National Teachers' Organisation (a Catholic primary school teachers' trade union) remembers how Father Troy burst into a staff meeting. He hurriedly told them the news and there was a moment's silence, says Bunting, broken only by the sound of children's laughter from Wheatfield school across the way. One of the teachers broke the silence, saying how bitter she felt that children there had not a care in the world while those at Holy Cross were in fear of their lives.

There were some good days. They were all invited to Connemara on the west coast of Ireland and Grainne remembers the bus being too wide to get up a narrow lane. When the children got out and walked up the road, local people formed a guard of honour and applauded them all the way. The national chairwoman of the teachers' union spent a day at Holy Cross and the kids had fun trying on her chain of office. Its southern branch invited the teachers to a weekend in Dublin. It was a huge morale-booster.

Although some parents are critical of a perceived lack of action by all the churches, including the Catholic hierarchy, Grainne says their local clergy were towers of strength.

"Father Troy didn't put a foot wrong. He was the right man for the time. Anne Tanney once said 'Cometh the hour, cometh the man' and she was right."

Although many parents criticise the Dublin government for its perceived inertia, the children met the Taoiseach, Bertie Ahern, and President Mary McAleese and were "treated like royalty", she says. As for the response of politicians and government, "It was as if the people in Ardoyne were expendable. Their fathers were not lawyers or doctors and weren't going to sue anyone. It wouldn't have been allowed to happen anywhere else."

There is also anger that, although they persuaded the authorities to find extra money, the same benefit went to all the other nearby schools, penny for penny.

"We lost our netball court, we lost our front playground when it was made into a car turning circle. Hardly anyone skips up to school now, they have to be bussed in and out. You feel so cheated," says Grainne. "We had to sit in Holy Cross, afraid to put our toe over the door and watch as their schools were transformed, their new pitches and new windows and new shutters."

All schools in North Belfast benefited from the Holy Cross dispute. Extra money was granted across the board, although Holy Cross got a little additional funding for counselling and extra staff. Some of the Holy Cross teachers were disappointed at the lack of support from their professional colleagues at Wheatfield, where teachers decided not to make a public statement for fear of attracting criticism from their own community. It was, perhaps, an understandable decision, but as Frank Bunting of the INTO puts it, "There comes a time when you have to stand up and be counted."

Grainne says, "Whatever grievances the loyalists had, real or imagined, they should never ever have expressed them in that way. They say they never intended to hurt the kids. That might have been understandable on the first day, but after the first minutes, when they realised what was happening, it should have stopped immediately. I am not the same person I was before the protest. It's like coming through a bereavement, but at least you can work through a bereavement naturally.. It has come to a point where people don't talk about it."

Anne Tanney won a "Lifetime of Achievement" award from her peers in June 2004, the same month she retired from her beloved school (although she's hoping to maintain links in a voluntary capacity). She is looking forward to spending more time travelling and painting. Her successor, Betty Quinn, who has taught at the school for ten years, has specialist training and experience in counselling.

Every now and again, there is a bomb scare at Holy Cross. The police are sent out to search the grounds and hedges for devices. To avoid frightening the children, the teachers tell them the police are "looking for dead birds".

Chapter Nine

THE POLICE

It appears the police were more concerned about placating the loyalists than protecting the schoolchildren. Martin Morgan, SDLP councillor

The police and British Army made the parents and children queue up like Palestinians at an Israeli checkpoint.

Mickey Liggett, Ardoyne Focus Group

The loyalists shocked us, despite what they had done over the years, but the police were worse. "Miss E", parent in legal challenge to police operation

Laws are enacted by democratically elected representatives to protect rights and prevent people coming to harm. The police enforce the law. It seemed to many in Ardoyne in autumn 2001 that there was no law and no policing. Day after day, scores of heavily armed police officers stood and watched as adults, many masked, threw not only verbal abuse but missiles, scalding water and urine at small children and their parents.

The police were, supposedly, the most sophisticated riot control officers in the world with over thirty years experience on the streets of Belfast. It was not a one-off attack, giving them at least the excuse they were not forewarned. The abuse happened at fixed times, at least four times daily, every single school day for three months.

The law protects people going about their legitimate daily business, which includes walking children to school. The law also, of course, protects the right to protest, but within legal limits. Trade unionists, for example, are proscribed from intimidating strike breakers for entering their places of work. Racists are not allowed to picket Muslim mosques or shout abuse at those entering them. Anti-Semites are not allowed to throw missiles at Jews going to their synagogues. The police would not be slow to act if any of these groups broke the law in virtually any circumstances.

The law tries to set down fair rules to balance the right to public protest and the right not to be harassed at home, work or school. The best known example in the North is between the rights of marchers to public assembly and the rights of residents not to have unwanted marches within their sight or sound. The position in North Belfast in 2001, however, was so complex. The rights of the child take precedence in human rights conventions, international and, in theory, domestic law over virtually all other rights. What then happened in North Belfast in 2001 that allowed the unthinkable to take place repeatedly, publicly, in front of the eyes and ears of the watching world? Did law and order, effectively, break down?

Halfway through the dispute (November 4, 2001) the rusty old Royal Ulster Constabulary became the shiny new Police Service of Northern Ireland. The police had few enough supporters in Ardoyne before the protest but even fewer after it. Did the new police force waste an invaluable chance to convince nationalists it was a genuinely reformed service? The police case, so far upheld in the courts, is that they took every reasonable measure to protect the lives of the parents and children, commensurate with lawful protest. They also have a strongly held belief that they did all they practically could to prevent harm to the children.

Others disagree. There is a strong view in Ardoyne that the police feared if they confronted loyalists effectively, it might lead to a Drumcree-style stand-off, with loyalists flooding into North Belfast from as far away as Portadown and Ballymena.

The view of one insider, a policing professional who does not wish to be named, is, "The police feared if they were perceived by some loyalists as too aggressive, the trouble would spread. They were afraid that loyalists could set up half a dozen flashpoints across Belfast. It was a matter of risk assessment. I know that that was part of the thought process."

This view is critical as it confirms the view of the Holy Cross parents that the police were unwilling, or unable, to stand up to loyalist aggression, a central problem at the root of nationalist grievances against the state since its inception. Former Assistant Chief Constable Alan McQuillan, then Belfast's most senior officer (now head of the Assets Recovery Agency), accepts that some within the UDA were trying to engineer a Drumcree-style stand-off in the heart of North Belfast.

"When the protest began, there were UDA people who wanted to draw in support from other areas, but very few wanted anything to do with it."

McQuillan categorically denies, however, that this influenced policing. "The reality is my officers had pipe bombs thrown at them by loyalists. They were shot at repeatedly by loyalists. My officers frankly had every reason to hate loyalists because nightly they were under attack. If you are trying to get children up a road, equipped with a shield and a helmet, and you see how abusive the mob is, you have very little love for them, no matter what your political views are."

The parents' case, though, begins with their complaint against the ineffective "anti-spit screen" (literally, a screen intended to stop people spitting at the parents and children), partially erected on the first day of the 2001 autumn term.

Lynda Bowes says, "The police suddenly said we would all be going up in one group. Anyone left behind wouldn't get through. They had had two months to prepare for this but they were now freaking out. In my naivety I thought that we would be walking up the middle of the road away from the houses and the nastiness. I walked in and a cop immediately shouted at me, 'Get the fuck on the footpath'.

"Then I saw the plastic screen and the jeering crowd that I had been listening to earlier. I was now walking beside them. The screen gave out. In theory there was a line of policemen, but there were only a few who all shouted at us, 'Fucking keep moving'. We couldn't go back because we were all being pushed forwards. Much later we discovered that the volume of protesters had prevented them from building the screen all along the road. It was in that knowledge that they took us through. I don't know if they thought it was the lesser of two evils. It was like a game somebody in an office was playing, giving orders to say it didn't matter if the screen was finished, just push them through anyhow."

Alan McQuillan accepts that the anti-spit screens were ineffective but, he says, the loyalists had promised a peaceful protest.

"We wanted the operation to be as low-key as possible to avoid frightening the children. The police in Derry had had some success with the anti-spit screens at Apprentice Boys' parades. It was a long distance to protect so the idea was to create a corridor. If we'd saturated the area with police, it would have built up tension. The screen should have protected the kids, given a peaceful enough protest. The difficulty was, as soon as we tried to put the screens into place, the loyalists began to attack us. We got a large section in place but the screens only work when both sides are willing to behave lawfully. What rapidly became apparent on day one was that wasn't the game."

Given the failure of the screens, the police changed tactics on day two and formed a corridor down the middle of the road with Land Rovers.

A second complaint from parents is that police were rarely willing to make arrests, even when they co-operated by pointing out offending protesters. Martin Monaghan claims they were fearful of going too heavy on them. At a meeting with police, he says, he was told that arresting more would make it worse for the parents. "How much worse could it have got? These people had, after all, thrown a bomb at our kids."

There were many similar claims. Monaghan's wife, Pat, says, "People were allowed to go free who were clearly guilty of major offences. If anyone in Ardoyne had been doing the same, they would have been put away for it. Every law in the book was broken but few were prosecuted."

Parent Sean Carmichael says he was "amazed" there was not more arrests, even when fireworks were thrown over the shoulders of RUC officers. "Many protesters covered their faces with scarves or hoods or masks to protect their identities, that was never challenged by the police."

Lynda Bowes says, "If you saw someone clearly breaking the law, you would turn to a cop beside you and ask if he saw it too. He would confirm he had and advise you to tell a senior officer. When you told the senior officer, he would ask the junior one for corroboration who would then deny seeing anything. Cops who had witnessed things were denying, to your face, that they had seen anything. That was commonplace."

One day on the road Lynda spotted a man whom she knew had been charged with shouting abuse and given bail on condition he stayed away from the protest. He was pointed out to an officer but he declined to make an arrest. She quotes him as saying, "We can't arrest him, there are too many of them in the same boat and it would start a riot. If you have got a complaint, take it to Oldpark Police Station."

Lynda adds, "If people did go to Oldpark to make a complaint, they would be asked to go to the man's house and identify him to the police, physically point him out. Who would be daft enough to go into Glenbryn and do that?"

Chief Superintendent Roger Maxwell, then head of policing in North Belfast, says the theory that policing was affected by fear of a loyalist backlash is "nonsense, it was never a consideration".

He insists that people were to be arrested if they were seen breaking the law. In which case it might be thought that with people throwing hot water, holding up defamatory placards and using foul language, there should have been hundreds of arrests, at the very least for behaviour likely to cause a breach of the peace? Maxwell says that would have been difficult.

"Let's take throwing tea. First you see someone throwing tea, then you have to get to them physically, while the children are passing. Do you start a melee there and then? Trying to get to that person? Secondly you have to maintain eye contact with the arrested person virtually throughout in order to connect them back to the original incident, otherwise you haven't got a legal case. Officers know only too well the difficulty in making arrests under those circumstances. Nationalist politicians have been the strongest critics of that kind of arrest. They have exploited it repeatedly over arrests for riotous behaviour."

McQuillan agrees, adding, "If you have a crowd of 150 people facing you and some of them are shouting sectarian comments constituting an offence, to make an arrest, the police officer has to prove he saw the person who shouted the comment. We tried to use a video but it was of limited use in those circumstances because it doesn't record voices very well."

Maxwell derides loyalist claims that police went softer on them after the September 5 bombing. "No we didn't. Absolute nonsense. What we tried to do was groom the loyalists, push them certain ways. The idea that they dictated terms is an absolute nonsense."

The police made eight people "amenable to the law" (loyalist and republican) in connection with Holy Cross between June 19 and 30, 2001, after the "man and ladder" incident, and a further 29 between September 3 and the end of the main protest in November. "Amenable to the law" can mean either arrested or cautioned or brought before the courts.

Then there was the alleged lack of sympathy shown towards the parents by police officers and British troops. Parent Sharon McCabe accuses British soldiers of failing to shield her when under attack.

"A lady behind me was hit in the head and blood was gushing everywhere. The funny thing was there were two soldiers in front of us and they pulled their shields over themselves, like a roof, so the bricks bounced off. We were left there totally defenceless."

Tina Gallagher says, "Their attitude throughout the protest was stinking. We were treated like muck on their boots. It seemed to us that we were mere inconveniences. If you asked a policeman a question, he would just reply that he didn't know the answer and was only standing there because he was being paid. There was no compassion from any of them for the children. They just didn't care, full stop. More understanding was shown to the protesters, who were abusing both our children and ourselves, mentally, physically and emotionally, than was ever shown to us."

Alan McQuillan, however, says, "Quite frankly, when officers were taking those children up the road, or their parents back down again, knowing they were passing the mob, they were petrified. So of course they would look grim. They were continually expecting attack."

Parent David Lindsay also claims the police were "not in the least bit neutral". He insists they were not providing a policing service but were "pro-protester".

"The police said at a meeting they wanted to make the route less of an ordeal for the children. The next day, as we neared the school, there was a length of road, about 30 to 40 foot, with no protesters or cops on it. We began walking on the pavement, hoping this was the normality they promised. Next thing, a cop jumps out and shouts, 'Where the fuck are you going? Get on the road now', before grabbing me and shaking me about.

"All this as I held my daughter by the hand. Only for Father Troy arriving, God knows what would have happened. They started to manhandle me but Father Troy ran into the middle of them and pushed us away from them."

Maura witnessed the same policeman later that day, shouting to her husband, in front of Sinn Fein's Gerry Kelly, that he would "see you again, don't you worry about that, boy". It seemed to her like a threat. The incident happened on November 5, the day after the official name of the police changed from "Royal Ulster Constabulary" to "Police Service of Northern Ireland".

Lynda Bowes, as usual, has an interesting angle. She also attended meetings with senior officers during the dispute. "They were damn stupid. I couldn't believe that these men, high ranking officers, had absolutely no concept of how people think."

She had asked a police officer if they could be more polite in the morning when mothers and children waited to be allowed through the British Army barricade. The police response was that they had to get their officers in place.

"I told him that we were not daft, we could understand that. But to approach a Land Rover and have its gates slammed in your face with not a word, how the hell did he think that made us feel?"

The police officer repeated his mantra about getting his men in place, but Lynda also persisted, saying she was not stupid and she didn't want to proceed if there were only ten policemen on the road. She merely wanted the police to refrain from slamming doors wordlessly in the parents' faces every morning. How would he feel if he had a door slammed without explanation in his face every day? The officer replied he had never really thought about it that way. The redoubtable Lynda replied, "That is the problem – you don't think."

"I could not believe that these men had been in control of the country for so long and still didn't have a clue about what was going on in our heads. It was also the way they looked at you: their looks spoke volumes. The best one ever was the day one loyalist shouted to a cop beside me that not too long ago he had been giving the protesters our names. Now, the loyalist complained, the police were protecting us instead. The cop didn't react, he just kept walking. It was obvious the loyalist had hit a raw nerve."

Frances Doherty, a voluntary interface worker with regular dealings with the police, says, "I expected much more from the RUC. They saw what our kids went through and knew we had done nothing wrong. The way they spoke to us and our children throughout the protest was out of order. As soon as the protest was called off, the same officers who had been treating you like a doormat were saying, 'Good afternoon madam, and how are you today?' It was as if the whole thing hadn't happened."

This, they say, was in stark contrast to the friendly relations the police had with the loyalists.

Liz Murphy says, "In the mornings the protesters would have tea and coffee on a wee card table on the side of the road. When they had finished, they would give the cops the nod and the police would open the gates to let us through. The tea and coffee that wasn't drunk got thrown at us. The police knew we would get the dregs but they did nothing to stop it."

That attitude irked many parents, including Judy Haughey. "The RUC stood and had tea and a wee natter with the protesters. They waited until the Protestant kids got into Wheatfield and then opened the barricades."

Lisa Irvine, also accusing the police of being over-friendly with the protesters, says, "The RUC were working alongside them. In the mornings, as you stood freezing waiting for the gates to open, you could hear the protesters asking the police to wait until they had finished their tea. The police told us once to hurry back down from leaving the children off at school because the protesters were complaining they were getting cold having to wait to abuse us coming back."

Tina Gallagher says the parents were forced to stand at the barricade "like cattle" until the protesters were out of their homes or cars and were in place, ready to shout at them. Parents were, she says, treated with "absolute disdain".

Elaine Burns corroborates this claim. "The police would wait until all the loyalists were in place before they opened the gates every morning. People could hear the loyalists shouting to the police to 'Wait until so-and-so had arrived' to join the protest."

Asked about this claim, the Police Ombudsman, Nuala O'Loan, suggests that what the parents might have heard were shouts between police officers, checking with each other that they were all were in place. She adds, however, that she would normally have expected them to use their radios to do this and that, if the parents claims were true, "it would be terrible".

Chief Superintendent Maxwell is adamant that none of his men felt any sympathy towards the protesters.

"Some officers would come to me on a daily basis and say they couldn't go back, they had had enough, they were sick and tired of it. On a number of occasions I had to talk them round, not quite counsel them, but talk them into going back because of the personal abuse they had taken from the protesters. Claims that we drank tea with them could not be further from the truth. It is absolute nonsense."

If parents heard police officers asking others if they were "ready" before opening the gates, says Maxwell, it was to ensure they themselves were co-ordinated.

"We were trying to get 200 children and adults up 300-odd metres of road where there were people who hated them, two or three times a day. Up and down. We had to make sure we had all of our ducks in a row, that we were absolutely watertight."

There were also complaints about the supposed barricade separating the children and parents from the protesters. The Land Rovers were never bumper-to-bumper, leaving gaps through which the protesters shouted and threw missiles. Father Troy had to contact the police every morning to get an up-to-date security assessment. He repeatedly asked the police to improve the quality of the barriers between the loyalists and the children but was told the protesters had the right to see the people they were protesting against.

"On the Twelfth of July," says Tina Gallagher, "people in Ardoyne can't leave the area. The roads are closed off and the world comes to a standstill to let the Orangemen walk past. I could never understand why the police couldn't have done the same at Holy Cross. Why do it for them and not for us? I was never a really bitter person, but I can tell you, I am bitter now."

Holy Cross politicised many parents. Liz Murphy, an attractive, chatty, warm woman was one who, for the first time, defied the police that year during an Orange parade.

"I was so angry and hurt, I thought to hell with this, I am going out to give them a drop of their own medicine. A crowd of about 50 of us got on to the Crumlin Road before the police sealed it off. The cops told us that if we weren't off the road within a minute they were going to beat us off and we would be arrested. Why did they not tell that to the loyalists on the Ardoyne Road? I didn't see anybody being beat off that road or told to get off it or be arrested. They were using one law for us and another for them. If the RUC had done the job we taxpayers pay them for, the protest would have ended in 24 hours. They allowed the UDA and the residents of Glenbryn to dictate to them."

Maxwell says he had considered using the British military screens deployed at some Orange marches – but where?

"Did we use them at all the junctions on the right as well as the left? There weren't enough screens to go the full length both sides of the road. The Wheatfield children use that road and they had to get to school as well."

McQuillan agrees and says, "Unless you use 10 to 15 foot tall screens, which you can't because the engineering doesn't work, people can still throw stuff over. There were two-storey houses along the road with people up at the windows shouting. It was virtually impossible to stop them."

Maxwell says that removing loyalists from the front gardens would merely have shifted the problem elsewhere.

"Where would the protesters go? Into their houses. Can we legally justify going into the houses after them? If they go upstairs, can we follow them and beat them out of their front bedrooms? How far could we go? Can we do this in every house along the entire 300-odd metres?"

He also says the critical difference between policing Orange parades and Holy Cross was the dimension of time. "Orange parades are relatively short-term affairs. Successive Twelfths of July at Ardoyne are difficult but short-term. Holy Cross went on for months."

The parents also say that loyalists were allowed to travel from other parts of Belfast and even further afield to take part in the protest. Liz Murphy says, "The RUC should have ensured that no one from other loyalist areas got near the Ardoyne Road, but they allowed busloads of people to arrive and swell the numbers."

There was also anger that the police and protesters appeared to be able to video-film the parents with impunity, while the parents could not do likewise. Lynda Bowes is just one of many parents who make the claim.

"As we made our way through the British Army gates, an RUC man would be standing with a hand-held camera focussed on the parents' faces. The police explained this was to see where missiles fell, not who threw them. The loyalists were openly filming. One day, after the police had taken film away from a couple of parents, we saw a massive camera in the upstairs window of the house where the Glenbryn residents met. We told the cops filming wasn't being allowed but they sent back word it was just a television crew. It was blatantly obvious it was no film crew, they were normal people with cameras. We were later told the Glenbryn residents had still photos taken from film of the parents and had put them on display in community centres throughout loyalist areas of Belfast."

The Glenbryn residents also created a website and posted photographs of individual parents and residents on it. Many parents said it was extremely disturbing to know that the UDA had instant access to your photograph. Roisin Kennedy, spotting a loyalist taking her photo, confronted a police officer.

"The more he ignored me, the more angrier I became. I tapped his shoulder and asked again but he said if I had complaints I should go to the Ombudsman."

She took his number and made an official complaint, but heard no more. Protesters, without police intervention, she says, openly filmed parents, who for obvious reasons couldn't cover their faces.

Sean Carmichael claims the protesters used photos of the parents, surreptitiously provided by rogue officers, for a photomontage stuck onto a board in Glenbryn community centre. (This very serious claim is unproven, but partially corroborated by an anonymous loyalist source.) What is undeniable is that the loyalists were able, somehow, to identify the parents by name, even those who had never given interviews to the press. They would single out individual parents on the Ardoyne Road and shout personalised threats at them using accurate names.

After the bombing on September 5, there was a temporary

improvement in policing standards, according to Lynda Bowes.

"If anything good came of the bombing, it was that the police and British Army were much more alert than they had been. Before, they had thought it was just going to be shouting and verbal abuse. Once they saw some of their own men injured, they realised it was out of control and they were more on their toes. The first couple of days, their attitude had been that they didn't get paid enough for enduring this crap, but after the bombing they realised they were in danger themselves."

The parents' complaints about the police, then, are:

- They failed to put up high enough screens
- There were too many gaps between the police vehicles, allowing protesters to throw missiles and shout abuse
- They failed to prevent outsiders coming into the area
- They allegedly did not arrest those perceived to be breaking the law
- Their attitude to parents was unsympathetic
- They facilitated protesters by waiting until they were ready before opening the British Army barricade every morning
- They filmed the parents and allowed the protesters to do the same while not allowing US observers or parents to film the loyalists.

The police believe they can give reasonable explanations for every charge made against their operation at Holy Cross but many complaints are backed by both the SDLP and Sinn Fein, who were also on the ground daily monitoring events.

"If the police service had done their job properly they would have arrested key loyalists," says the SDLP's Martin Morgan. "In July 2001, the police brought in water cannons, British Army snipers on the shop roofs, police dog teams, 1,500 officers – all to facilitate the return route of about 50 Orangemen through Ardoyne. The police beat the tripe out of the Ardoyne people. The Taigs were being put off the road. They then took a conscious decision, less than three months later, not to deal with the Holy Cross protest the same way, contributing to the endangering of those children and their parents.

"The police pander on the streets of this city to the loyalists. They assessed where the greatest paramilitary threat lay and gave in to it. It was better to annoy republicans than loyalists because the republican ceasefire is more solid. When the police take a conscious decision to steward a protest adequately, they can do it. On the Ormeau Road in 1997, to facilitate another Orange parade, people weren't allowed past a certain point if their name wasn't on the electoral register. The police appeared to have no problem there in restricting the free movement of nationalists. There was no attempt to do the same with loyalists in Glenbryn. How in the name of God could they justify that?"

Alan McQuillan says, however, that it didn't take nationalists long in places like the Ormeau Road to "work out a way around" the restrictions based on the electoral register. "They just came in the night before and stayed." Loyalists would have done the same in Glenbryn, he says, adding that the area is in any case far more porous and easily accessed than the Ormeau Road. "People can come through Deerpark and across the playing fields at Ballysillan. It's not bounded, like the Ormeau Road, by a river."

Morgan is adamant though. "The police failed. There can be no excuses. They had the opportunity, it was wasted."

His view is shared by the principal of Holy Cross Boys' school, Terry Laverty. "If the shoe had been on the other foot, if Catholic parents were stopping Protestant children going to school, what would the reaction of the police have been then? My own view, and I say this categorically, is that the protest wouldn't have lasted more than a day or two. Any Catholic crowd who had behaved that way on the Ardoyne Road would have been battered off it."

Brian Barrington, SDLP leader Mark Durkan's special adviser, says, "We weren't suggesting there should be brutality or breach of anyone's rights. What we were suggesting was better protection for the kids and a tougher approach by the police so that people couldn't get near them."

Durkan agrees, adding, "We didn't see a proactive policing approach. How could the police allow themselves to be mute witnesses? How could they fail to actively try to apprehend people who were attacking children going to school? There was no real policing challenge to the protesters, their role was limited to providing a corridor instead of tackling the reason the corridor had to be there in the first place. Rather than dealing with the people responsible, they ended up becoming part of what was a very ugly scene. Fair enough, they didn't want it to escalate, but you cannot tolerate the law being broken. Where were the arrests, pursuit, follow-up actions? We could never get adequate answers to those questions."

This view is shared by Sinn Fein's Gerry Kelly who says, "It was abominable. It was sectarian policing at its worst, pitiful. They didn't hold the blockaders back far enough and instead facilitated the protesters by holding back the parents and children until the loyalists were in place ready to abuse them. In nationalist areas, the police immediately push people off the streets. Orange parades are a good example. People are kept well back to force parades through. The police keep people at bay for hours until the parade has passed."

Not all the parents' comments on the police were wholly negative, however. It would be unfair to both sides to say they were. Colette Cassidy noticed a slight change at one point.

"I was a voluntary interface worker, trying to stop trouble. The police did begin consulting a bit with us on how we could co-operate. It worked for a while until Stormont was suspended. Within 24 hours, we had crazy cops out on our streets again and there was no consulting anymore. They were back to being heavy-handed. The change was amazing."

Donal Flanagan, chief executive of the CCMS, has some sympathy for the police. "I suspect the police were in a no-win situation. There was a genuine, but inept, attempt to provide security on the first day but it improved. In defence of the police, if you have a complete lockout, does it become permanent? Does it become a new peace wall? I suspect that was part of their thinking. I don't think policing was perfect; I couldn't say it worked well at any stage because the demonstrators were able to breach security, but I think they made reasonable efforts. Was their intent good? The answer is 'Yes'. Was it planned properly? The answer is 'No'."

Parent Liz Murphy accepts that the police were frightened. On the day of the bombing, she says, "The cops were in a panic too. I remember one just shouting for everybody to run."

Liz also remembers the day loyalists threatened to have a sniper on the rooftops of Glenbryn and then threw firecrackers. "We started to run and a cop grabbed my arm and said, 'Run as fast as you can, run quick.'

That cop was either a very good actor or he thought they were shooting at us."

David Lindsay remembers the police being terrified when they found themselves in the line of fire of loyalists throwing bricks and bottles at his home.

"One of the cops shouted, 'Get out' and they all started running. I was that angry that I grabbed one and said to him, 'You're going nowhere.' The cop was nearly crying but I wanted him to see what we had to put up with. These were the police whose jobs were to protect us, but once the loyalists began attacking, they ran away more concerned about their own safety than trying to catch the people doing this every night."

Roisin Kennedy, another parent, says, "I am sure there are Catholics among the police and some days you caught a genuine look in their eyes as if to say, 'This is unbelievable'. Some of them would hold their shields as tight against you as possible and try to gently reassure you. They would say, 'Don't be worried, nothing will happen', but you never knew if they were genuine and in any case it only happened once in a blue moon."

There are some, although fewer, complaints from loyalists about policing. Most of the protesters claimed police unjustifiably beat them. In the months June to November 2001, there were 120 complaints from North Belfast made to the Ombudsman's office, most during July and September, and the majority from the Protestant side of the community alleging unreasonable use of force.

Ronnie Black claims his advice to the police was ignored. "We warned the police that if they tried to push us back into side streets, they would create a riot and the children would get caught up in it somewhere down the line."

Jim Potts complains that, when trouble began, the police would move in and push loyalist crowds back, using the space gained as a "sterile zone". They would then man the zone with British soldiers, preventing loyalists from "offering protection". The families who lived in the houses inside the zones would apply to move out permanently, says Potts. He gives the example of an elderly resident, who had lived in Glenbryn for 50 years, being forced to move out and a young couple who also left home.

Loyalist community worker Anne Bill blames Chief Constable Sir Ronnie Flanagan for what she believes were the police failures at Holy Cross.

"Not the police on the ground, because they were just doing what they were told. On the other hand, they could be quite vicious, some of them enjoyed venting their frustrations. They would put their shields up and kick people from underneath them where they couldn't be seen."

Like Potts, she complains that protesters were pushed down side streets, off the main Ardoyne Road, or into gardens. She also complains that she was man-handled on at least one occasion when she was trying to keep the peace.

"You were there trying to keep the thing calm, not with much effect, but at least not causing anybody any harm. The police could have worked with us. There were plenty of tactics they could have used but didn't."

Lollipop lady Amanda Johnston believes the police used at Holy Cross were specially drafted in from outside Northern Ireland. "They were huge, I'd say they were soldiers. They had obviously been trained to deal with mad riots and were hyped up. If you went anywhere near that road you were beaten."

The UDA also issued sporadic threats against the police. In one threat it said it was prepared to retaliate if "heavy-handed RUC tactics" continued and loyalists were beaten up. The UDA also threatened policemen's families on one occasion saying, "We will go to the doors of police officers involved in these attacks on the loyalist people. The protests will be peaceful, but we will make life very difficult."

Ulster Unionist Fred Cobain, a Policing Board member, defends their record. "The police are piggy in the middle. When you look at the thing in five or ten years' time, I think you will have to conclude that the police did as good a job as possible. Protestants, not Catholics, felt the brunt of it. A lot of Protestants felt the police intimidated them and most of the brutality was aimed against them."

Nuala O'Loan herself initially decided not to observe the protest officially, to avoid giving the impression that she was, by her mere presence, criticising the police. Finally, she felt she had no alternative. "It came to the point where I had so many complaints, I had to go. I had to know what it felt and looked like."

She was undoubtedly shocked at what she saw, not least because she had personal experience of something not dissimilar at the Catholic church she attends at Harryville, a suburb of Ballymena, County Antrim. In the late 1990s, loyalists mounted a protest against the re-routing of an Orange parade nearby, yelling sectarian and sexually explicit abuse at Mass-goers, including O'Loan's family, over a 79-week period. She took her seven-year-old son with her to Mass one day. When the little boy got back into the family car, he sweetly asked his mother, "Mummy what is a fucking Fenian bastard?" She never took him again. This does not mean she necessarily believes the Holy Cross parents should have taken the alternative route. "It was a different situation. It was a horrendous decision for them. If they had used that route, I think Holy Cross would have closed."

After observing the protest, she went to see Anne Tanney, the children and the staff before controversially saying that her personal view was that the protest should not be taking place at all. "I thought it was absolutely terrible, outrageous. There was such a small area in which it all happened, the very close proximity of police officers, protesters and children. There were literally feet between them."

Whatever her personal views, in 2001 O'Loan's powers were limited. "The only thing I could do was to research matters evolving from individual complaints which didn't allow me to examine policing decisions."

Asked if she had the powers then that she has now whether she would have initiated an inquiry into policing at Holy Cross, her response is an unequivocal "Yes". She does, however, feel the problems were difficult. "If they had cleared the protesters off the road, undoubtedly there would have been massive trouble across Ardoyne, with Catholics suffering at the hands of loyalists possibly even more than they did."

She suggests that if the police had baton-charged the protesters off the road into their gardens, it would have been even more terrifying for the children.

"They would have been stuck in the middle. I think it is very easy to be wise in retrospect. I am quite sure that if they were policing Holy Cross now they would have learnt a lot. I wouldn't like to second-guess the man on the ground faced with ordering a baton-charge while getting children out of the way. You can't baton-charge people who are just standing there. You have to have a reason. They have got to be disorderly. It was all so complex and so hideous and the answers aren't simple.

"My perception of watching it, and I did watch it with almost despair, was that they tried different methods of policing but nothing worked. Nothing really saw those children up the road safely except Aidan Troy. I think I would probably have been more robust but the police were making operational decisions and I was not. I remain uninformed of all the intelligence they had which informed their decision-making."

O'Loan has spoken to individual police officers and says they found it "enormously difficult".

"A lot of their sympathies were with the children and I don't think they were just saying that."

She also met both Ardoyne and Glenbryn residents. Those present at the Glenbryn meeting, where about 200 loyalists packed into the local community centre, say it was "hot and heavy". O'Loan suggested the protest was not a good way to air their grievances and that the police were quite within their rights to prevent spitting at little girls. Towards the end, the atmosphere took a downward turn when a woman quite baldly told O'Loan that "the only good Taig was a dead one". Then they offered her a cup of tea.

Long before then, however, a mother at Holy Cross had decided to take the initiative. The mother, known only in the courts as "Miss E", challenged the police to justify their actions in Ardoyne. Before her case concluded, however, there was an unseemly row involving the then Chief Constable, Sir Ronnie Flanagan, the chief commissioner of the Human Rights Commission, Professor Brice Dickson, and other commissioners. In the great scheme of things, the row was of far greater import to the diminishing credibility of the Human Rights Commission than the story of Holy Cross, but it was deeply hurtful to the mother involved and arguably damaged her court case.

The Commission had originally taken legal advice on whether a challenge to the policing operation at Holy Cross had a reasonable chance of success. The reply was that it probably had not. A Commission sub-committee, charged with deciding whether individual cases should be financially supported, then received a request from "Miss E" (who will subsequently be referred to as "Martha") and approved funding. This infuriated Dickson, who regarded it as subverting the previous decision taken by the Commission as a whole. It later emerged that Dickson, with the backing of three commissioners, wrote to Flanagan in December 2001 informing him of their opposition.

Martha and the other commissioners were unaware of the letter in which Dickson wrote that he did not believe her case had any merit and that the decision to fund had not been unanimous. Dickson also said in the letter that he was "strongly of the view that the policing of the protest at the Holy Cross Girls' school had not been in breach of the Human Rights Act".

Flanagan, unsurprisingly, seized on this sign of weakness and wrote back that his lawyers were "anxious" that Dickson's letter be disclosed. "You are aware of my reluctance to do this but equally I have a duty to the court and the wider public," said Flanagan. Martha, her solicitors, other commissioners, the SDLP, Sinn Fein, the Committee on the Administration of Justice (the North's civil rights watchdog) and others viewed Dickson's intervention as a breach of confidence undermining the legal challenge. Subsequently, the Commission said it was "regrettable" that procedures had not been in place to ensure that such differences of opinion were dealt with internally, adding that Dickson had been "mistaken" in believing the letter to Flanagan was appropriate. Dickson himself admits he was mistaken. Not because his views had been revealed to the Chief Constable, but because he had expressed them in a letter, rather than allowing them to be published first on the Commission website.

"It was wrong to write the letter," says Dickson, "because that gave him (Flanagan) the views of only four commissioners. What we should have done was to record our views in the minutes and put it on the internet so everybody could see them."

There was, and remains, huge bitterness between members of the Commission over the case. Leading trade unionist, Inez McCormack, for example, says it was bizarre there was ever a question mark over funding the case.

"If you're a Human Rights Commission and the primacy of the interests of the children is not incorporated into domestic law, it is egregious. You have to stand up for those rights. If they had been my members going to work, and had suffered that kind of racist, political or sexual abuse, those responsible would have been prosecuted, even without allowing that these were children."

The day before Halloween, Inez McCormack had walked back from school with the children. She was chatting to a child, trying to distract her from the abuse, and the two were smiling at each other when "a big gob of spit hit the child right on the temple".

Mark Durkan's adviser, Brian Barrington, is also critical of Dickson. "It was one of the more interesting out-workings of the Holy Cross episode, one that I found particularly depressing. It showed a weakness in Northern society. Here you had a Commission of people of goodwill, charged with standing up for human rights, yet some just couldn't do the right thing."

The row, while hugely damaging to the Commission, did not affect the funding of Martha's case. When that was dismissed, however, some blamed Dickson's intervention for holing it below the water line. Martha herself says she was devastated by the revelation.

"It was like a defence barrister giving information to the prosecution to further their case against me. Brice Dickson had given practical and moral support to Ronnie Flanagan and supplied him with a way of undermining our case. It was a massive breach of trust and we were shocked and very angry."

Martha, for whom the Holy Cross protest was a defining moment, is one of thousands who believed in a new dawn when the Agreement was signed in 1998. She says the case was taken on behalf of all the parents.

"Anything was better than the past. The way we had lived, seeing people murdered, was no kind of life to bring a child into. For me as a child growing up, what the RUC said went. It didn't matter if they beat up your mother or your aunts or any family members, it just happened and you had to accept it. It was degrading but that is the way you were treated. You were scum. You were below them. They could walk all over you and that was the way you lived your life. Their actions forced you to take sides in the conflict.

"I knew the Human Rights Commission was part of the Agreement. We were going to be given equal rights as everyone else. This was brilliant, this was going to be different. I had a son in 1992, a daughter in 1994 and another wee girl in 1998. My children were going to have equal rights and be treated properly. The Human Rights Commission was part of the new beginning, to ensure fair and equal treatment. The Agreement meant it wouldn't matter where you came from, you were going to have a chance and not be looked down on. It was about an end to all that was rotten in this society. I know that sounds foolish, naïve and 'pie in the sky', but that was how our family genuinely viewed it.

"How dare they say they were 'policing' the protest? They might as well stand alongside the protesters in civilian clothing rather than portraying themselves as 'caught in the middle'. Our expectations were high. After all, the eyes of the world were on the protest. You tell me how letting gangs of loyalists within feet of school children and their parents is doing their best? We asked them once if we could get through the gate because it was so cold and they told us it would annoy the loyalists if we were let through before they were ready.

"The police knew there were guns and bombs in Glenbryn, yet all they put up on September 3 were useless spit-screens. They knew people were coming to stop us walking, but they weren't even able to finish putting them up. They allowed children as young as four go up, knowing what was waiting for them. They thought if the protesters had free rein the first day, we wouldn't want to go up a second. They were hoping we would take the tough decisions for them. My child changed from being a fun-loving little girl to a wreck, afraid of the least thing. She wouldn't leave my side. To witness pure hate-filled sectarian abuse was one of the most terrifying experiences I have ever endured. We were standing with our mouths open. To be honest, the police attitude shocked us more than the protesters did."

The bomb was the turning point, she says, in making the parents decide to act. They met a solicitor and Martha made a personal decision to allow her own case to be used.

"I had never been in a more dangerous position in my entire life but it had to be stopped. The British government was doing nothing about it and the Irish government was saying it had nothing to do with them.

This was the Commission's first major test case against the RUC. We were hoping it would be a lever to get the police to do their job. I talked it through with my partner. We were worried. The Red Hand Defenders had warned people who'd spoken out they would be 'executed on sight'. We weren't sure if our anonymity was guaranteed.

"We were thrilled when we heard that the Commission was backing our case. It meant we weren't on our own, somebody was taking us seriously. It was like an endorsement. When I heard about the letter to Flanagan I was confused. This was Brice Dickson, head of the Commission, writing to the people we were taking legal action against? Were they all working hand in hand? The initial joy and happiness over the Commission taking the case was shattered. It was a huge blow."

"We felt betrayed and badly let down," says Martha, adding she believes Dickson should have resigned. "How in the name of God was he allowed to stay there?"

Her strongest fear was of loyalist attack if her name was released but by then her barrister had told her that in order for the police to respond to their affidavits, the Chief Constable and the Northern Secretary would have to know her identity. Then she discovered that her name was included in a police affidavit. "I have no idea why or how my name was made known to other people, other members of the RUC – it certainly should not have been."

The next development was even worse. Going into court to sign some papers, she was confronted by some of the protesters, who had been charged with public order offences.

"They were on the other side of the street and they kept shouting out my name and saying, 'There is Miss E'. So the loyalists knew my identity also. The information could only have come from the police."

The loyalists began shouting out, "Miss E" at her on the road to school. The ones responsible were the "real hardliners", says Martha. "I don't think I could have felt more frightened."

Martha eventually decided to move home. She lost her case against the police.

In his ruling in June 2004, the Lord Chief Justice of Northern Ireland, Sir Brian Kerr, said the Holy Cross protest was one of the "most shameful and disgraceful episodes" in the recent history of Northern Ireland.

"The sheer weight of evidence about these terrible events permits no conclusion other than many of those involved in the protest had as their purpose the terrorising of these innocent children and their parents."

But that sense of outrage could not be allowed to substitute for a dispassionate and scrupulous examination of the legality of the policing operation, he said.

"That appraisal must take place within a well-defined legal framework. Having conducted that assessment, I have concluded that the policing judgements made have withstood the challenge that has been presented to them," stated Sir Brian, finding in his 22-page judgement in favour of the police.

Chief Superintendent Roger Maxwell, he said, had convinced him that the police had done everything possible for the children's safe passage. There were constraints, including the risk of even greater injury, he said.

"Throughout, the safety of the children remained the paramount consideration of the police. More aggressive police tactics would undoubtedly have led, Mr Maxwell believed, to even more serious public disorder and the probable involvement of loyalist paramilitary organisations."

Not everyone was convinced. The Committee on the Administration of Justice (CAJ) said it was extremely disappointed that the judgement did not engage with serious questions raised by the challenge. Where, it asked, was there any ruling on the principle of the primacy of the "best interests of the child"? The ruling had also disregarded the vital role the law played in holding senior police officers to account. A case in which families had experienced "inhuman and degrading treatment" had offered no effective remedy, it said, arguing the police could not just blame both protesters and parents while absolving themselves from responsibility. The ruling also, said the CAJ, interpreted the right to education in the narrowest sense in saying that the efforts of parents and teachers had ensured the children had continued to learn.

The SDLP's Martin Morgan says it was patent nonsense for the police to claim they had done all they could.

"The same year they used 1,500 police with dogs, water cannon and military backup to force an Orange march past Ardoyne. Claiming that they exercised restraint in order to avoid paramilitary involvement is even more ludicrous. Just who did the police think made and threw the pipe bomb? The UDA were involved from day one in engineering the confrontation. It appears the police were more concerned about placating loyalists than protecting school children," he says.

Sinn Fein said the outcome was "undoubtedly influenced by Dickson's letter".

Martha is appealing the verdict and her solicitors were preparing a case in the autumn of 2004. "I was expecting to lose but still felt disgusted," she says. "I still hope something can come out of it. It just goes to show the police, the courts and the judiciary – they're all covering each others' backs."

The gulf between Ardoyne and the police over Holy Cross will probably never be bridged. The police have an answer for everything, plausible or otherwise, while Ardoyne has supplementary questions. Both Alan McQuillan and Roger Maxwell undoubtedly faced a uniquely difficult policing problem in Ardoyne. Both men appear genuinely disappointed, but not surprised, at the response of the parents to their efforts. Alan McQuillan says policing the dispute almost brought his force to breaking point. One thousand officers were injured that summer in North Belfast, 41 of them at the Holy Cross protest.

"I doubled the number of officers on public order duty in Belfast. We were drawing people every day from as far as Fermanagh and Derry. We even set up a temporary dormitory. It wasn't just Ardoyne, there was nightly rioting across the city. Holy Cross was a drip, drip, drip of poison that spread across North Belfast. We had violence on a nightly basis."

Martha, whose life was turned upside down by Holy Cross, says the police operation convinced her the Agreement had not resulted in any improvements in policing.

"You hoped the RUC wouldn't let them do anything to hurt the children. The eyes of the world were on them. But they did. I just couldn't comprehend it. It was the same old RUC. Nothing had changed."

Chapter Ten

LOYALISTS

The UDA took a decision to make a stand in Glenbryn. They were dogged by media reports about their drug dealing and wanted to portray themselves as the saviours of the loyalist people.　　　　Sean Carmichael, parent

There was no influx into this community. The only people who left the Shankill were the UVF. Why would they come into a UDA stronghold? That theory is totally unfounded. We had support from the lower Shankill but they didn't live here.　　　　Jim Potts, CRUA spokesman

Many nationalists paint a pre-2001 picture of Glenbryn as an ageing community, relatively quiescent and relaxed about living along the peace-line with Ardoyne's Holy Cross school in its midst. Relations between the two communities were, if not cordial, at least not overtly hostile. Sure, there were regular arson attacks on Holy Cross and the odd riot on the Ardoyne Road in July – but Glenbryn was largely left alone.

Father Kenneth Brady, the Passionist priest at Holy Cross before August 2001, and his Church of Ireland counterpart, the Rev Stewart Heaney, for example, were, and are, brotherly friends and their congregations shared services. Wheatfield (the local Protestant primary) and Holy Cross Girls' schools had a flourishing cross-community relationship, with joint trips and visits, thanks in the main to a determination by their two principals. Bar the odd tense marching season, everything in the garden was, if not a bowl of cherries, at least not a bed of nails.

Those who emerged during the Holy Cross protest as spokesmen for Glenbryn, however, paint a dramatically different picture. They say Ardoyne had, for many years, subjected them to vicious and sustained attacks. Loyalists complained of pensioners intimidated in the Post Office and the chemist at the Ardoyne shops, of schoolboys assaulted at bus stops, of nightly riots and attacks on their homes. And of sectarian abuse being shouted by Catholic parents collecting their daughters from Holy Cross school, even deliberate targeting of Protestant residents by parents picking their children up after classes ended.

They speak of endemic economic neglect, of politicians' broken promises, lack of investment and a general sense of decline. They also, even more seriously, speak of a growing fear that burgeoning Ardoyne wanted to roll back the peace-line and take over their homes. There was fury in Glenbryn when large, handsome houses sprung up on the Catholic side of the peace-line, on the old bus depot facing the main road to the shops. There was more anger when their front doorsteps overlooked the Ardoyne Road. Glenbryn residents would have preferred to walk past their back doors. They said they were promised the houses would face into Ardoyne. Now it meant Protestants had to walk past the new house-fronts on their way to the shops.

Ardoyne's population, however, already feels caged inside its peace-lines. Why shouldn't the houses face outwards, asks republican Mickey Liggett. "What gives them the right to design the houses we live in?"

There is also a loyalist sense of resentment about Holy Cross Monastery itself, its bulk looming over the hotly disputed corner where nationalist Ardoyne meets the loyalist Woodvale and Twaddell Roads (the latter named after a unionist shot dead in the 1920s).

Dr Peter Shirlow has studied the demographic make-up and shifts in population in North Belfast for many years. He says Glenbryn, like other Protestant working class areas of Belfast city, has had its intellectual capital "hollowed out". Most people who can, he says, have left, aspiring to own their own house and garden in the better-off suburbs. He sees violence and paramilitarism as further powerful incentives on upwardly-mobile Protestants to get out of Glenbryn.

"Within unionism, there is a definite dislike of violence, wherever it comes from. Many people moved out to get away from the UVF and UDA, they did not want their kids to get involved. In the 1970s, Boys' Model (the largest school serving the Protestant Shankill Road area) won the Ulster Schools (Rugby) Cup. There is no way it could win it today, they couldn't even get a team together."

The same school in the 1970s, he says, was sending a respectable number of its teenagers to university. Last year it sent two.

"There was a slow burning fuse of resentment in Glenbryn at the superior quality of life loyalists believed was being enjoyed by people in Ardoyne. The June 19 incident finally lit the tinder."

As ever in the North, perception is reality, no matter how inaccurate. In reality, Ardoyne suffers multiple deprivation on the same level as Glenbryn although, as throughout Belfast, Protestant residents are less organised to take advantage of grants and incentives for community development. Anne Bill, a community worker from Glenbryn, says that until the protest, she had tried in vain to get people organised. "There was so much apathy. We organised meeting after meeting but people just didn't turn up."

Stuart McCartney, another loyalist from Glenbryn, has a diploma in psychology from Queen's University and has been involved in community work since his early 20s, mostly with young people in North Belfast. He joined the PUP (linked to the UVF) in 2002 and voted, for the first time in his life, in favour of the Good Friday Agreement. He is proud of his anti-sectarian credentials.

"When my son was aged nine or ten, he came to me and asked what a Prod was? I was very proud. I've gone out of my way to teach my children not to tie labels onto people."

Another major player on the loyalist side of the community is Jim Potts, who was born and brought up on the nearby Crumlin/Shankill Roads before marrying and moving into Glenbryn in 1998. As we walked, on our first meeting, through heavy metal railings around a run-down local park, towards a dingy-looking white low-level building, he confided that this was his "little bit of heaven". I was surprised when he explained that, since October 2001, he had turned what had been a former children's nursery into a flourishing youth club, by dint of hard work and determination, "to get kids off the streets". Inside, Potts organises pool, darts, table tennis, music, cultural awareness, art and cross community projects with local young people. The group has visited Malin Head and Culdaff in County Donegal and Carlingford in County Louth on cross-border trips. This is an unseen side to the man most nationalists only identify from the angry face he presented to the television cameras on the first day of the school term 2001. Potts was filmed shouting loudly at the cavalcade of parents and children walking to Holy Cross and was later charged with causing an affray and ordered to keep off the road unless travelling to his then place of work in Glenbryn.

In all, six loyalists had been arrested. Potts' address in court was given as Dover Street, off the Shankill Road. (A co-accused, Stephen Bell, was also charged with possession of an offensive weapon, namely a golf club.)

Potts describes himself as a loyalist and a unionist. Correctly or otherwise, he is regarded both within his own community and Ardoyne as being close to the UDA. Like the UDA, he believes too much has been "given to republicans" during the peace process and as a result of the Agreement. But the protest would probably have happened anyway, he says. The state of the peace process was not critical.

Another loyalist, Ronnie Black, a 42-year-old Shankill man and taxi-driver who has lived in Glenbryn since 1973, agrees. Glenbryn was always fertile ground for Ian Paisley's DUP and the parties linked to the paramilitaries, he says. Emphasising the dilapidation of the area, he says people felt neglected and ignored by the main political parties. Like others, he insists that the protest was not directed at the school children.

Like Black, Michael Cosby, another long-standing loyalist, only became politically active through the Holy Cross protest. He is particularly proud of the architect's drawings on the wall of CRUA's office showing what the new houses in Glenbryn will look like. Cosby, like Potts and Black, accepts that once the current redevelopment has finished and the new Glenbryn has risen from the ashes, it will be a challenge to persuade former, or new, residents to move back.

The question, which would later become critical, of where to make their protest, says Anne Bill, was a "simple reaction".

"People felt that they needed to protest on the Ardoyne Road because they saw that as their first line of defence."

All the loyalists interviewed agreed there was never any conscious democratic decision to block the road. No strategy was discussed or vote taken; it developed spontaneously.

Anne Bill says, "We had been pushing for years for a security gate between us and Ardoyne. In 1997 we were even told it was going ahead. The moment Sinn Fein heard about it, everything changed and it never happened."

Faced with the prospect of the 1997 gate, she says, the violence from Ardoyne was turned off like a tap. "Every time we asked for the gate, it would calm down. It was clearly orchestrated - they could stop and start it just like that," she says, clicking her fingers.

For an explanation of the tensions that led to the protest, loyalist Stuart McCartney argues there is a refusal by nationalists to accept their own sectarianism. He says nationalists are incapable of conceiving that Protestants fear them, telling of how a Sinn Fein Assembly member once lectured him about Catholic fears in North Belfast, without mentioning Protestant fears.

"That told me Sinn Fein didn't give a shit about my son's safety, that I had wasted my time bringing him up in a non-sectarian manner, teaching him to respect others. If I feel that way, how much more does the normal Joe on the street feel? I'm not asking Sinn Fein to change their politics; I am just asking them to make a little more effort to win the hearts and minds of my community and show us that they can be trusted with our future."

Potts says the protest was against parents or guardians involved in "targeting people and the daily intimidation we were tolerating". The people in Ardoyne were simply not prepared to address those concerns. Glenbryn was under siege. It was about our homes, the streets, the bad conditions. Catholics saw our area becoming run-down and began to feel they had the right to move in."

There is a widespread belief in Glenbryn that there was an elaborate Catholic strategy to push the peace-line back. "Ardoyne is a far larger community with the capacity and experience of 30 years of conflict to over-run a small Protestant enclave," says Potts.

If nationalists have their theories on why the protest started, so does Glenbryn. Some loyalists now believe their anger was exploited, or deliberately provoked, in a republican plan to shift the focus off the political stage where Sinn Fein was under pressure. Hesketh resident and former Holy Cross lollipop-lady, Amanda Johnston, a supporter of the Glenbryn protest, certainly believes so.

"Their gameplan was to divert attention from IRA decommissioning and Colombia," she says. (On August 11, 2001, three republicans were arrested in Colombia travelling on false passports. There were claims, since rejected by the Colombian courts, that they were training FARC guerrillas in bomb making. It caused a major international political storm.)

"Republicans also wanted to cause a diversion because the IRA was under pressure over decommissioning. They had to distract attention and give a reason why they wouldn't disarm. So it was IRA propaganda from the beginning. And what better way to do it than with schoolchildren, to attract media attention? Of course, they also want the peace-line moved," she says. "They still want to move into Glenbryn. If you look at a map of Belfast 30 years ago and then at how it is now and you colour in orange and green, and put them on top of each other, you'll see how the green has progressed."

Anne Bill also believes that the Colombia Three affair played a part and subscribes to the "peace-line pushback" theory. "They thought if they took one street off us, they could move in and get the next street. Why should this area become nationalist?"

Michael Cosby is of the same opinion. "Their gameplan was to take over this area. That's why Holy Cross was built there, along with three or four other Catholic schools. Our Lady of Mercy, a Catholic secondary school, is in the heart of Ballysillan and it's even more loyalist than Glenbryn," he complains. (This school has also, however, suffered repeated loyalist attacks, most recently when six teachers' cars were smashed with baseball bats in September 2003.)

"How can you move Catholics into a Protestant area? You just can't do it. You can't," protests Cosby, sitting in the old CRUA committee headquarters, looking over the old, flattened houses.

Loyalists deny nationalist claims that reinforcements were bussed in to swell the numbers at the daily protests on the Ardoyne Road. Hard evidence either way is difficult to come by. There are very few links between nationalist Ardoyne and the loyalist Shankill, but one Ardoyne parent has cousins living there. They rang her the night before the main protest began, warning her to be careful as supporters were being bussed in.

Holy Cross parent Elaine Burns, who has a wide circle of contacts from her community work background, says that she recognised faces in the protesting crowds. "The majority were from Tiger Bay, the Shankill, Ballysillan. They weren't Glenbryn residents that I recognised."

Rev Stewart Heaney also claims outsiders regularly came to the protest. "I saw big burly men arriving, four and five in a car. They came from everywhere."

Sharon McCabe, a Holy Cross mother, remembers the morning she spotted a minibus taking loyalists back to nearby Woodvale and the Shankill. On another occasion there was a busload of Scottish people. "You knew by their brogue. I was amazed they were bussing them in from Scotland."

Such views are hotly contested by others. Anne Bill, for example, denies claims that protesters were bussed in from other loyalist areas. "On the first day there were people coming from everywhere, including the Shankill. I remember a crowd arriving and I didn't know one of them. But after the first few days, they never came back."

Liz Murphy disagrees. "We saw for ourselves, cars coming up from the Shankill. They parked up from the school and came down to protest. No cop ever told them to clear off because they weren't from Glenbryn. They did as they pleased."

The counterpoint to Glenbryn's conviction that Ardoyne is determined to roll back the peace-line is the widespread theory on the nationalist side of the peace-line that the UDA/UVF feuding in 2000 in the Lower Shankill led directly to the Holy Cross protest. The theory goes that some UDA men, loyal to Johnny Adair, decamped to Glenbryn to avoid the unwelcome attentions of the other main loyalist grouping, the UVF. Martin Morgan, the local SDLP councillor and former Lord Mayor of Belfast, believes this theory has credibility.

"Clearly some of the UDA activists in the area originated from the lower Shankill," he says. "There were frequent occasions when people in Ardoyne identified individual loyalists on the protest; there is that kind of familiarity at conflict points. I firmly believe the UDA inspired and maintained the violence, the Glenbryn community was put up to it."

Rev Norman Hamilton, Presbyterian minister in Glenbryn, disagrees. "Those (UDA) influences were there, but to what extent is another question. My clear perception at the outset was this was a protest by everyone, including folks from outside who were now part of the community. Of course there were people in Glenbryn who were horrified; of course there were people who were intimidated. But how do you measure the relevant influences of these groups?"

It is a theory with no support in Glenbryn and evidence both for and against is inconclusive, but one credible first hand account comes from Ardoyne couple Chris and Rita McDonald. The good relations they had with their Protestant neighbours in Glenbryn in the early 1990s, they say, gradually deteriorated during the worst years of the Drumcree stand-offs in 1995-6. This coincided with older people leaving the area. Houses started becoming vacant, they say, with a lot of families drifting in and out. "A lot of the older generation seemed to be moving out or passing away and being replaced with a different kind of person," says Chris.

The McDonald home began to come under attack. "The police told us those responsible were originally from the Shankill, Ballysillan and Glencairn (three staunch loyalist areas nearby)," Rita McDonald says.

"You would hear them having all-night parties with loud music across in Glenbryn, which was something that you would never have heard before. Some of the houses you could only describe as drinking dens for partying all night. In the old days, you would call the police if someone was making a noise at 8 o'clock at night, that's how quiet the place was. Now there were all-night parties and cars constantly driving around. It was just a totally different kind of estate. It went from one extreme to the other. It was frightening."

Rita says the feud in the Shankill accelerated the change and the attacks became more organised. When they first moved in, she says, there was no painting of kerbs or UDA flags. When that began, it symbolised the change that had come over Glenbryn.

"We knew things were getting worse; you could nearly taste it in the air. The whole atmosphere was changing. From older people going to the shops, there were youths of 16 and 17 hanging about instead."

Sean Carmichael is another Ardoyne resident who is convinced the feud played a role. "The UDA took a decision to make a stand in Glenbryn. They were being dogged by media reports on drug-dealing and wanted to portray themselves as the saviours of the loyalist people."

A third Ardoyne resident, Judy Haughey, says, "It erupted when people moved from the Shankill to Glenbryn during the feud. The Shankill crowd had never seen Catholic kids before. They just couldn't accept it or cope with it."

Jim Crawford, a Holy Cross parent, says a close friend in Glenbryn told him that, just before the trouble really started, the UDA were visiting houses at weekends inviting donations of £5 for loyalist prisoners. "If you didn't give it, you were threatened or burnt out," he says.

Long-time community activist, Elaine Burns, says she was so worried about the obvious influx of loyalists in Glenbryn that she contacted the Housing Executive.

"We warned them there was going to be trouble. The ones arriving had always lived in the middle of a loyalist area and were not used to seeing Catholics about, whereas Glenbryn people have always had to interact with us because of sharing the shops, doctors' surgeries and so on. They couldn't stomach seeing 'Fenians going up their road'. The whole environment changed, even the pillar boxes were painted red, white and blue. In the old days, you would see flags going up in July – but in 2001 they started in March. One chimney pot even collapsed under the weight of flags."

Dr Peter Shirlow believes the exodus of UDA men from the Shankill to Glenbryn played a significant, perhaps critical role.

"Glenbryn had the odd paramilitary but it didn't have any hard core of loyalism until that small group of people arrived who had never lived close to Catholics. The wall on the Shankill/Falls interface is so high they never saw people with Celtic shirts walking about. They didn't know a world like Ardoyne existed just two miles up the road with Irish flags and hurley bats and kids in GAA tops. They would have stiffed (murdered) anyone who wore a Celtic top on the Shankill. Now they were seeing them every day. It played upon their sense of being taken over. UDA members are not the world's sharpest intellectuals, but they do know how to manipulate. In Glenbryn, they found a vulnerable community, a fertile ground of fear and prejudice."

Asked about the Ardoyne theory of "UDA exiles" and gradual demographic change, however, Jim Potts just laughs, although he admits the area has a strong UDA element.

"There was no influx of families into this community," he insists. "We had support from some of Adair's people in the lower Shankill but they didn't move in to live here."

Adair, a heavily-built, right-wing UDA assassin, initially supported the protest from within his prison cell. References and photographs of Adair appeared repeatedly at the protest. Sentenced to sixteen years for "directing terrorism" (police officers had tape-recorded him boasting of his murderous exploits), he was released in September 1999 but re-imprisoned in August 2000 after his involvement in the loyalist feud. One protester created an Adair mask and would stand on the road, lifting it up from time to time and shouting, "Boo" at the children. Another held aloft a picture of Adair taken in jail with the slogan "Trick or Treat" on it. These were the words shouted by UDA gunmen as they murdered seven Catholics and one Protestant at Halloween in Greysteel, 1993. Later, however, Adair said the protest had "run its course" and that loyalists were "being made to look bad in the eyes of the media".

Chief Superintendent Roger Maxwell is also sceptical of the notion that the UDA had planned to expand its sphere of influence into Glenbryn. "That theory is predicated on the notion that the UDA has a strategy. The UDA has no strategy. It is a loose collection of criminal gangs."

Anne Bill also decries the theory that the UDA was behind the protest. "It's just plain not true. There was movement of people but none came from the Shankill into Glenbryn." Potts, McCartney, Black and others also disagree.

UUP councillor Fred Cobain, while conceding that some UDA men had moved into Glenbryn in the summer of 2001, doesn't believe it was critical. He also agrees there was a power struggle between the UDA and UVF in the area, but says it was over by the time of the protest.

"I don't think they (the UDA) were trying to show their muscle. I think they were establishing a power-base long before. There were tensions between the UVF and the UDA. Years ago, in the 70s and 80s, Glenbryn was a power-base for the UVF but that's been turned round and it's now clearly UDA-controlled."

Neil Jarman says the theory is "too superficial an explanation" for the dispute. "The movement of significant UDA people to Glenbryn from the Shankill was a factor, but it didn't erupt out of nothing; there were tensions in the area for the previous few years. It wasn't completely trouble-free and suddenly the UDA arrived."

Former Assistant Chief Constable Alan McQuillan tends to agree with Jarman. "There are very close family connections between Glenbryn and the Shankill, including UDA connections, but there was no evidence we saw of a huge influx of people from outside."

But while the UDA did not plan the Holy Cross dispute, McQuillan says, it certainly fitted into the general drift of its activities at the time.

"There was a conscious attempt by the UDA to stir up sectarian hatred; they didn't like the way things were going politically. Their own political hopes had just been wiped out, if they ever had any. They decided to go back to their core business, a faction of the UDA who said, 'Let's go kill a Catholic to show them we're not happy', but I don't think there was anybody sitting back with a clear conscious strategy to focus on Glenbryn. It happened during a period when the UDA was quite clearly behind large numbers of pipe bomb attacks on Catholic homes, not at the Glenbryn/Ardoyne interface but in other parts of Belfast. Adair was back out of jail and there was a sudden increase in activity clearly associated with 'C' Company. I have no doubt there were leadership people within the UDA in the lower Shankill who were perfectly happy to try to re-ignite sectarian violence."

Maxwell agrees. "Some of the protest's leaders would have had connections with the UDA, which is different from saying it was the UDA that led the protest."

McQuillan's belief that the UDA "piggy-backed" on the Holy Cross protest is, ironically, precisely what Gerry Kelly of Sinn Fein says.

"The UDA didn't plan the Holy Cross protest but it certainly ran with it," says Kelly. "It opened up a chance for the UDA to present themselves as the protectors of the people. If there's fear of Catholics, it was implanted and I blame the UDA which is a sectarian and criminal organisation. You can't blame Ardoyne for that. The UDA relishes situations like Holy Cross to cover its criminal activity."

Kelly believes the UDA uses its fearsome reputation, along with its claim to be the defender of the Protestant working class, as cover against police action against its endemic drug-dealing and racketeering.

"If the police ever went into loyalist working-class areas and really took on the drug-dealers, ordinary people would applaud it. The UDA knows that. If they went into the same areas and took out the same people, charging them with sectarian attacks, the outcry would be huge, unfortunately. So the UDA use their anti-Catholic sectarianism to persuade the community to tolerate their drug-dealing."

He agrees that people in Glenbryn feel ignored and forgotten, but "not because of sectarian attacks from Ardoyne".

"I'm not saying there were no sectarian attacks, but even the RUC admit that the majority are against Catholics. Were there attacks on Glenbryn from Ardoyne? Yes there were. But you have to look at the proportionality."

Another theory mooted in Ardoyne is that the protest was a UDA/UVF test of strength. Dr Peter Shirlow believes there's something in it. "You had the more progressive elements within the UVF on one side and the louts on the other side."

Potts says the opposite. "We were just coming out of the feud and the Holy Cross protest actually brought the two groups together. The UDA and the UVF stood together on the Ardoyne Road in support of the community. There was no rivalry," he says determinedly.

This appears, on the face of it, to be a tacit admission that the paramilitaries were involved, but Potts denies that also.

"OK, we had meetings with the Loyalist Commission (an umbrella group of loyalists, Protestant clergy and unionist politicians) for updates about the protest. The paramilitaries were kept up to date but they recognised it was a community problem and could only be sorted out by the community."

Potts adds that CRUA turned down several offers of paramilitary muscle. He says loyalist paramilitaries were so concerned at how long the protest was dragging on and the attendant negative media coverage that they asked the Glenbryn residents to call it off. However, "Stephen" (not his real name), a member of CRUA who wants to remain anonymous, says there were internal rivalries. A republican intermediary within Ardoyne contacted him to set up a meeting over Holy Cross, but CRUA vetoed it.

"I was very keen to meet him (the republican)," says Stephen, "but I couldn't meet anyone without the committee's permission and I wouldn't go behind their backs."

Stephen also says the CRUA committee always included two people who would report back to the UDA and UVF through their own contacts as well as the Loyalist Commission.

According to David McNarry, a member of the Loyalist Commission, a Glenbryn loyalist threw a handful of coins onto the table at one meeting – shouting angrily at David Trimble for failing to back the protest sufficiently and demanding he take his "thirty pieces of silver".

"I can remember those conversations very clearly because I was one of those who went to speak to the Loyalist Commission," says Potts. "Our response to their request was that we wouldn't call the protest off until we had meaningful dialogue to resolve the problems that had caused it."

Ronnie Black gives the same response. "CRUA spoke for the community not the paramilitaries. The offer of help was there but the community was against it. Not that we didn't need the paramilitaries – every community needs them – every community runs on paramilitaries. But I think the community felt the paramilitaries would discredit them."

It is widely believed in Glenbryn that Stuart McCartney, aligned with the PUP and regarded during the protest as a moderating influence, distanced himself from CRUA when it began to be perceived, rightly or wrongly, as overly UDA-influenced. He doesn't admit that openly but shrugs and admits he had "concerns" about some of CRUA's tactics and personnel.

Billy Hutchinson, the PUP Assembly member for North Belfast, says rather opaquely, "There would have been PUP up there and the other side of the loyalist operation. I never saw anyone from the UPRG (Ulster Political Research Group, linked to the UDA) up there and I never saw one Ulster Unionist. The only politicians there were myself, Nigel Dodds and Nelson McCausland (both members of Ian Paisley's DUP). I didn't speak unless asked and I was certainly not involved in any power struggle. I had plenty of other work to do. I didn't need to be stuck every morning at a protest. Certainly some people were unhappy at my presence but we don't need to identify who they were. They didn't like people who were articulate, but that's their problem not mine."

Shirlow believes the arrival of the UDA in Glenbryn undercut people like Hutchinson and the UUP assemblyman for the area, Fred Cobain.

"Until 2001, they, along with church leaders had been able to control sectarian tensions by promising to intercede with people in Ardoyne and so on. They were supplanted, wiped out, when the UDA arrived because it promised something far more direct, the rule of force. I think the protest cost Billy Hutchinson dear because he was seen as too ready to make concessions."

If in a similar situation, says Shirlow, a republican took the same risks as Hutchinson over Holy Cross, his electoral fortunes would soar as his electorate would respect his leadership, whereas many loyalists looked at Hutchinson's role and merely saw him as a coward, a traitor and a "Fenian-lover".

"There can be no doubt that anybody within the Protestant community with a calm voice was damaged during Holy Cross," says Shirlow.

Michael Cosby says CRUA actively decided to "keep outsiders away".

"It was for Glenbryn people to stand up and say our area was falling apart, not for people from the Shankill or Portadown or Ballysillan."

If they had wanted to, he says, they could have drafted in thousands. He admits that outside influences, including the paramilitaries, tried at different times to muscle in, but that CRUA wanted to do it for themselves, the way "they thought was right".

"This was a peaceful protest, to let the world know that we were crying here, we needed help."

Anne Bill concurs that the paramilitaries were "kept out" and that there were no rivalries between the UDA and UVF.

"That was at least one positive thing. Everybody was united, it didn't matter if you were a paramilitary, and it didn't matter which paramilitary you were, because we all stood side by side. People said they didn't want violence. Well, certainly the UVF leadership was saying it didn't want violence. The paramilitaries didn't cause violence really, other than that first day, September 3, 2001, and everybody was involved in that."

Others disagree, including the Rev Heaney. "The residents' association included some hard men. They had a lot of power. None of my parishioners was ever invited to the community meetings, so I don't know how representative they were."

He says the UVF and UDA were jockeying for position and criticises mainstream unionist parties for not "weaning people away" from the protest earlier. The CRUA leadership was "not terribly politically perceptive", he says, and did not realise how much damage they were doing themselves. Heaney still had paramilitary contacts from his school days in the area and began a series of conversations with people who, he says, "had clout" within the UDA and UVF.

"I told them the protest was absolutely morally wrong. They were not terribly sophisticated. They didn't have the foresight to see the damage it was causing and where it was leading. Some of them were more criminally than politically motivated."

He doesn't know, to this day, if he managed to exert much of an influence.

"You never know how much the other party takes on board. Eventually, though, the penny dropped. A UDA leader I spoke to, at a later stage, admitted to me it was a disaster. After several weeks they realised it was a mistake. They had taken on, not only schoolchildren, but the police and the establishment."

The Holy Cross protest, however, did indubitably take place in the context of innumerable UDA pipe bombings throughout North Belfast. Many nationalists saw the protest as an extension of that campaign and poured scorn on loyalist claims that the two were hermetically sealed from each other. The most powerful evidence of paramilitary involvement in the protest came on September 5, the day of the pipe bombing as the children walked to school. No one denies the UDA was behind that. In the immediate aftermath, Billy Hutchinson caused quite a stir when he said he was "ashamed to be a loyalist". Although he appeared to retract this admission on that evening's local television news, he now says he stands by it. His eyes blaze as he explains that attempts to claim the bomb was "aimed at the police" fail to justify it.

"That doesn't make it okay. I said on the day that I was wasting my time trying to explain why the protest was taking place if I couldn't be heard for the sound of bombs. After the bombing, nobody listened to us, nobody could hear our grievances. It undermined the protest, no question."

No question, either, about whom he holds responsible. "It was Johnny Adair's people, up to their necks in it." He alleges that the police did manage to arrest those responsible as they returned to their lower Shankill lair (known locally as "Little Beirut").

"The police went mad that day. One particular police officer, who was well-known for coming down hard on loyalist paramilitaries, went after them. He caught up with them in the lower Shankill and was removed from his position," alleges Hutchinson.

This surprising claim is based on a widespread belief amongst some loyalists, as well as republicans, that the Special Branch had infiltrated the lower Shankill UDA to such an extent that they effectively controlled them. Hutchinson, however, is more concerned to push home his belief that the bombing destroyed any chance the Protestant community had to get their viewpoint across.

Ronnie Black says be believes the UDA "moved back after the pipe bomb, after all the media attention and the blame being put onto the paramilitaries".

"They backed off and told the community to sort it out on their own," he says.

Anne Bill shares the Hutchinson view, that the bombing was a disaster for the protesters. "I was gutted. It was just madness, stupidity when we were trying to get our grievances heard."

Stuart McCartney was close to the explosion and it "scared the hell" out of him. "Regardless of the chaos, however, it was still our community. I'm not saying paramilitary organisations don't have integrity, some of them do, but at the end of the day this was us fighting for our identity and we didn't want it shanghaied."

Parents of children at Holy Cross do not accept that the bombing was aimed at the police, not the children. Liz Murphy is typical. "They knew we would be returning back down the road without the children, so why didn't they wait and throw it then? They shouldn't have done it at all, but given the choice, why do it when the children were there?"

Whatever divided the protesters, something did unite them 100 per cent. That was their firm contention that their actions had nothing to do with the children, were not aimed at the children and should never have affected the children. Jim Potts, asked if they were trying to frighten the kids because they couldn't frighten the parents, says, "There was no intention to scare anyone, that was not part of our protest. But if you are asking me, was I human? And if I had any feelings for the kids going up and down the road? Of course I did. I have two young children of my own. But I think the overriding thing for me was the parents didn't choose to go up the Crumlin Road. That would have created a breathing space for us all to resolve it. If the shoe was on the other foot, we wouldn't be allowed to build a school in Ardoyne and move up and down freely. We had allowed them access to their school for 30 years with very little hindrance."

Billy Hutchinson agrees, despite his criticism of some of their tactics. "The protest was never about the children, the protest was about people acting as guardians who were intimidating that community. These were people who used the children for propaganda purposes."

Put to him that, even if the protest had been silent, it would still have frightened the children, he says that would have been fair enough, "As long as the children weren't being harmed or intimidated or threatened."

Even if such a protest inevitably results in large numbers of police in close proximity to the children? "You didn't need the police there in the first place. For years, Protestant people had protected the children from other Protestants who wanted to abuse them."

Hutchinson goes further and accuses the Holy Cross governors and its principal of "not being clean in all of this". His reason? "Because the governors used the children to get extra grants for their school.

"They were quite happy about the protest. It was a disgrace." There were a number of opportunities for the church to give direction to the parents but it didn't. That meant parents were left to decide themselves whether to walk up the road or not," he says.

Jim McClean, the "man up the ladder" during the initial June 19 incident, now lives in a bleak, pebble-dashed street high above the city looking over his old home in Glenbryn. He is proud that he never missed a day of the protest, saying, "It was never against the kids. They were used as bait, propaganda for the republican movement."

When loyalist Ronnie Black saw the effects of the protest on the children on the nightly news bulletins, he says he was "sad" that they were caught up in it, but that it had to "reflect back on the parents". If they had negotiated, he says, there would not have been a protest.

Amanda Johnston says, "You put a few crying schoolgirls out there and you're going to attract media attention. The world couldn't believe how bad we were to those children but a hair was never touched on any of their heads."

Defending the loyalists, Ballysillan Presbyterian minister, Norman Hamilton, says the protesters believed, at first, that after a few short days they would get into talks to resolve their problems.

"One of them (protesters) put it in a memorable one-liner that I have used many times, 'Sure, we have lost everything, so what the hell?' But I don't want to defend the indefensible, or try to explain the inexplicable."

The Holy Cross parents reject loyalist claims that the children were not their target. "If they had protested for 12 hours a day; if they had protested when we were walking back from the school without our children, maybe," says Lynda Bowes. "But they didn't. They came out for an hour in the morning, when the kids were going to school, and an hour in the afternoon, when they were getting out of school. If they had just protested against us, OK. They could have shouted and screamed all they liked. They never made any attempt to show that it was not against children. They did everything to prove that it was."

Another accusation made against the protesters was that they threw urine-filled balloons. No loyalist accepts this happened. Anne Bill, for example, says the claim is "absolute nonsense, the balloons only contained water".

Ronnie Black says he checked out the claim and, "according to the wee lad who threw them", they contained only water.

"We can't stop them claiming there was urine in them, but as far as we're concerned there was none."

Jim Potts agrees. "Tell me this – can you actually envisage someone trying to fill a balloon with urine? It would be quite a difficult thing to do. I don't accept it. The individual who threw the balloons anyhow was not the 'full shilling' (Belfast slang for mentally impaired)."

One of the most disturbing tactics of some protesters was the use of pornographic language and images. Whatever the provocation, most adults would regard the use of sexually explicit language in the presence of children aged four to eleven, as reprehensible. The loyalist representatives interviewed here accept that abusive language was used and say they disapprove. On the use of pornographic photos, most deny it happened. Anne Bill, for example, never saw any pornographic photos but she did not agree with some of the abusive language used. "I don't think that shouting out 'Fenian whores' or 'sluts' was necessary," she says.

Loyalists regularly referred at the protest to the two priests of Holy Cross, Father Troy and Father Donegan, as paedophiles. While clearly not believing it to be literally true, they still attempt to justify it. Anne Bill concedes there were placards held up claiming Father Troy was a child abuser.

"That was because he had called the people of Glenbryn 'child abusers'. I thought he was silly to do it, especially where he was coming from," she says. She doesn't condemn the placards, though, "because he brought it on himself".

Potts says, "with hand on heart", that he didn't see pornographic photos. On swearing, he says, "If bad language was used, it was by both sides. I witnessed many individuals going up and down the Ardoyne Road using abusive language. I remember a young Protestant girl being attacked over the front of a police Land Rover. It was a shouting match, one was as bad as the other. Then a Catholic parent lunged across with an umbrella and tried to hit the young girl who was shouting at her. The media latched on to the claim that we used abusive language against the children and then everybody accepted it. It totally sickens me." He claims it was never widespread and, in any case, mutual.

Amanda Johnston says that claims about pornographic photographs and urine balloons were "lies if ever there was lies".

"They tried to make everything out as bad as it could possibly be. I know that for a fact that is the biggest load of lies I ever heard in my life."

Stuart McCartney was not at all happy about the use of foul language, saying there was "no call for it" and even going further, saying it was "unjustifiable and unforgivable".

"They shouldn't have used those words. These were children. You could use that language against the parents but not the children."

Does he accept that his community was dehumanising itself and should someone not have intervened to stop the worse excesses of the protest? McCartney, as he answers, becomes visibly upset.

"I don't think ... I don't think a lot of people are that deep. Their backs were against the wall. To do that would have required self awareness and self judgement. That doesn't come naturally to a lot of people."

As McCartney continues speaking, his distress becomes deeper. He recalls listening to the language used during the protest.

"I'm not saying that people are stupid, but I was crying. I stood there in tears. There was absolutely fuck all I could do about it," he says. "I could understand the anger, the hurt, the resentment, the bitterness. I had chosen to fight their corner but I felt like choking a lot of people. I couldn't condemn them because I understood. I condemned what they had done but I couldn't condemn the reasons for what they done. I condemn the target of what they did. Those children should never have been exposed to it. It's like every community. You've got the very well thought-out careful people, then the morons and the die-hards."

No such concerns trouble Ronnie Black. "Every day the nationalists came out with a new story for publicity. One day dogs' dirt, then urine, then porn magazines; half of it didn't happen or we would have seen it."

When it became obvious, though, that the tactics being used were losing the propaganda war and alienating the very people they were seeking support from, did the protesters consider alternatives?

Jim Potts said they did. "We didn't want to inflict any hardship on the kids so we turned to the idea of using whistles to stop people from shouting by giving them an alternative. It was then agreed that we would be silent while the parents and children were walking towards the school in the morning, but to make as much noise as we could on the return trip without the children."

McCartney, however, rejects the idea that CRUA should have considered the possibility that their tactics were self-defeating.

"That's looking at it as though it were a game, a political game. People had their backs to the wall. They didn't give a damn what some homeowner in Canada or Washington or Berlin thought. We had to live here. This wasn't a political sales pitch. To be honest with you – to have turned round and said we should stop now, we're on a hiding to nothing – I would have considered that actually offensive, because this was people's lives. The amount of trouble I got in trying to stop the language, serious trouble! But, at the same time, it was awful, it was terrible, it was out of line, but I understood why it was happening, why they were angry. They had been betrayed, nobody gave a damn, the papers were hammering them. What was the point? Nobody had given a shit about the community for years. If I had had my way, it would have been a dignified protest. If I had that kind of power, I would have insisted that anyone who couldn't behave would have taken themselves off. All I could do was to try to calm people down. I'm amazed I don't have major dents in my head, because a lot of the time I jumped in between people."

CRUA appointed McCartney and others as stewards and issued fluorescent orange bibs to try to control the protest, but with only limited effect. "The condemnation of the world was awful," says an anguished McCartney, "but we thought, hang on, we have our grievances too ...."

He recalls Sinn Fein's Martin McGuinness once being asked to condemn rioters and replying that riots were "the cry of the oppressed". This, says McCartney was Glenbryn's cry.

"If the world didn't want to hear it, fine – but we were being bullied by a much larger community and nobody gave a damn, not even the police."

Potts says that although they were clearly losing the propaganda war, CRUA felt it couldn't back down. "We knew the consequences of the protest would be the world's condemnation, although I don't think we realised how bad it would be. We were in a corner and we couldn't get out."

Billy Hutchinson, who is more media-savvy than Potts, points out that, three days after the bombing, they changed tactics dramatically to "using whistles or silence".

Ronnie Black says it was more sophisticated than that. "We tried to have a different theme a day, to show we weren't bad guys. There was one day we all dressed up as Mexicans in sombreros. The idea was to lighten the tension for the children."

It did not have the desired effect. No one on the nationalist side could figure out what they were trying to do, ending up concluding this was some sort of attempt at political commentary on events in Colombia.

Anne Bill, contrastingly, says they never discussed changing tactics.

"People began to get angrier because, no matter what we tried, the Catholics were always portrayed as the victims."

But, when your enemy uses your tactics to defeat you, is it not time to change your tactics? "You can say that, and we might have done if it had been a military operation, but people were just swept up in the emotion of the moment. If parents wanted to trail their kids up the roads through the protest, fair enough. We didn't ask them to do it."

Amanda Johnston says that by the time they realised what a bad press they were getting, it was too late to change tack. "There was nothing else we could do. We had tried everything else – talking to MPs, media, nobody seemed to listen. We felt we had no alternative."

As the protest continued, it fell into a routine that some Glenbryn protesters said was not entirely unpleasant. A creche was even set up in the local community centre to care for children before parents left to take part in the protest.

"I had never seen this in all of the time I had worked in the area or lived in it even before that," says Anne Bill, approvingly. "I could not believe that this many people had reacted, ordinary people, a lot of them were pensioners. They had had enough. They couldn't take anymore. Someone had to listen."

Ronnie Black says he can never remember Glenbryn being so galvanised. "It became a way of living – from early morning up on the road, having a smoke and a banter. The community was bonding. We were all on the same wavelength. The protest was positive from our view, everything was positive. The feeling of everyone in it together and no one walking away, although it got harder and harder as the winter came in and it was freezing and raining. The fact that people didn't drift away gave us a bit of clout. If it had started dying, we would have been a laughing stock. OK, outsiders mightn't have had a good perception of us, but we had to try to make something out of it. People had to understand."

Michael Cosby, on the other hand, says the community gradually began to realise they could not win. There was a public meeting just about every night, he says, with angry people feeling increasingly powerless. "We gradually realised we were never going to win it – that we were never going to get much out of it."

There are strong arguments each way on whether CRUA was genuinely representative of ordinary people's views in Glenbryn. The Rev Heaney got into hot water by alleging that CRUA was not truly representative. "The CRUA committee was not democratically elected. I couldn't say anything else because it was absolutely true."

The police warned him not to appear on the Ardoyne Road after he spoke out and from then on he would make pastoral visits to Glenbryn for bereavements and marriages only between the morning and afternoon protests.

"I felt there was a moral issue here, that this was child abuse. I knew people in my own parish didn't support the protest and I condemned it outright. That led to some of my congregation, who supported me, having stones and eggs thrown at their homes. So, we were suffering alongside the nationalist people."

After the attacks, he says, those who opposed the protest kept their heads down because they were frightened.

"Our Mothers' Union wanted to stand on the road to support the parents but didn't for fear of violence. The vast majority of people in Glenbryn did not want to be involved. I was going in and out of houses in the area and I never met many who supported it. Every house I went into, people were very depressed about it. It was awful. People were sitting in their homes, feeling terrified, and no one was speaking out for them. There was a very powerful minority who were pushing their own views. The homes of those who disagreed were being pelted. There were remarks passed at them going to church. I had no dissenters (supporters of the protest) from within my own congregation. I wonder if the nationalist people in Ardoyne realised they had more friends in Glenbryn than they knew. There were folks from Glenbryn right throughout the protest who still went to the Ardoyne shops and never had any bother."

Amanda Johnston, however, says 95 per cent of the community were behind the protest. "The other five per cent were too elderly – but no one opposed it. It hurt me to see a Christian woman like Irene (her fellow lollipop-lady) squealing at the top of her voice, sinning her soul with language. I saw a middle-aged lady once, a well-dressed, lovely lady, running through an entry (alley way between terraced houses) carrying stones and saying she never thought she'd see the day she'd be doing this."

Michael Cosby says, "I never saw Glenbryn rise like it. Some of the protesters' backgrounds would have amazed you. There were ex-police officers, ex-prison officers, nurses, doctors. Yeah, they were all on the road in the protest."

Such views are not shared by all. Patricia Monaghan, whose daughter goes to Holy Cross, tells a heartbreaking story of an elderly Protestant married couple in their 80s, related to her through an aunt. They ended their days in a nursing home, she says, after being forced from the home for refusing to support the protest. In the first week of the blockade, she says, the UDA ordered them to put a flag out in support. "It was a black and yellow paramilitary flag. Peggy said she'd lived there all her life and would have none of it."

The UDA offered the flag to the elderly couple at the cut-down rate of £20 because they were pensioners. "She told him that they were putting no flags out. He said if they didn't, her old man would be thrown through the window. The incident happened in June and the couple moved out in July. They couldn't get re-housed and they ended up in a nursing home. The elderly man has since died."

Philomena Flood remembers returning from the school run and seeing a "wee woman from Glenbryn" hiding in the hedges. "She said that she was afraid in case the crowd saw her and she said, 'I am very, very sorry' and she was in tears."

Liz Murphy, who had an uncle living in Glenbryn until recently, says, "There are still decent people up there. Unfortunately, out of pure fear, they just closed their blinds rather than come out and condemn it publicly. At times I would have been critical of people like that, but then you remember what the UDA are like and realise it was either keep quiet or face them down. As we know, the UDA are capable of anything, even to their own."

Dr Peter Shirlow speaks of widespread intimidation in Glenbryn by those behind the protest. "The UDA were going round and demanding £20 from everybody for flags. People were being told to turn up and protest; they weren't allowed to sit in the house or show disapproval by not attending."

Sean Carmichael also says some Glenbryn residents, "decent people", wrote letters and phoned Anne Tanney to apologise. "Obviously they were powerless to stop it for fear of being put out of their homes."

Maura Lindsay, from Ardoyne, has evidence that not all Protestants supported the protest. "I once saw a woman from Glenbryn drive into Alliance Avenue and jump out of her car, crying her eyes out. She told me how sorry she was and how ashamed she was to be a Protestant. The woman said flyers were put round all their doors telling them to get out and support the protest. People who opposed the protest, their windows were broken."

There is evidence of at least three known actions taken by loyalists to persuade other Protestants that Ardoyne posed a threat, attempts to divide the two communities even deeper than they were already. Maura and David Lindsay believe they witnessed one such attempt on a Sunday afternoon in summer 2001. Maura heard an elderly woman screaming over the peace-line in Glenbryn. Looking out of her bedroom window, she saw four young men standing just on the Ardoyne side of the peace-line. They were throwing stones at the elderly lady's home in Glenbryn and yelling, "Orange bastard".

Maura heard them shouting, "You dirty Orange whore, get into your fucking house or we'll kill you" before hitting her with stones and bricks. "She was shouting back, 'You fucking green slugs'." Maura watched as the men, tiring of the attack, then surreptitiously moved back across the peace-line into Glenbryn. "These were loyalists pretending to be nationalists. They tried to make that woman believe they were from our side."

There were other incidents. In October 2001, the police blamed the UDA for mailing anonymous threatening letters to elderly people in Glenbryn, signed "Catholic Reaction Force". The letters demanded loyalists end the Holy Cross protest "or you will be targeted by the North Belfast Catholic Reaction Force". The police at first took the letters as a genuine republican threat. Then they became convinced they were a clumsy attempt by the UDA to turn back the tide of international condemnation. A senior police source said at the time that they did not believe the "North Belfast Catholic Reaction Force" existed.

The *Sunday People* quoted a police source saying, "The UDA have been oiling up their PR machine in the last few months and they see this kind of thing as one way to counteract their appalling image. I've no doubt at all, not one shred, that this is a UDA idea and it's not the first one like this which we've seen. These were drawn up by hand, with some kind of stencil. These have not come from the Catholic community. We're looking at loyalist PR disaster number two."

One 76-year-old woman, living on her own in Glenbryn Parade, said that when she opened the letter, "I just couldn't believe it. I nearly died. I am afraid and scared."

The then president of the Methodist church in Ireland, Dr Harold Good, says he knows of at least one elderly lady who was terrified when she read the letter. Dating back to pre-Troubles days, she had friends in Ardoyne and felt very distressed that she was no longer welcome. Good was never told that the police believed the letters were hoaxes. "I didn't know who wrote them or who sent them and the police had a responsibility to make that known publicly if that was the case."

Loyalists were also behind another crude bid to paint the Holy Cross parents as Sinn Fein ciphers. In October 2001, a memo, supposedly from "Members of Oldpark and Ardoyne Sinn Fein", began circulating in loyalist areas. It claimed Sinn Fein was manipulating parents at Holy Cross to distract attention from demands for IRA decommissioning by coercing them to take their children to school via the usual route.

The memo read, in part, "It is up to all party members to do there (*sic*) upmost (*sic*) to ensure that the media are given full excess (*sic*) to the parents. Please remember to impress upon the media that the parents only want excess (*sic*) to the school via Glenbryn. Also inform all parents that they must say they use this route every day. On Friday 22nd June we will walk up to the (Brits) police line, please make sure that mostly party members and there (*sic*) children are at the front of the line.

"If the police batten (*sic*) charge do not fight back if the media our (*sic*) in the area. Our associate friends will stay about 100 yards away from the police lines. Our people will support us in different areas over the next week. We need to take the pressure of (*sic*) the party over arms and put the spotlight on the loyalists.

"In making statements to the media," the document continues, "be as graphic as possible and try to slant these statements in our favour and remember to pull in a witness or two."

The "memo" is littered with even more spelling mistakes and

grammatical errors. The hapless loyalist forger even spelt Sinn Fein "Sinn Fien". It convinced no one.

There is bitterness in the loyalist camp over how the protest ended. Some of the main players behind the CRUA campaign are now of the view they were wrong to argue for the protest to end. Amanda Johnston's opinion is a fair example. "The politicians promised us everything. We got nothing. We were promised a wall. We were promised the earth if we called the protest off. All we got were a few hanging baskets and a security camera that nobody watches. I don't call that very good security. Trimble and Durkan? I hate them. We got nothing except being turned into monsters."

Amanda's only regret is that the protest was called off. "They should have kept it going until the wall was built, until we got the promised chicane in the road. But again you're promised it by people who are in power and you treat their word as gospel."

But there is little evidence of regret in the loyalist camp, despite it all. "This community was backed into a corner," says Jim Potts. "A wounded animal will do things against its nature. The Protestants of Glenbryn are good people. You (the author) have told me about things that I never saw myself. You tell me people like Father Troy witnessed them. I am not going to go against the word of a priest. They were uncharacteristic of the people who live here. I think we were used by republicans. I was too caught up in things at that time to realise it. Looking back, I do honestly feel I was caught up in something I had no control over. It was very depressing. There was no joy in what was taking place. There was a sense of pride in sticking together but it was very, very, very frustrating that our voices were not heard through the media."

Ronnie Black says he has no regrets. "I knew in my own mind that we weren't targeting the children so I don't have any guilty conscience. The parents should have a guilty conscience though. If they were prepared to walk their children through that, why should I have a guilty conscience? I know it's a hard thing to say, but that's the way I get over it. I wouldn't put my child through it."

Rev Bill Shaw, the Presbyterian minister born in strongly loyalist Sandy Row, who acted as facilitator to the Ardoyne delegation at the final meeting of the summer of 2001, gives a very different Protestant perspective.

"It was horrific. I felt it very badly, both because of my personal involvement in the talks that had failed and because those involved came from the community I had grown up in. I felt almost a guilt by association, that this was 'my tribe'."

Did nationalists have any understanding or sympathy for the plight of the declining Glenbryn population who felt under such pressure? It seems whatever residual or potential sympathy might have existed was extinguished by the protest. Ardoyne mother Lynda Bowes says groups of parents would sometimes get together and try to figure out what was behind the protest, what was making the loyalists tick, so they could try to figure out how to end it.

Eventually, she says, she gave up. "I ended up not wanting to understand what way their minds worked. I was worried that if I understood them, I might begin thinking like them, and I wasn't going there."

Ardoyne resident, Tanya Carmichael, says the underlying problem was that unionism had "got its own way" for so long that it was a shock to discover that they had to campaign for better housing and schools. "They never realised the problem lay at the doorstep of their own MPs and their own councils."

Monsignor Tom Toner, the Catholic priest who co-chaired the post-protest "North Belfast Community Action Project", says he was shocked at the lack of cohesion and organisation in loyalist working-class areas of the city.

"When civil servants went to talk to people in Glenbryn about their problems, they found no one to talk to. They were so badly organised, there were about seven different groups all working against each other while nationalist areas were far more articulate and better at accessing funds."

Alan McQuillan was also shocked at the low level of organisation within loyalist ranks. "One of the biggest problems we had with the loyalists was getting them to articulate what they wanted. We tried asking them and all we got was the usual complaint that they didn't like Catholics and were opposed to them walking 'up our street'. But there was no coherent answer to the question of what they actually wanted."

Nationalist Judy Haughey says people in Ardoyne understood that their neighbours in Glenbryn had grievances, but there were other ways to protest. "I have six children in a three-bedroom house but you don't abuse children to get your point across."

The SDLP's Martin Morgan also has little patience with those who use social exclusion as justification for the Holy Cross protest. "There've been far too many occasions when loyalist grievances and associated violence are excused on the basis of deprivation."

Many, many parents say the protest left them embittered towards their Protestant neighbours. It appears that it had the same effect in the other community. Liz Murphy tells of how an elderly lady, who had come out on June 19 to remonstrate with her own community, became hardened as it went on.

"Come September, you should have heard the language she used to the same children. Someone had got to her. I have no doubt that she got into trouble for telling her own community off for stoning the children, but she ended up being one of the worst ones on the protest."

Is it fair to blame individual loyalists for their actions, or can they be excused on grounds of the increasing sense of fear and cultural/political vulnerability? Were they simply badly led?

Shirlow thinks that is a cop-out. "Nobody gave them pornographic magazines or put the words in their mouths. What is fundamentally wrong with loyalist paramilitaries, especially those attached to the UDA, is there is no rationale – it is simply made up as they go along. Loyalism is reactive; it is about maintaining boundaries. It is not about creating anything. Loyalism is in difficulties because it is trying to preserve the impossible.

"Here was a group of people, parachuted into a community that had never been organised, with vulnerabilities and stories to tell about being excluded, threatened and harassed. They manipulated it and copied what they'd already done in the lower Shankill, that is to bully and intimidate people and encourage sectarianism, thereby creating a new fiefdom."

At the same time, Shirlow explains the sense of isolation that motivated at least some of the protesters. "Republicans are confident because 40 miles down the road there are three million people who won't mind you joining them. Up here, there are over a million people looking across the Irish Sea to where Britain is saying, 'Go away'. I am not apologising for anything loyalists have ever done, but you have to grow up in that community to realise how different it is."

By late 2003, two years after the Holy Cross row, the upper end of Glenbryn, facing the Ardoyne Road, had been largely demolished in a redevelopment plan that pre-dated the protest by 11 years. New houses are due in the area by 2005, although whether those displaced by the redevelopment will return again is unclear.

Chapter Eleven

FAMILIES

The two of us fought every day, constantly rowing and shouting and falling out with each other. Even my mother asked if I was doing the right thing, so she and I fell out too.
Tina Gallagher, parent

We would argue irrationally. I would ask Gerald why couldn't he have done something to bring it to an end? All he could say was that this was one thing he just couldn't fix.
Sharon McCabe, parent

For obvious reasons, most sympathy and concern during the protest was focused on the children. But the initial June events, followed by the tense summer and 12 weeks of blockade also took its toll on parents.

Even families with no direct link to Holy Cross suffered as an already poisonous summer descended into localised violence, virtually unnoticed by those fortunate enough to live away from sectarian fault-lines. News organisations, even locally, regarded the nightly violence as so mundane that it went largely unreported. The peace process should have ended such endemic violence, but hidden from view a small number of families stoically struggled on, trying to live normal lives against overwhelming odds.

There were three times as many shooting incidents attributed to loyalists as republicans and fifteen times as many loyalist bombings (*see Appendix Two*, page 319). Those at the receiving end of the violence were mainly not politically involved and had done nothing to deserve the fate that history dealt them. Their suffering was acute and prolonged. Families along the peace-lines had to endure temporary separations. Parents under loyalist death threat would remain in their homes to do what they could to protect them, while small children were farmed out to relatives or neighbours for safety.

Those families who decided to brave it out together in their homes would often end up sleeping in different beds. Typically, the husband would sleep downstairs (as front-line defence in case of attack), children in rooms that did not face the peace-line and wives in whatever room was left. Often, baths would be filled with water before nightfall, to be used in the event of a petrol or pipe bomb setting the house ablaze in the middle of the night. The fear was, if the rioting was bad enough, the fire brigade might not be able to get through. Some families came close to breaking point. Others moved home. Both wives and husbands lost jobs. Some couples disagreed over tactics and marriages were put under intolerable strains.

Judy Haughey and her husband, Anthony, went through a rough time. "We were like yo-yos. One day he would say to me that enough was enough and the kids weren't going back. I would disagree. Other days, he was all for it and I was sort of backing down. Maybe it was a good thing that we kept the balance."

One parent, who cannot be named for legal reasons, was typical of many. Her father was a Protestant and she was singled out for special abuse as a result, with some protesters who recognised her, calling her an "Orange bastard". She worked for a mixed-religion company and says her bosses repeatedly and sarcastically referred to her appearances on television in front of co-workers. She resigned as a result of what she saw as a personal vendetta.

"I lost two stone in three months, I was skin and bone. I had no social life as I never went out, I was afraid to leave my daughter. Your whole life revolved around the protest. You got up in the morning and went to bed at night thinking about it. I remember driving past a bank once and spotting one of the protesters. I drove on with the tears trickling down my face. I was a nervous wreck."

She went to counselling and was prescribed tranquillisers but did not take them, believing it was bad enough having to face the protest as a nervous wreck "without being a nervous wreck who was high". She describes herself as being "weepy" all the time and eventually developed irritable bowel syndrome.

Other parents had problems at work, especially those in mixed-religion workforces such as Belfast city council, where protesters and parents sometimes worked in the same department. One parent, for example, recognised the boyfriend of a work-mate's daughter amongst the protesters, and was himself spotted. "He had a scarf around his face and was standing behind two peelers (policemen), making a firing gesture with his fingers at me."

It did not make for harmonious workplace relations.

Some parents gave up their jobs to cope with the extra psychological strains on their children. Jim Crawford, for example, took three months off work because his daughter, Roisin, cried every time he left the house.

"I wanted to be there to protect her," he says, adding that his wife also resigned from her job during the protest, so the whole family suffered because there was very little money coming in.

Marriages like Sharon and Gerald McCabe's were put under tensions. "We were fine as a couple throughout the protest. Then, when it ended, we weren't," says Sharon. "We were physically together but emotionally we were apart, which is unusual for us."

Sharon worked as a cook at Holy Cross Monastery. As part of her normal duties, she would answer the phone. There were dozens of threatening calls coming through for Father Troy, but they wouldn't wait until he got on the line. The strain of listening to the threats herself was too much to bear and she resigned. To alleviate the stress, she thought about joining a gym but, on her trial night, she recognised a protesting loyalist at the gym. So that was out. On a shopping trip to a local mall, she and Gerald were spotted by another loyalist who recognised them. The family went into Belfast city centre another day and a man smirked at her. It dawned on her he was another protester. Sharon, a quiet woman and loving mother, suddenly snapped.

"The thought came from nowhere that I wanted to kill him, to go right for his jugular, and I started to panic. My daughter fetched my son from another part of the shop and he dragged me out. After that, as far as going into town was concerned, that was me finished. I had nightmares where I was always running to get to the kids and hide them. Aliens were chasing me."

As well as losing her job, she began attending counselling and taking tranquillisers. "I went through a phase of asking myself if I had done the right thing – a guilt complex – but when Gemma looks up at me, I know we did. She has to believe that she did nothing wrong. She was just going to school and they had no right to do what they did."

The McKernans also had a difficult time. Dee McKernan had a nervous breakdown and had to give up work for six months. "He just couldn't handle it. He isn't a violent person but he wanted to go and kill them all," says Jeanette. "He ended up on anti-depressants and our relationship was falling apart. He drank more than previously during the protest and that played a big part. It was his way of coping."

Their arguments always ran along the same lines. "If I had a bad day, I would tell him about what the protesters had been throwing at us and he would reply that I should take the kids out of 'that fucking school'. I would tell him that was the easy way out and that I didn't want to walk away after all we'd been through. The relationship became very strained. I reckon that if he'd gone back to work, he would be in jail now for killing one of them."

Some of Dee McKernan's work colleagues were protesters. "He couldn't handle going into work every day and seeing them, knowing what they were doing to our kids, having to look them in the face and be civil."

Liz and John Murphy also went through difficulties, rowing over trivia. Their son, Martin (10), felt neglected with the household revolving around their daughter, Niamh. "I would snap at him if he asked for anything, complaining I had enough to worry about already, and he would withdraw into himself. Towards the end our elder children finally told us what they had been going through, watching us, and only then did I realise what the other children had been going through."

David Lindsay says his family was on the point of breaking down during the summer of 2001. They lived on the long Ardoyne/Glenbryn peace-line which runs at the back of their garden. David sat in the dark, night after night, protecting his home. "We were constantly at each other's throats. You waited on every wee sound, sitting in your kitchen listening for them coming. At times you would wait for hours and nothing would happen. Then it would start as soon as you went to bed."

Dereliction caused by Glenbryn's re-development caused serious problems for people living along the Alliance Avenue peace-line. Loyalists were using the empty homes as makeshift arsenals and firing points.

"They went up into the attics, broke slates and put up paramilitary flags. Then they'd smashed the slates up and spend nights on end, at their leisure, throwing the pieces against our houses," says David Lindsay. "Some of them must have worked in the shipyard because we also found lots of heavy metal pieces, all cut into small but thick sizes, strange and ragged shapes, so if they'd hit you, they would have done real damage."

The timing of the attacks settled into a pattern. "It would start about 11am and last for an hour. They had a break for lunch and it then started again. After suppertime, you would hear them running up and down in our back gardens, bottles clinking and dragging stuff. You could hear their voices talking to each other. I got a load of sheets of wooden fencing and stuck them along the back wall to make it higher, a bit more awkward for them to get in. We got a security camera."

Maura, his wife, says the loyalists would get so close to the house that she could hear them moving about in the garden outside her kitchen.

"One night, there were a lot of wet leaves, and one of them slipped and fell right up against our kitchen wall. All the streetlights were broken so it was pitch black. The two girls and myself ran out of the house, hysterical. David and a few others went to see what was going on but the loyalists had already jumped over the wall and run away. People were living on their nerves every night, not knowing what to do. You couldn't put the lights on at the back of your house. As soon as they saw a flicker of light, they attacked."

Under attack one night, David heard the sound of police officers running around behind his home. Going out to investigate, he asked them why they were leaving when loyalists were pelting his home with bricks and slates. Their reply was hardly confidence inspiring. The police were fleeing themselves from the hail of missiles. Lindsay says one policeman was on the point of tears, explaining he could hardly be expected to stick around.

There was no escape for the Lindsays. At 3pm one Sunday afternoon, a pipe bomb came through their front window. If it had exploded, they would all have been killed. As it was, a large piece of shrapnel landed close to their daughter, Kirsty (12). "She was very lucky she didn't get it in the face."

They called the police but they did not arrive to examine the evidence for two weeks. David handed them the components of the pipe bomb and the police left, admonishing the family for interfering with evidence.

The Lindsays could overhear the loyalists bantering as they perched on rooftops attacking their home. From such conversations, they learned that the nickname of one of their tormentors was "Mousey". They told a police officer, hoping for an arrest, but the official response was only that Mousey was "well-known" but they couldn't touch him as he was a "slippery wee frigger". The Lindsays could even identify different attackers by their voices.

Maura says, "You would have heard the older ones, in their forties, with deep husky voices giving orders and then the younger ones would start throwing. After that summer we knew that it was only a matter of time before we moved. We had stuck it out long enough. David was sleeping on the settee down the stairs. The two girls were in our bedroom at the front of the house, and I was in the back bedroom. We lived like that for over a year."

As well as living under siege, Maura Lindsay had to cope with walking her Amy to school every day. Terror was a constant companion. "The fear was unbearable every morning. Once I nearly passed out walking through the British Army barricade on Ardoyne Road. I had to stay in the school that day. I couldn't face walking back down again. It took me over."

For parents with the courage to speak out publicly, the threats were personal and very nasty. The main RTE spokesman, Brendan Mailey, was instantly catapulted from relative obscurity to become a regular TV performer. Elected by the other parents, and like dozens of other men in Ardoyne, Mailey had spent years in a prison cell serving a life sentence for his part in the IRA killing of a policeman. As a representative of the parents, his name was on all the letters sent requesting meetings with politicians. He got his reply from Ian Paisley during the Stormont debate in September.

"I have no intention," said Paisley, "of obeying the summons from a man by the name of Mailey who has told me that, as a leader, I must go to a meeting. A man who shoots a policeman dead is not a man with whom I do business."

Mailey had other problems. His daughter, Rachel, refused to return to Holy Cross after the first day of the protest on September 3. As the parents' spokesman, this posed a personal dilemma.

"Every parent sat down with their child and asked them what they wanted to do. Some children were stronger than others. Some were more determined than others, some were wiser than others and some were more scared than others. The decisions being made were massive. I believe every parent's decision was respected by everyone else, irrespective what it was. With Rachel not wanting to go back, I felt I should offer my resignation to the committee. Most, although not everybody, wanted me to stay, but should I still speak to the press? My child was not going up the road with the rest. How could I speak on behalf of the parents who were? We all discussed it and it was agreed that I was still going up to the school with the rest and there was no real problem. I was still representing all the children and their parents."

Rachel Mailey, though, never went back to school via the Ardoyne Road after September 3. Although Mailey retained overall support, there was one hurtful episode. A local woman complained to the *Irish News*, Belfast's nationalist morning paper, that as his daughter was no longer walking to school, he should not be speaking for the parents. Whatever her reason, he says, he deeply resented the intervention.

"The loyalists began shouting things like 'Your fucking kid is not here, why are you?' Sick, but it was the only time I can recall any disunity amongst us. We had our differences, people had different opinions, that was fair enough. At the end of the day we stood by each other. We had a sense of pride going up and down that road."

Only at night, says Mailey, was there time and silence for parents to think over the events of the day and question whether they were on the right road.

Philomena Flood was another RTE committee member who was prominent on television in the early days. With a mane of blonde hair, she became the target of much loyalist attention. Lynda Bowes was one of many concerned about her safety. "She took constant, personalised abuse on the road. The scariest thing was they knew exactly where she lived and threatened to kill her on a daily basis."

Going up to school on September 4, a loyalist shouted to Philomena that she would have a bullet through her head that night. The following afternoon, just hours after the pipe bomb was thrown, she was in her garden when the police arrived.

"They said the Red Hand Defenders had decided I was to be executed on sight. I cannot explain how it devastated our family. In that moment my life changed forever. I had to send the children to live with family and friends for weeks. I would see them, perhaps, once a day to give them their tea and then they'd sleep in someone else's home."

Eventually, Philomena took matters into her own hands and approached a Protestant minister to see if he could intercede with the UDA to lift the death threat.

"He said he would do what he could, but only if I would agree not to give any more TV interviews or speak out against the protest." Philomena turned down the offer.

There is one other incident that bears witness to her extraordinary strength of character. It happened one morning, as the parents and children arrived at school. The press corps would follow them in and then, when they were all safely inside the gates, would turn back down the road and interview the loyalists. One journalist, however, got stranded inside the locked gates and heard what Philomena said that morning. Some of the parents were cheering and clapping but she turned on them angrily.

"I don't want to see anyone punching the air," she declared. "This is not a victory. All we've done is vindicate our rights. Those people out there, they are our neighbours and we want to live in peace with them."

It was one of those moments when an ordinary person manages to lift themselves above their own miserable surroundings, above the hate and abuse, transcending and conquering their own suffering.

A friend offered Philomena the use of a holiday home in Ballyhornan (a seaside resort in County Down) for a weekend's break with her children. Before 24 hours was up, however, a policeman rang her mobile phone. He told her that a loyalist had spotted her and there were plans to kill her over the weekend. The family returned home to Belfast immediately. Philomena still wonders how the policeman got her number.

"The threats kept coming. I would sometimes see a strange figure outside the house, in the early morning or late at night. It all got too much. I was fed up with living without my children. In October, we applied to be re-housed. They put us in two rooms in a hostel on the Cliftonville Road (an arterial road through North Belfast). We lived there until early December when they found a house for us in the Short Strand (a Catholic enclave in East Belfast). Unluckily for us, the house was the first door over the peace-line – but for the first five months it was peaceful. We had a good Christmas and Eirinn started at a new school."

In May 2002, though, loyalist violence started up along the Short Strand peace-line. Philomena's house, being the nearest, came under attack. On May 11, two pipe bombs were thrown at the house and loyalists tried to smash down the front door with a hammer. The police came to her home and Philomena assumed, wrongly, they were investigating the bombs.

"Instead they raided our house, claiming to be looking for explosives."

Later, a loyalist community worker shouted her name and said she would be shot dead. That was the end of the family's peace. They stuck it out, but in May 2003 the loyalist side brought out a video giving their side of the Short Strand violence. Philomena featured in the video. "They claimed I was the 'key instigator' of the trouble at Holy Cross and I had been sent by republicans to stir up trouble in the Short Strand. We had to move again."

Philomena has had another baby and still lives in the Short Strand, although not at the peace-line.

Hers was not the only family to sell up and move out of Ardoyne. After months of enduring attacks, in September 2001, Holy Cross parents Rita and Chris McDonald decided they could take no more. When they originally moved in, Chris and Rita, a couple who regularly look at each other when talking, seeking assurance and always finding it, used to exchange gardening tips and football chat across the peace-line with Glenbryn. They were relaxed enough about it to install wooden decking and enjoy summer evening barbecues. It was their first home and they were delighted with it, but life began to go downhill fast around the Drumcree stand-off in 1995. Nationalist and loyalist youths began clashing at the top of their street.

The following year was far worse, with sustained attacks on the back of their house with sticks, bricks, bottles, ball-bearings and marbles. The children were sent to their granny. After Chris was beaten in his own garden, he and Rita also left home for a while. Loyalists had surged through the hedge from Glenbryn, smashing up a wooden fence and shouting at each other to poke his eyes out. As they jabbed at him with the pieces of broken wood, he held on to one of them for grim death. Chris managed to break free but the family dog got left behind in the rush. Returning to retrieve it, there was one of those black Belfast moments.

Chris was on crutches from a previous beating and was hobbling up the garden path to fetch the dog. As he arrived at the front door, a would-be defender rushed around the gable end from the rear with a pitchfork, thinking he was a loyalist. Chris raised a crutch in self-defence and the two sides landed a couple of blows with pitchfork and crutch, before realising the mix up. "I dropped the crutch and he dropped the pitchfork and both of us ran like hell."

A couple of days later, Chris and his father went to the local police station to make a statement and ask what they proposed doing about the continual attacks.

"My father is very diplomatic, it's a mixed marriage. He asked what protection they could offer and the police admitted they had lost control in North Belfast. The desk sergeant said his advice was to go home, lock the doors and hide in the bedroom. My father looked at me and said, 'In the name of God, we are all paying taxes and this is what we are told'. It scared the living daylights out of us. If the police tell you they can't protect you, what are you to do?"

Routinely, Chris would appeal to policemen sitting in the Land Rover parked outside the house to arrest those visible across the peace-line, pelting his home. The bored response was invariably that reinforcements would be called in. Nothing ever appeared to happen. It was time to move.

Like other home-owners, the police had first to certify the McDonalds were under threat. Then the family had to negotiate a sale with the Housing Executive under the SPED scheme (Special Purchase of Evacuated Dwellings – set up to buy the homes of people under threat). It was all a huge struggle. Initially, the police refused to sign the required certificate.

"They said they'd lost my original statement and had no records of any assault, even though I got a £1,000 out-of-court compensation payment," says Chris. "I suggested they get the Mater Hospital medical records. In the end, they gave us the certificate – but by that time we were tied in a financial knot because neither of us could work. We were losing money and struggling to get a mortgage."

Rita says they effectively lost their family life for two years. "We weren't coping very well towards the end. You slept whenever you could. There was no home structure, no routine." Chris's business closed because he "just couldn't work".

"I was physically and mentally burnt-out. We were up all night with the slightest noise and once you woke you were awake the whole night."

A friend says Chris looked so worn-out at the end of this ordeal that his friends thought he was seriously ill. "I had thought he had cancer but it turned out to be lack of sleep. He had failed away to nothing and his eyes were all bloodshot."

Sleep was at a premium. Chris says, "Rita would get a couple of hours if she was really lucky. I would get a couple during the day and that would have been it. We were sleeping in shifts with one doing look-out."

So they moved, but Rita still misses her old home. "We had to get out of a house that we didn't want to leave. It really gives you no hope for the future of the North."

Claims by families like the Lindsays, the McDonalds and the McGrandles that law and order didn't exist in Ardoyne in the summer of 2001 are rejected by the police officer in charge, Former Assistant Chief Constable Alan McQuillan.

"Neither we as police officers, nor the government, can ever allow law and order to break down but it was certainly the most difficult summer I spent in North Belfast in a variety of different ranks."

Physically, he says, there was nothing the police could do to protect nationalist families on the Ardoyne/Glenbryn peace-line.

"We tried to keep a sterile area between the two communities, but we couldn't do anything for those who lived inside that zone. Our people were in there too, with others trying to kill them. Nobody was killed in a riot by the other side. People were injured, including many of my officers. If we hadn't been there, there would have been dozens dead."

Whatever efforts the police did or didn't make, normal domestic life was put on hold for scores of families that year. Jeanette McKernan says that, for the whole 12 weeks of the protest, her house wasn't properly cleaned once. Her husband would "tidy up, but he doesn't clean like I do".

"He did most of the cooking too. I tried to keep things as normal as possible. If I had to cry I waited until the girls were out. My son suffered too. It was his Eleven Plus year and I wasn't there for him. I couldn't sit and help him with his work. My head wasn't my own. But we kept the kids' bedtime routine as normal, 7.30 every night. Their dinners were also on the table every day at 5 o'clock. I made them do their homework after school whether they liked it or not."

Jeanette, like many parents, resisted giving her children sedatives, although she took them herself because she was "walking about not knowing who I was".

"The mothers found that after we had left the kids at school we felt at a loss. Elaine Burns decided to start coffee mornings. Father Troy gave us the big living room at the Monastery and we could meet there for a cup of tea. We counselled each other. We sat there day after day, crying our eyes out, talking. As soon as we heard a siren going, we would panic and phone the school to check."

Some parents lived in fear and dread of the protesters. Others, like Tanya Carmichael, a normally laughing woman with long auburn hair, managed to block them out of their minds.

"I never feared those protesters. I was angry with them. It was the adrenaline of the anger that pushed you forward. It got to the point that you could actually block the protesters out, noise and all; you just totally blanked them out of your mind."

Anger was a common thread amongst the parents. Tina Gallagher says she "raged" at both the protesters and police every day. "I thought, 'Well fuck them! They are not scaring me or my family off the road.' At the same time if my kids had preferred not to go up the road, I really wouldn't have forced them. No parent could force any child up through that."

Tina had three children at the school, whose leaving times were staggered, so she had six journeys to make each day.

"As the protest went on it got harder and harder though. For five days a week, for 16 weeks, I had to walk that road six times a day, 30 times a week. The scariest day was the day of the sniper. I was totally petrified. There were three woman standing together that day, one of them a woman who'd been named in the Sunday papers as Johnny Adair's ex-girlfriend."

One of the three women threw a firework at Tina. For an instant, she thought she'd been shot. "It freaked me out. I had a huge umbrella and I began beating the three of them with it. One of our own people had to drag me off. I thought he was a peeler (policeman) so I beat him too."

Tina was advised not to walk back down the road after the incident as she might have been mobbed after the umbrella incident. "I don't think I could have taken anymore that day. Walking up that road was like walking to the gallows."

Community worker, Elaine Burns, is a strong woman but even she took a tranquilliser on September 3. "I stood in the kitchen and sobbed my heart out that grown men and women could do that. I felt so useless that I couldn't protect Niamh."

She and her husband, Danny, talked about it through the night. "He was very focused, saying Holy Cross is where I had gone to school, and my sisters, and that they weren't going to stop her."

The couple concluded that Niamh and Leona should walk to school the usual way and the tranquilliser was a one-off. "I never took anything like that again. I tried aromatherapy, massage and alternative ways of reducing stress."

Elaine was due to fly to America a week after the protest began in September to visit a friend in Pittsburgh. Her mother insisted she went, throwing her clothes into her suitcase. There was a storm that night in New York and the onward flight was cancelled. The next morning, she was on the runway at La Guardia waiting to take off when the two planes hit the World Trade Centre. Elaine watched the smoke billowing out of downtown Manhattan. All flights were grounded and she was stuck in a hotel for a full week before she could reach Pittsburgh. Then there was trouble getting a flight back home. Her mother could hardly forgive herself.

Many parents only realised the extent of their stress after the protest ended. Some, like Lynda Bowes, lost weight. Her husband Dougie says, "Everybody who knew her kept commenting about how much weight she had lost and how frail she looked."

Some parents had violent mood swings. One, who for her own sake should remain anonymous, admits that before the summer, she wanted the men from the district to "go and kill those protesters".

"I wanted them to ignore all the good advice and just do it. But over the summer we had time to calm down, sit back, go on holidays and see what would happen in September."

Nothing, however, prepared her for the start of the autumn term. At first, she swore she would never again go up the road but then changed her mind. "I was adamant that I would be back up that road, even if I had to fight my way up. I went from being very frightened to very angry and then defiant. Even if my daughter didn't want to go back up that road, I was going."

After the bombing on September 5, she and other parents gathered in the "parents room" at the school. "After we all calmed down a bit, the craic was ninety (Belfast expression for lively enjoyable conversation). That probably sounds strange in the middle of that nightmare, but it was our way of coping."

She found herself hating the loyalists more and becoming even more determined to stand her ground. "It caused friction in our home because I was constantly fighting with my husband. He didn't want our daughter going up. It made me into one hard and bitter person. Now, I couldn't see any good in the people living in Glenbryn, even if they did good. No matter what they say or do, I always suspect there's an agenda behind it."

She was working at an insurance firm but left because she was working beside Protestants and "just couldn't face seeing them".

"I began getting panic attacks. One day, a couple of girlfriends told me my skin was turning bright red. It wasn't until I looked in a mirror that I saw I had cuts all around my neck where I had been picking my skin."

And her daughter? "The things she used to say frightened me. She was frightened that men in masks would come in the middle of the night and kill her mammy and daddy. I started to question my own judgement then and wondered if I was doing right."

"As things dragged on," she says, "you went into a robot mode. You got up in the mornings, went up and did the walk through the usual abuse and then came back down. You took it. The days when my husband was there were the worst. He was a man having to listen to what they were shouting. He began shouting back. I advised him not to; by that time I had learnt to control myself. Everybody has his or her own opinion at the end of the day. I did what I believed to be right, but personally I don't think I would be ever able to do it again. I wouldn't have the strength."

In the McCabe family home, as in many others, parents Sharon and Gerald had long talks with their four children, who were terrified their parents would be killed during the protest.

"We sat and talked it over with them," says Sharon. "I was absolutely terrified about walking up the road, but at the same time what was I to do? Did I sit back and let someone tell me that my child couldn't go to school? I had to do some serious reflecting on what my whole life was about. The most important thing for me as a mother was to get my children educated. It's the key to life. One of them was on the verge of going to university. That was what we wanted for all of them. Education starts at primary school. I knew we had to stick it out for their own sakes."

The stress got to parents in different and unpredictable ways. Lynda Bowes, for example, reacted well on the road itself but then broke down completely in the middle of town after a protest rally in support of the school. The rally was dispersing and a group of parents were walking back up Royal Avenue when a loyalist woman started hurling abuse because of Amanda's Holy Cross uniform.

"She was shouting that we were 'Fenian bastards' and I just lost it. We had planned to take the kids to Burger King but I had to get home. I suppose it was normal to hear it on the Ardoyne Road, it wasn't normal in the centre of the town. When I got home, I told Amanda to 'get that bloody uniform off'. After that, she would cover every little bit of red uniform she could with her coat when we went out."

Sinn Fein's Gerry Kelly says, "The parents, whoever they were and whatever their political affiliation, behaved with principle, restraint, impeccably, through a massive personal dilemma. They listened to everyone; to us, to the teachers, to the clergy and to their own consciences. Then they made their decisions. Out of that we got a very sensible approach. Some of the parents' meetings were angry. I had to advise them to be disciplined. I knew the protest was unbearable, that it was hard, but I still argued against retaliation.

"When I heard some of the things they went through, I don't know if I could have done it myself. You're talking about children from the age of four. I have children that age, wee girls. I don't know if I could have dealt with it. It would have broken my heart. Some of the fathers, they were tough, they were afraid of nobody. They held together and didn't retaliate because they did not want to sully or confuse the issue. But I tell you this, at times it must have been almost impossible. I'm not one for crying, but was I emotionally affected? Yes absolutely. It was heart-rending."

Despite everything they went through, the vast majority of Holy Cross parents never retaliated and resisted sliding into bitterness. Pat Monaghan tells how she and a small group of Holy Cross parents once went to a nearby Protestant school to nip a potential counter-protest in the bud. Local nationalist teenagers, she says, had begun to lurk about to see how the Protestant parents liked a dose of their own medicine.

"We told them that it was as simple as this. We had come down from Holy Cross Girls' school and they were not going to do to other children what was being done to ours."

Stewart Heaney, the Church of Ireland minister at Emmanuel church on the Ardoyne Road, cannot speak highly enough of them.

"I remember Maureen (his wife) and I going into the school and talking to some of the parents. We were received so graciously. I hope they knew where I stood, they were so nice to me. I really did feel sorry for them."

Heaney also tells of an act of kindness from the parents for one of his congregation, an act never publicly known about before.

"An old couple in Ballysillan were burgled and I was interviewed on television about it. The next day, the parents' group came to the rectory with a present and asked me not to say where it came from."

The gift was a new video and television that the group paid for out of their budget to replace those stolen from the elderly couple.

Chapter Twelve

POLITICIANS

It turned my very guts when the politicians told us to consider the 'bigger picture' while our children were being terrorised. We were begging for someone to stop it, but nobody did. No one really cared.

Maura Lindsay, parent

A lot of politicians should be hanging their heads in shame. Even the Irish government. They used the children as pawns, to score points. When their day of reckoning comes, when they face God, they will be judged.

Patricia McAuley, parent

Politicians are probably the group that comes out worst from the Holy Cross dispute but, as ever, there are two very different accusations made by the protesters and the parents. Did, as the parents claim, unionist politicians refuse to use their influence to end the protest? Did Sinn Fein manipulate the protest for electoral gain, as protesters claim? Did nationalist politicians in general fail to address the fears in Glenbryn? Or must they all be given the benefit of the doubt, bearing in mind the first rule of politics is survival. All politicians were repeatedly entreated by both sides to come to their assistance. Did they respond in a responsible and courageous way? Or did they pander to the worst instincts of their followers?

Not long after the Right to Education group was hurriedly formed in June 2001, its members sent out letters to every political party in Ireland, north and south, asking for meetings. The letters were followed up by phone calls. Liz Murphy, a parent, personally phoned them all. "We wanted support and advice on how to resolve it quickly." Not all the parties replied, including the local MP, Nigel Dodds of Ian Paisley's

Democratic Unionist Party.

The DUP "totally ignored us", she claims, until she spotted Dodds standing amongst the protesters on Ardoyne Road. The parents then quickly made and displayed posters accusing Dodds of taking the protesters' side and, not long afterwards, he met them on October 30, 2001 – two months into the protest.

"When we asked him why he hadn't responded to our letter, he said he hadn't seen it."

When the parents did finally meet Dodds, it was hardly a meeting of minds. Martin Monaghan was in the parents' delegation and says Dodds, at first, professed sympathy about their plight.

"I told him that couldn't be true because he was standing amongst the crowd while they were abusing our children. He said that people had a right to protest. I pointed out he had accused us of being in Sinn Fein's pocket but that it had nothing to do with Sinn Fein, nothing at all, it was about children's rights. We hit him with all of it but he brushed it off and didn't want to know."

Parent Lynda Bowes was there too. "It was the biggest waste of time. He shouted at us that the protesters had problems, which we accepted but said that our children had not caused them. He was the minister responsible for housing at the time. I asked Nigel Dodds why weren't the Glenbryn people knocking on his door and demanding he did his job? He didn't like that one bit. He went on to praise Billy Hutchinson and I reminded him that Gerry Kelly was doing good work too."

Dodds at that time was proposing a shuttle-bus to bring children to school as a temporary measure. This was opposed by the parents who feared it would inevitably become permanent. He assured them that no extra public money was being spent on Glenbryn as a result of the protest.

Tina Gallagher says Dodds' appearances on television "drove me demented".

"He even said the bombing was 'a cry for help'! When a Protestant school was attacked, there was Nigel Dodds holding forth and condemning it as a disgrace. Yet at Holy Cross, it was our entire fault as far as Dodds was concerned. It really sickened me. That man let our children down. In fact, I feel he let himself down."

Dodds also attracted parent Lisa Irvine's anger. "This was our MP, yet he stood chatting in a relaxed way with the protesters, some of whom were wearing masks and hoods, as they screamed abuse at our children."

Some unionist politicians, like Fred Cobain of the UUP, knew they were on a losing wicket. Before the protest got into swing in September 2001, he had made vain efforts to persuade the CRUA leadership to drop the idea.

"The difficulty was that tensions were high and sectarianism runs very deep. People just went for the protest without thinking it through. Like all these things, once it got off the ground, it was very difficult to keep control of it."

Cobain is highly critical of his own party leadership, both over Holy Cross and more generally.

"I have said this to Trimble (David Trimble, party leader) before. The Ulster Unionist Party is middle-class. The people who live in these areas are people who are economically and socially bankrupt. We don't do anything to help. We had an internal debate within the UUP about university students' fees. The vast majority of kids I represent leave school with no qualifications. Some of them have numeracy and literacy problems. I have explained all of this to the party leadership. They don't listen. They have no experience of it. You go into these areas and the age of alcoholism is dropping, kids in their early twenties are drinking out of control.

"People who are dependent on drugs are fair game for the paramilitaries. There's prostitution and young girls pregnant with kids to two and three different fathers. I am sick telling people about it. The social and economic issues are being swept under the carpet and nobody gives a damn. The peace process should have been about all boats rising at the one time, but it isn't. The poor are getting poorer. I listen to people saying the unemployed are doing well on benefit. It's a lot of crap. Go into some of these areas and see the social difficulties some of these people are living with."

The SDLP's Martin Morgan echoes Cobain's views on social deprivation in Glenbryn, but says one cause is the continual in-fighting between unionist/loyalist politicians.

"There were about five distinct different unionist factions in

Glenbryn, all desperately fighting for votes, even between elections. There's no political or social cohesion. That's not creative tension."

He also criticises unionist politicians for failing to speak out against the protest. "There was no categorical condemnation, although in private conversations at City Hall and elsewhere, they told me they knew it was a disaster. Unionists have always found it difficult to condemn attacks on nationalists. There was no political leadership on their side. They were simply not prepared to put their real views on record. They never are. If they want to get their own way, over Orange parades for example, they do show an ability to organise, but on Holy Cross they chose not to – they were all over the place."

Morgan accuses unionists of milking the dispute for electoral gain while unionists make the same claim of Sinn Fein.

Fred Cobain says, "Sinn Fein was in charge; they knew from the beginning they would win the propaganda battle and dominated the parents from Holy Cross."

Sinn Fein's Gerry Kelly denies this. "That argument doesn't hold water because it assumes republicans knew in advance that a long blockade was inevitable. I've been around a long time, but not in my wildest dreams did I ever think anyone, to be frank, would be so stupid as to blockade a school. Sinn Fein doesn't gain votes because of events at interfaces. Our vote is growing because we are good at negotiating. The softer vote is the one that is increasing, so we didn't gain electorally. If you look at constituencies where there is no interface violence, like Mid-Ulster or West Tyrone, the Sinn Fein vote is going up. Holy Cross was of no benefit."

Cobain's arguments cut no ice with the parents either. They say unionists focused on the wrong question. Pat Monaghan says, "They accused us of abusing our own children. Why didn't they ask the statutory agencies, the government, the politicians, if they were doing their duty to prevent the children being violated? The only politicians we got support from were our own. We didn't want to take sides and we told that to all of them, including Sinn Fein and Gerry Kelly, who only did what we asked. All decisions were made solely by the parents. If Sinn Fein or any other party didn't like what we decided, tough."

Pat's husband, Martin, once asked Martin McGuinness why he didn't support the families by walking up to school with them, just one time? McGuinness explained if he did, the protest would be politicised. The loyalists might even try to shoot him, which would put the children at risk.

"I was happy enough with that," says Martin. "Gerry Kelly was at the barricade every morning arguing with the police and he also said it would be wrong to walk with us. That was fair enough."

Not everyone was happy with McGuinness, however. Judy Haughey, for one, felt he should have walked with them to school.

"Fair play to Gerry Kelly, but we wanted the likes of Martin McGuinness. He was the Minister for Education. McGuinness did speak out, but he should have been up there with us. If Nigel Dodds could be there, why not Martin McGuinness? He probably thought it would be too political. To me, he made the wrong decision."

Tina Gallagher also criticises McGuinness. "I think he should have shown his face, even just the once. He should have confronted the head of the RUC and had it out with him. I don't think any politician or trade union did enough to help. We were let down by everyone."

Gerry Kelly (who, like McGuinness, never once walked the road) sometimes regrets his decision. "I told the parents I would be proud to walk with them. At the same time, I had to advise them it would be used against them. Some parents said I should walk up anyway, but eventually it was agreed that I shouldn't, which I have to say, I sometimes regret."

Martin McGuinness defends himself against those who believed he should have walked up the road by explaining he had instinctively wanted to do so, but had been asked not to by a representative group of parents.

"There is nothing I wanted to do more than be with them on the Ardoyne Road. That was my first and enduring political instinct. But I believe, absolutely, that for the sake of children and for their parents the decision not to was the right one."

Personally, he says, he was outraged by the protest but did not want to engage in a "superficial political gesture" that could have made the situation even worse. "My presence would hardly have deterred the loyalists. The protest was a disgrace, a shameful and heart-breaking episode in our history."

Some parents felt that more could have been done. Roisin Kennedy says, "I was fond of Gerry Kelly and Alban Maginness (SDLP) but at times I got very angry with them because I thought they weren't doing enough. I don't know what went on behind closed doors but I got annoyed at times and wondered if they were fighting as hard as they might."

Another parent, whose views mean she must remain anonymous, says she wanted the Provos to "go up and blow that place to smithereens".

"If the UDA is going to bomb us, why can't the IRA at least threaten them? People told me the loyalists were trying to get the IRA to break its ceasefire but I still wondered why the IRA could sit back and watch our kids being tortured. They weren't doing anything. I saw Gerry Kelly standing there and thought he was doing fuck all. But as the weeks went on I calmed down a bit and realised you couldn't do such things. I now know Gerry Kelly was right; but when it was happening, you thought, 'screw the ceasefire'. Looking back now, I see where Gerry Kelly was coming from. The loyalists were going on and on about ex-IRA men's kids going to school. Even if you're an ex-IRA man, your kids still have to go to school. We even wanted the INLA to intervene, anything to stop the agony. I remember a former IRA man saying to me that, if he knew he had only six months to live, he would have strapped a hundred bombs on himself and gone up and blown Glenbryn to pieces."

Gerry Kelly saw the same picture from the other side. "I fought with people because I took an unpopular stand at times and argued against taking on the Glenbryn community. They were saying daft things, like go in and shoot them. I argued that we needed to talk to them instead. I was the one who prevented people from doing mad stuff and I'm supposed to be the militant one. But I was elected to talk, no matter how difficult it was, and not just to the British government, to the loyalists. Generally they came round.

"I don't think the same arguments happened on the loyalist side. I don't think people of influence stood up and argued there had to be talks. The position of the DUP was deliberately against speaking to Sinn Fein. I think they have to take some blame for what happened. The people in the UUP weren't much better, but at least people like Fred Cobain and Billy Hutchinson saw it needed to be sorted out."

Support for Sinn Fein's insistence that it was not manipulating the parents comes from an unusual source – former Assistant Chief Constable Alan McQuillan who, at the time, was in overall control of policing in Belfast.

"The nationalist side did have a coherent leadership, but it would be wrong to believe Sinn Fein was in total control. They were not. The reality was that community tensions were so high that some people were virtually out of control. If I put myself in the position of being a Catholic parent taking my kids to school every day, I can see why."

Another police source claims that feelings in Ardoyne were running so high after the bombing that Gerry Kelly was forced to leave a meeting in the community centre for his own safety. The author also once witnessed a woman in Ardoyne angrily asking Kelly one night why the IRA's guns were not coming out.

Sharon McCabe says Sinn Fein never tried to take decisions for the parents. "If we needed any explaining, they did their best. If we were taking decisions, they helped us explore the options. We were just a bunch of parents who didn't know anything. The loyalist protesters soon forced us to learn."

Lynda Bowes says she never knew a thing about politics until "this all kicked off", but believes Sinn Fein acquitted itself well.

"Gerry Kelly told people who wanted him to walk the road that if he did we would all be branded republicans. And he was right. You needed that type of guidance. The SDLP locally were hopeless. All they did was moan about us taking advice from Sinn Fein. One of them complained that only Gerry Kelly was invited to meetings, which was pathetic because they were public meetings, anybody could go. Gerry Kelly was the only one turning up. We made a point of faxing the SDLP a letter after that, telling them when the next public meeting was. They still never turned up."

The SDLP was punished at the November 2003 assembly elections when it lost a seat in North Belfast.

Gerry Kelly believes neither the British government nor the power-sharing Executive did enough. "The Office of the First Minister and Deputy First Minister (OFM/DFM) got involved relatively late, perhaps because they believed the nonsense about republicans winding it up."

Mark Durkan, the SDLP leader, however, was determined to end the protest, although when he was elected Deputy First Minister he had other, personal, problems to face; his mother had been diagnosed as terminally ill on the previous day. The Holy Cross dispute took up far more time than anyone realises, he says, fearing his effectiveness was limited partly because his office had little significant leverage over other ministers who guarded their turf jealously. The British government also retained all authority over policing and security, a key factor in the Holy Cross dispute.

"There was also," he says, "a readiness by the UUP to understand and explain the protest – which was not where the SDLP was coming from at all. I have difficulty in dignifying it with the term 'protest'. It was an attack on children and their parents going about their rightful business."

Durkan accuses the DUP of being more outraged by what became known as "the brawl in the hall", when politicians jostled each other after the formation of the new Executive, than the scenes at Holy Cross.

"There was certainly a unionist reluctance to call Holy Cross for what it was. If they didn't condone it, they bordered on excusing it. The protesters certainly felt they were condoned which encouraged them to keep it going. The UUP only really came out and condemned it once there had been universal criticism from every other quarter. Trimble's primary reaction was to give the protesters their gate but we argued strongly against that with the British government."

Durkan also had difficulty meeting the Glenbryn residents. "To be honest, I had to bite my lip when listening to what amounted to an awful load of old crap. Some of them, including their pastors, were coming out with nonsense and lies, as if the protest had nothing to do with children and they had been in an impossible position with no alternative. Total reality reversal. I was more concerned with what we as an Executive could do with our limited powers to get a complete stop to it. The Glenbryn side kept on changing the agenda from gates to social deprivation to something else. They added on to it all the time."

Durkan also criticises the role played by David McNarry, Trimble's special adviser. "He was behaving in a completely inappropriate way. As an adviser to David Trimble, he was engaging in a partisan way with the

Glenbryn people and making tactical suggestions. He was promising them things he had no right to promise and confusing his role as Trimble's adviser with being a supposed official within OFM/DFM and with his membership of the Loyalist Commission (an umbrella group including paramilitaries, politicians and clergy). At no time did he have any authority to act for the OFM/DFM, making promises and side deals."

Durkan's own special adviser was Brian Barrington, a Dublin-born barrister originally hired by Seamus Mallon. He also found meeting the Glenbryn protesters an eye-opening experience. "It was shocking, the way they tried to say it wasn't about the children," he says.

Barrington confirms the problems Durkan had with unionist politicians "understanding" the reasons for the protest.

"Anyone who tried to excuse or minimise what was happening gave the protest oxygen," he says. "One comment you regularly heard was, 'It's just that the loyalists have no media skills'. Media skills were not the issue. Sectarianism was the issue. Naked hatred was the issue. You don't need media skills, you just need decency."

The SDLP disagreed with some in the UUP who said the Executive should not condemn the loyalists because it would reduce their value as mediators. "We didn't accept that because of the barbaric nature of what was going on."

It exposed a fault-line in the power-sharing structure of the OFM/DFM. One could not move without the other. If Durkan or Seamus Mallon (the previous Deputy First Minister) wanted to take more robust action and David Trimble resisted, it was impossible for Durkan or Mallon to act unilaterally. As for the argument that the Executive should have put forward a united front by travelling to Ardoyne as a single unit and calling on the loyalists to halt the protest, Barrington says Trimble would not have agreed.

"We were always trying to get Trimble to agree stronger wording to condemn the blockade. In those circumstances we didn't have a mission of getting Trimble walking up the road with us, it just wasn't going to happen. If we had SDLP ministers walking up on their own, the impression would have been given that not only had the loyalists divided the community, they had completely divided the Executive."

Durkan points out that the protest came to an end just three weeks after he became Deputy First Minister, on November 23. He had moved as fast as he could, he argues.

If the Ardoyne parents felt let down by some of the politicians, it was the same over in Glenbryn. Although the parents were given constant advice from "their" politicians, there seems to have been a political vacuum on the Protestant side of the peace-line. After his entreaties against the protest fell on deaf ears, Fred Cobain stayed away.

"I felt torn in two directions. These were my constituents and look what they were doing to themselves! It was very painful to watch, knowing that at the end of it – and all of these things end – they would be rejected and portrayed all over the world as monsters. I suppose the totally unacceptable was allowed to happen but I don't think any one political party was responsible. The paramilitaries had a big say, whether you like it or not. There was the UDA and to a lesser extent the UVF, and the IRA was exploiting it. There was no way any of them wanted the protest to end."

The PUP's Billy Hutchinson did speak out at the final November 23 meeting in Glenbryn in favour of ending the process, but with many other unionist leaders it appears to have been a case of "Where my people are going, I will follow."

In Ardoyne, the parents fulminated against the presence of unionist politicians on the road to school. Parent Judy Haughey said she was maddened that Nigel Dodds and Nelson McCausland, a DUP councillor, were standing alongside the protesters.

"They were backing the protesters every step of the way. Shame on them. Unionist politicians didn't give a toss about our children. As far as they were concerned we had no rights. We expected nothing more from them. They were just there to get the support of their voters and had to be seen. They gave no political guidance."

Billy Hutchinson wrote declining an offer to meet the parents, saying it would be "unwise" to do so "outside the parameters envisaged by the (Glenbryn) community".

Parent Pat Monaghan wrote back saying he need not inconvenience himself; she would meet him where he stood on the road every morning, standing with the feared protester known as Spiderman. Hutchinson would move about the road, she says, between groups of protesters from day to day, depending on which group he found favour with.

"As the mood swung this way or that, as splits began, Billy would stand in different places according to which faction supported him."

There can be little doubt that the dispute polarised loyalist/unionist opinion in North Belfast, to the DUP's electoral advantage. A UUP politician interviewed, who wants to remain anonymous, believes that the DUP anticipated and exploited this.

"The DUP were happy to sit back and let the protest continue indefinitely because it pushed the community into its arms. People became more hard-line and believed the DUP represented them better than the UUP. The Holy Cross protest delivered nothing for the working class Protestants of Glenbryn and made them even more disillusioned with mainstream unionism."

The majority of Glenbryn protesters interviewed for this book said they had supported the Agreement, but now oppose it. Most complained about the way it had been implemented, giving "too many concessions to republicans". Most also felt the general sense of loyalist disillusionment fed into the school dispute. The views of Jim Potts, the main CRUA spokesman, were typical.

"I voted 'Yes' in the referendum – now I have reservations. I wouldn't like to say I would vote 'No' but I would like to see the Agreement re-jigged so there was a better balance between both communities. Everyone expected not only peace but benefits after the ceasefires. That's what we were all told. The government promised to change people's lives with job opportunities, but it didn't happen."

There was one set-piece two-hour debate on Holy Cross at the Stormont Assembly on September 10, a week after the protest began. It created more heat than light. Gerry Kelly of Sinn Fein tabled the resolution: "That this Assembly supports the right to education of schoolchildren attending the Holy Cross Primary School in North Belfast."

"Last week," were his opening words, "the entire globe watched a single image of Belfast. What can only be described as one of the most frightening and depressing episodes in the past 30 years was witnessed from every corner of the globe."

Disregarding repeated unionist interruptions, he went on, "Politicians should call for the blockade to end. If they do anything short of that, they will let the bigots off the hook and provide them with political cover for their attacks on young children."

Danny Kennedy, education spokesman for the Ulster Unionist Party, tabled an amendment adding the words "all schools throughout North Belfast", which meant it included condemnation of alleged intimidation against Protestant schools. Calling Kelly's speech a "republican rant", Kennedy also said that many scenes at Holy Cross had been "unedifying and undoubtedly appalling" while criticising those responsible for "verbal abuse" of Protestant schoolchildren. Accusing Sinn Fein of using the school dispute for political ends, he echoed the protesters in suggesting it was being used to distract attention from matters in other parts of the world such as Colombia. Skirting the main issue, and again echoing the protesters, Kennedy linked Holy Cross to the annual row over the Orange Order's Drumcree parade in County Armagh, saying he welcomed Kelly's support for the right to process along a main route, "particularly with regard to the rights of Orangemen in Portadown".

Alban Maginness, a North Belfast SDLP Assembly member, said the "so-called protest" at the school was not a protest at all. It was a blockade of the school and had "no moral or political justification".

Then it was Nigel Dodds' turn. He began by reminding the house of the recent death of a Protestant teenage boy, knocked off his bike after throwing a brick at a woman driver (Dodds referred to it as a "cold blooded murder").

"We have heard much talk about the suffering of the children. No one has yet mentioned that the only child to have died in this recent period was a Protestant child, murdered as a result of sectarian hatred in North Belfast."

Reminded by Alban Maginness that the case was sub judice, Dodds finally spoke about Holy Cross.

"To see Sinn Fein/IRA nauseatingly exploit this situation for their own narrow political ends is sickening in the extreme. We have seen people who have been engaged in taking the blood of innocent people coming to speak about education rights and the rights of children. I have a list of people – schoolteachers, principals and school bus drivers – who have been murdered by IRA/Sinn Fein. The Minister of Education (Martin McGuinness) and his colleagues condoned it and egged them on, and indeed, in many cases, took part in murders."

When it came to the actual protest, Dodds appeared to defend those responsible. "This is a community that has suffered at the hands of IRA/Sinn Fein for years. Their concerns, injustices and inequities have been ignored by the media, who are now up there in their thousands."

A second unionist Assembly member for North Belfast, the independent, anti-Agreement Frazer Agnew, went even further. Ignoring police statistics, he opined, "All the violence that we have seen in North Belfast in June, July and August has come from one source."

Referring to events on September 3, the first day of term, he said, "What we saw was a parade of Provos into a Protestant area. More Provos have walked up Ardoyne Road every morning, taking children to school, than have schoolchildren. That is a fact."

Again appearing to defend the protesters, he said their grievances had been ignored: "They cannot go to the post office to collect their pension; or to the library in Ardoyne; or to the shops to buy groceries."

Perhaps because he had been himself misled, Agnew said that only 12 children had regularly been using the front entrance to Holy Cross school, with the rest using the rear entrance "which is handy for car parking".

"It is all about ethnic cleansing. They want the Prods out of upper Ardoyne, and they want those houses for their own people."

Billy Hutchinson claimed parents accompanying the children to Holy Cross Primary School had acted in "a sectarian manner", and physical and verbal abuse had been doled out.

Jane Morrice, of the Women's Coalition, was one of the few politicians who expressed any sense of personal responsibility about the dispute. "I rise with a feeling of terrible shame," she said. "It is based on the obvious fact that we as a people, as politicians, as mothers and fathers and as a society have not done enough for our children."

Robert McCartney (an anti-Agreement unionist), while condemning the protest, said the blame lay at the door of the "bogus peace process" which, he said, had "segregated and divided the communities into their respective ghettos".

Ian Paisley, the DUP leader, criticised "thugs and bullies who terrorise little children", but claimed, "The Provisional IRA has targeted children to a greater extent than Protestant paramilitaries."

Gerry Adams, president of Sinn Fein, said, "Those who have made their political careers from sectarianism – most famously the previous member who spoke, Ian Paisley – must reflect on their roles since the 1960s in creating the depressing situation and difficulties that are visited upon all of us.

"At the same time," he said, "it is important that republicans listen to what the unionist and loyalist people of North Belfast and other places are saying. They clearly suffer the same social deprivations and disadvantage as people from the nationalist parts of Belfast."

During the debate, the UUP Assembly member for North Belfast, Fred Cobain, was taken ill. A colleague delivered his speech, which spoke in generalities about deprivation in North Belfast but did not mention the school. Martin McGuinness, then Minister for Education, made one of the most memorable speeches of the day, condemning minor violence that week against Protestant pupils travelling home from Cliftonville Primary School in North Belfast.

"Let us be clear and unequivocal – protests affecting schoolchildren, whether they involve throwing bombs or missiles, sectarian chanting, blowing whistles, letting off klaxon horns or turning backs, are completely unacceptable and must stop."

Schools, he said, had generally been considered inviolable during the Troubles and it was regrettable that Holy Cross and Wheatfield, opposite each other, had not been accorded the same immunity.

"Who could ever forget the appalling scenes of terrified children aged four, five and six screaming in fear and clinging to their parents? Tears were streaming down their cheeks, while grown adults screamed sectarian abuse, spat and threw missiles at them.

"There is," he said, "a responsibility on politicians and community leaders, particularly those representing the local area, to get discussions going and reach an accommodation. This is a task for local politicians and community leaders. It is not a task for children, schoolteachers and boards of governors, who must immediately be relieved of the terrible pressures that they face every day."

Gerry Kelly, the resolution's proposer, criticising in particular Frazer Agnew's contribution, said he had taken an "exceptionally, unbelievably dangerous attitude" in calling all the parents "Provos".

"That is the position of the UDA, and under the name of the Red Hand Defenders, the UDA has made death threats against all the children and the parents. He should withdraw it because it turns people into targets. He is saying that they are all republicans; they are not."

The amendment was passed by 48 votes to 43, with the entire unionist block supporting it and the SDLP, Sinn Fein and Alliance opposing. The motion, as passed, read, "That this Assembly supports the right to education of schoolchildren attending all schools throughout North Belfast."

The parents also asked for help from Dublin but are generally underwhelmed by the response. They faxed and wrote to the Taoiseach (Irish prime minister) and, at first, got no answer despite phoning his office on numerous occasions. Liz Murphy then sent another letter to Bertie Ahern's office and followed it with phone calls. She still got no reply.

"Then I got through on the phone to his brother and he said that he had no knowledge of the letter. I told him I had received a stock reply telling me it had been received in his office, yet I was still being told they hadn't got it!"

Martin Monaghan was another parent who felt angry with Dublin. "Ahern's office just wouldn't respond at all. The Irish Labour Party said they couldn't come up to support us either."

The Taoiseach, Bertie Ahern, finally met the children in February 2002, three months after the protest ended. He was photographed with them at the Smithfield Observational Tower in Dublin. One of the children gave him a white teddy bear.

President Mary McAleese, whose mother went to school at Holy Cross, and who had lived around the corner in her teenage years, having once been forced out by a loyalist gun attack, was desperately concerned about the children. She met many of them, along with Anne Tanney and Father Troy, on November 9 at Holy Cross Monastery. A month later, she hosted them at Aras an Uachtarain, the Presidential residence in Dublin for a Christmas tree-lighting ceremony.

Speaking of how the protest had "torn at her heart strings", she went on, "I shared your hurt, confusion and that of your parents, friends, teachers and all right-thinking people. I congratulate you for displaying so much courage, patience and quiet resolve over these weeks. The dignity of the parents, the forgiveness of the children and the tremendous efforts of so many has earned respect the world over. Never again must people resort to tormenting children as a means of protest."

She and Father Troy were in regular phone contact and the President made her own views known in characteristic uncompromising terms, given the exigencies of diplomacy and protocol. On a visit North, she said the protest was depressing, counter-productive and taking a huge toll on parents and children alike. On Irish state radio, she called for the protest to end. Her own children might have gone to Holy Cross had fate not dealt her a different hand, she said.

"The children have done nothing to incur the protest, they own nothing that can provide an answer. This has always been a place where territory has been marked in ways that are so inhumanely indecent and so awful."

President McAleese also appealed to nationalists to have the forgiveness needed to begin dialogue with their Protestant neighbours to find a way they could all live comfortably together.

The Taoiseach, Bertie Ahern, today condemns the protest without reservation. "Young children and their parents should not have been subjected to such appalling sectarian abuse and worse on their way to and from the school. There never was any justification for the protest," he says, adding that the government in Dublin had been "deeply shocked and dismayed".

From the very start of the protest, he says, he had personally raised it with both Tony Blair and John Reid.

"No grievances or wrongs, real or perceived, could justify such disgraceful treatment of young children. We accepted that the residents of Glenbryn had concerns about their security and the need for more facilities for their community, just as the residents of Ardoyne had similar concerns. We stressed, however, that the problems of Glenbryn would not be resolved or alleviated by terrorising children."

The Irish government, he says, was in continuous touch with many interested parties, including parents, the Board of Governors, local representatives and the British authorities. In the course of Dublin's contacts with loyalists, the government's view on the protest was put forward, while listening to their concerns.

"I myself met Father Aidan Troy in October 2001 and discussed the dispute with him in some detail," says the Taoiseach. "Achieving an end to the protest as swiftly as possible was my key concern."

Neither the protesters nor the parents speak warmly about any British minister. Both sides felt they were self-serving and dishonest. When Holy Cross hit the headlines, the then Northern Secretary, John Reid, hurriedly cut his annual vacation by three days to return to Stormont where he set up a "task force" to tackle the problem. Reid had left the North just after deciding against specifying the UDA as a group not on ceasefire and, in a move that did not endear him to the parents, had drawn a distinction between the loyalist protest and other acts of UDA violence. Reid had said that people were "entitled to protest" and that, in his view, the protest was "different from acts of terrorism".

Parent Gerald McCabe said that if Reid had seen the terror in the children's eyes, he "would change his tune". McCabe was one of a delegation from Ardoyne who met Reid in October. None of them were impressed. "He was the Secretary of State, the man in charge, but what did he do to get the loyalists to stop?"

He says that, within five minutes of the meeting starting, the parents knew they were going to walk away with nothing.

"The atmosphere was strange. Reid told us he knew some of the CRUA people were known UDA and UVF members and that their top people would have to put pressure on the lower ranks to get it stopped. He wanted us to see him as a good guy on our side. That's fair enough but he wasn't doing anything to help us other than talk. He acted like he was our best friend, he was really laid back, talking as if he had known us all our lives. He gave the impression that he viewed us as educated people with right on our side and the Glenbryn people as uneducated 'thickos', just a bunch of thugs, buttering us up while putting them down. He may well have said similar things about us to the loyalists."

Parent Sean Carmichael claims Jane Kennedy, the then British security minister in charge of policing, once told him that she believed the children should be taken through the back door of St Gabriel's, a key demand of the protesters.

"By expressing that view, she was in effect backing the loyalists from Glenbryn. She was saying that we should have stopped what we were doing and stepped back," he says.

Gerald McCabe also crossed swords with Jane Kennedy during a meeting at the House of Commons in London. It was their first face to face contact, despite repeated attempts to speak to her. All the parents had got out of her until then were statutory two line responses saying that she was "looking into" how the protest was being policed. But she could not hide when they met her in the committee room at Westminster. John McDonnell, a British Labour MP, chaired the meeting.

McCabe was overjoyed. "I thought, if nothing else comes of it, I am one happy man for capturing her attention, just this once."

The meeting went well. McCabe put on a video showing what was happening on the Ardoyne Road. Jane Kennedy was sitting beside the TV.

"When the video stopped, somebody had to break the silence. I had it in my head then that I had to speak to her, I had a captive audience, I needed other people to hear what I was going to say. Somebody in the audience asked about policing. She said she was dealing with it. I interrupted her and said, 'Jane, our kids are getting abused on that road every day and we see you doing absolutely nothing about it. I want to ask you one very, very simple thing. Get the RUC to stop treating us like animals, lining us up and herding us up and down the road. Get those gates open and let the RUC deal with the protesters and let us take our kids to school normally.'

"She looked at me and said she would most definitely be taking my request on board. The following Monday, the police opened the gates early. Father Troy had been demanding it too. I don't care if it was him or me who managed it. It was done and we were happy."

There was support for the parents from unexpected quarters. Of all people, the Tory MP Quentin Davies walked the road with the children one afternoon. The author was there and witnessed Mr Davies getting severely abused by the protesters. Parent Tanya Carmichael says that when Davies got to the gates of Holy Cross, he broke down and cried. She said he could not believe the abuse the children had to go through.

Other politicians who "walked the walk" alongside the parents included Liberal Democrat spokesman, Lembit Opik; British Labour MP, Kevin McNamara and Fine Gael MEP, Mary Banotti.

Liz Murphy says the Alliance Party's Eileen Bell gave support. Monica McWilliams from the Women's Coalition, she says, was also very helpful and "couldn't do enough".

"She condemned the protest and offered us any help we wanted."

Chapter Thirteen

CHURCHES

On the day the bomb went off, the last two boys to get off the road were two priests. No one can ever challenge the fact that we literally put our lives on the line for the children.
Father Gary Donegan

Statements issued by other churchmen only made it worse. I wasn't going to join the party. Far better to talk to people rationally, to try to persuade them they were going about their cause the wrong way.
Rev Norman Hamilton, Presbyterian minister

Sitting in the Passionist Monastery on the Protestant side of the interface between nationalist Ardoyne and the loyalist upper Shankill, it is impossible not to imagine how vulnerable the priests inside must feel at night. UDA flags flutter defiantly on the lamposts behind the monastery. Part of it is derelict after repeated arson attacks. Over the monastery roof, British Army helicopters buzz back and forth, night and day.

The monastery is a place of echoing stone corridors, high ceilings, Spartan refectories, ghosts of the past. It is also home to Father Aidan Troy.

If anyone came out of the dispute with an enhanced credibility as far as Ardoyne was concerned, it was Father Troy. When he arrived, the community treated him like a ticking bomb. By the end of the protest, he could do no wrong.

He was a gift for the media, a priest straight out of central casting. Tall and photogenic, the camera loved his craggy face and anguished brown eyes. It also helped that he was articulate and totally unfazed, at least publicly, by his predicament. If he was frightened, he did not show it. If he had doubts, he kept them well hidden. He followed the first rule of public relations and kept his message straight and simple.

The children's safety was his priority. The children's school was his responsibility. The children's parents had his allegiance.

As for the protesters, if they believed they had genuine grievances against Ardoyne, then Ardoyne must accept they had grievances and treat them seriously. But he was uncompromising about the form their protest took. Like many others, he found it deeply disturbing that people could hate so much and vent that hate on innocent children.

For the local press, more familiar with priests and bishops who remain aloof in their palaces and presbyteries, Father Troy was a breath of fresh air. He talked to us. He treated us like human beings, not piranha.

The Catholic Church might not realise it yet, but Father Troy was an able shepherd whose example persuaded at least some of its flock to return or remain loyal to the faith of their fathers. A lesser man could have alienated the entire congregation. As it is, he is respected in equal measure by Sinn Fein and SDLP voters alike, no mean feat in such politically charged territory.

Father Donegan, Father Troy's friend and deputy, quotes Sinn Fein's Gerry Kelly at one public meeting saying he would not want to stand in an election against either of "those two boys" (Fathers Troy and Donegan) because "he wouldn't win". Kelly was probably correct.

Father Donegan believes it ran even deeper than electoral politics – and that runs deep enough in Ardoyne. "Kelly was publicly acknowledging that there was another authority, other than Sinn Fein's, in Ardoyne. He was taken aback because it was non-militant but very strong."

One senses the church hierarchy would have preferred Father Troy to have taken a more neutral stand. As it was, the bishops were stuck with him. They could hardly sack him at the height of the protest. Ardoyne might have risen and mobbed the bishop's palace.

There was intense speculation in Ardoyne and amongst the journalists covering the protest that pressure would sooner or later be exerted on Father Troy to advise the parents to take the alternative route.

Monsignor Tom Toner, Chair of the Diocese of Down and Connor's

Social Affairs Commission, says that was never likely. He was himself chaplain to the 1981 hunger strikers, ten of whom starved themselves to death in jail for political status. There was intense speculation then that the Catholic Church might deem their deaths suicide. Yet, Father Toner says, he never came under any hierarchical pressure to withdraw the sacraments of the church to the dying men, despite the head of the church in Britain, Cardinal Basil Hume, publicly declaring they had killed themselves.

"The bishop left me to resolve it myself at the men's bedside. Neither he nor Cardinal Hume were there. I was. The bishop appoints a priest to a parish. He likes to know what's going on, but he doesn't tell him how to run it."

Was there criticism within the Catholic Church of the public way Father Troy went about his work? "He needed to go public, I've no problem with that. As to degree? Well, I wasn't in his shoes. I know we saw a lot of him, but he was there, carrying the can. He hadn't arrived long when the whole thing blew up. He had no road map. The bishop wasn't meeting the parents of little girls. I think we all felt, God help him, what a situation. Thank goodness it's him and not me."

If some in the Catholic hierarchy had reservations with Father Troy, they weren't the only ones. There were others who positively loathed him. The loyalists were furious when he accused them of abusing the children. Their revenge was to manufacture large placards accusing him of paedophilia which they waved in front of the cameras and children. It was a heavy personal cross to bear.

Father Troy's father was dying in a County Wicklow hospital at the time of the dispute. He would often make the long journey south in the evenings to visit him after a day enduring the protest. He was desperately concerned that his father's health might suffer from the shock of seeing his son on the television news, being described publicly to the entire nation as a child abuser.

Billy Hutchinson speaks for many in the Protestant community in accusing him of "failing to give direction" to the parents by advising them to take the alternative route to school. Father Troy himself has absolutely no doubt he did the right thing.

Born in Dublin in October 1945, he studied at the Passionist seminary in Crossgar, County Down, during the 1970s. Ardoyne was his first parish. For the previous 31 years he had either been a "church bureaucrat", travelling the world as a church inspector or preaching the gospel at missions. Latterly working for six years at his order's headquarters in Rome, he was in his final year studying for a licence to teach theology when the call came to take up a new post in Ireland.

"I assumed I would be based in Dublin, so when I heard it was in Ardoyne I was dumbfounded. I wondered why I had been chosen but I told them to give me 24 hours to think about it."

He finally agreed because he had never turned down an assignment in his life. "I had absolutely no idea what I'd be walking into. When the trouble first erupted in June I was thankful it would all be over by the time I arrived."

By virtue of office, he was chairman of the both the boys and girls schools' Boards of Governors. "I'm convinced now that God has a sense of humour because schools were the only thing I'd asked my superiors not to get me involved in – and they came up with Holy Cross. I knew nothing of the schools system. I'm not good at budgets, redundancies and school maintenance or things like that. It was like God saying, 'We're going to teach this guy a lesson'.

"If I hadn't had a single civil, political or media problem in Ardoyne, I would still have been a very fraught person. It was all so intense and so unfamiliar. I did realise, however, my priorities as a Catholic school governor and they were to care for the safety, health and education of the children. As parents are the first teachers of children, I had to respect their views also. I remember the very first time I walked into the Focus Group centre (Ardoyne community development group). The reaction could not have been stronger than if I'd walked into a brothel. I couldn't have caused more disgust in the eyes of some people."

When he learned of the Right To Education group, he immediately wanted to join although his membership was rejected as he was not a parent. It didn't take long, however, before he was embroiled in the dispute.

One of the parents, Roisin, describes his first public meeting in Ardoyne. "He was thrown in the deep end. He hadn't a clue. People were shouting, 'What are you going to do?' and 'You're only new here, you don't know what is going on'. All he could do was try to calm them."

On the morning of September 3, Father Troy woke very early and communicated with the police commander on the Ardoyne Road. Then he went and met the parents at the barricade before walking up with them.

"Fourteen children were taken out of the school in the first week. Some families even moved out of the area. Some chose the other route. But on the morning of September 3, 90% of the parents were there with their children."

That decision, and his presence on the road every single subsequent morning, earned their respect and their trust. His appearance at later public meetings repeatedly drew standing ovations. The protesters again and again made it clear they believed he should advise the parents to use the alternative route. In the event, Father Troy walked a tightrope, keeping himself in relatively good standing with the church hierarchy, while retaining the trust of his flock. Individual families, he said, had the right to make their own decisions. There was a principle also about the inalienable rights of children that could not be conceded.

"In any case, if I had called on them all to take the longer road, the protest would in all probability have moved around the corner. I left the decision up to them and most chose to walk the usual route."

Mickey Liggett, an Ardoyne republican and founder member of the Focus Group, admits a grudging admiration. "He effectively put his neck on the line. When he walked up, the children felt protected. The bishop was nowhere to be seen."

Father Troy was, and is, the target of innumerable death threats, many received personally by phone at the parochial house in Ardoyne. But he also has inter-denominational supporters throughout Ireland and the United States. One particular service, he remembers, was in Cork. "You could have heard a pin drop as I spoke about the lessons I had learned about the future of the church from the children of Ardoyne."

Although the weeks and months of the protest are still a vivid memory, at the time he says he hardly noticed what was going on. "I was so focused on the children that I never really noticed that my own name was vilified every day. I was following, the parents were leading. At the same time, however, I was genuinely worried that a child might be killed.

That was my constant fear and focus. I don't think that even now, three years on, the true extent of the damage has come out. We are hearing new accounts every day of mental illness, about young children still being counselled and taking tranquillisers.

"I was, and still am, angry about the way it was reported, as if there were angels and devils on both sides. This was not a 'on the one side this, and on the other side that' kind of story. Whatever grievances the loyalist protesters had, and I am sure they had some, they should never have used the children. The methods they used were totally unacceptable."

After walking to school with the parents and children, he regularly had to return to the parochial house to wash spittle out of his hair. He remembers the worst times. "The police phoned me one day to say the loyalists had threatened to put a sniper on the rooftops. I had to decide whether to tell the parents and possibly cause panic, or to keep the information to myself. I had no option but to tell them, but they still decided to walk up the road. That was a crucial moment. If we hadn't gone up the road that day, if we had broken, then similar threats could have forced us to do the same day after day – but it wasn't easy."

The very worst moment was when a little girl stumbled and fell on her way back from school, grazing her leg. "The crowd of protesters surged forward, cheering at seeing the injured child lying bleeding in the gutter. I simply could not believe it."

The child was Rachel Mervyn (6) who had stumbled as she walked to school with her cousin, Eimear (4). A loyalist had shouted, "You can't even walk, you stupid Fenian bastards."

Father Troy says there was a strong element of denial amongst the loyalist protesters. On one occasion, a group of angry women protesters called him over and politely told him to stop telling lies, denying that balloons of urine had ever been thrown. He knew differently. He had seen it and smelt it himself. "They had some fair points to make, but there's no sense in denying what everyone saw with their own eyes."

He says he would have acted sooner had he known how long the protest would continue. "I was always being told that there were big things going on behind the scenes, politicians working to solve it – the thing went on for far too long."

Finally, it came to him in the dead of night as he lay trying to sleep.

It all seemed to him like a well-rehearsed drama. The parents walking in tight formation to the school twice a day, clutching their children. The loyalists forming up and hurling abuse and anything else they could think of. The police in black riot gear and their imperfect barricade. The press filming and reporting the ghastly scene. He was himself an actor, walking up and down in his black "costume". Everyone appeared to be performing a role. What would happen if one side broke the stage directions? The thought coincided with the end of the protest. At his instigation, the parents told the police they would not co-operate any more. From then on they would no longer walk the children to school together in one group at a set time. They would walk as they always had, in ones and twos.

"The police were against it but I insisted. They accused me of withdrawing my co-operation, but I couldn't let it continue. I knew that the protesters wanted to it end as well."

The spell was broken. With hindsight, he says there are lessons within the Holy Cross story about how the Catholic Church might renew itself at a time when, he says, it is reaching "the end of an era". Father Troy says he understands for the first time what Christ meant about "becoming as a little child".

"The fathers were strong and the mothers didn't buckle either," he says, "but the children were the real source of power: their innocence, their singing, their good cheer. There must be a new partnership with the people, not just between the clergy and bishops."

Children and parents are partners, so the clergy and the people must be partners. "We ignore children at our peril," he says. "Theirs is the Kingdom of God."

But a Kingdom still needs a material home and for the last two years his time has been devoted to raising money to refurbish Holy Cross Church itself. In 2002, he had ordered that the church be painted for the first time since 1964, in time for its centenary. The contractor broke the bad news that Holy Cross was on the point of falling down. Fortunately, he was introduced to Dawson Stelfox, architect, conservationist and mountaineer, the first Irishman to conquer Everest. Phase two of the work began in June 2004, to reopen the old school on the site as a cross-community reconciliation centre with a door opening out onto the

Protestant Woodvale Road.

"It would be great to think that something good can be born out of the Holy Cross dispute," he says. "Somebody, some day will have to shoulder the blame for what was allowed to happen. There are people who are convinced that I am on an ego trip, but events dictated the pace. I wish some of my brethren could understand that."

Father Troy still believes the four main Christian denominations might have helped to end the protest earlier if they had made a joint statement deploring it. Certainly, this would have been welcomed by the parents.

"When politicians fail, the function of the church must surely be to step in. If it doesn't, there's no reason for having a church. The church will just have become another big corporation," he says.

This view is contested by Monsignor Toner, who chaired the North Belfast Community Action Project. "When you have the mentality of people who would attack children, are they capable of shame? If the bombing didn't shame them, what would? How can you shame people with no self-respect? I really don't believe the churches have that kind of influence. I don't know to which church the people in Glenbryn are aligned. I suspect it's minimal."

Other ministers, including the Presbyterian Rev Norman Hamilton and the Methodist Rev Harold Good, agree with Toner.

On the support, or lack of it, from the Catholic hierarchy, SDLP councillor Martin Morgan says it failed to support Father Troy adequately. "It was just him and Father Gary. Where was the bishop? Father Troy showed more leadership than anyone, including the politicians. He suffered because of it and it shows physically. The death threat still hangs over him. He looks drained, even this late on."

Donal Flanagan of the CCMS says that Father Troy's presence drew at least some of the venom away from the children. "He sustained abuse that would challenge any ordinary person, any extraordinary person, to the limit. I saw signs of Father Troy visibly wilting from the abuse he took."

Father Troy and Father Donegan might have walked through Gethsemane, but their sacrifice is not wasted on the people of Ardoyne. Parent Liz Murphy says she'll never forget what they went through.

"But they still held their heads up and told us to be calm and stay together. What they did is something you cannot explain, it was really and truly magnificent. The people will never forget him and Father Gary for it. They walked up and down that road twice in the morning and twice in the afternoon and sometimes three times. They took all the abuse. Not once did either of them turn and lash out."

Judy Haughey concurs, "The things that poor Father Aidan was called were disgraceful. God bless him, he couldn't have came into this district at a better time along with wee Father Gary. The strength they gave us was unbelievable."

Sharon McCabe, another mother, used to cook for the two priests in the monastery's kitchens until the number of threatening phone calls forced her to leave. "There were times I should have been working but I wasn't fit for anything. I would lie across the kitchen table crying for probably an hour. Father Gary tried to make light of things, they were both fantastic."

Father Gary Donegan is sometimes referred to locally as the "Forgotten Man of Holy Cross" because he kept so firmly in the background. One was aware of his solid figure on the road every day and the parents always spoke highly of him, but he never gave interviews. Expecting a reluctant and taciturn interviewee from whom words would have to be dragged, it was a pleasant surprise to find quite the opposite. From a farming family in Newtownbutler, County Fermanagh, he came to Holy Cross in January 2001.

"Building up towards the summer there seemed to be a lot of tension in the area. I was still finding my feet and very homesick. June 19, the start of the whole thing, was my birthday. It will always be remembered. One wee woman told me I must have put a hex on the place because it was dead quiet until I came."

When he greeted Father Troy off the Dublin train in August 2001, he told him in no uncertain terms that the Holy Cross dispute had to be top of his agenda. Three nights later, while the two priests were out at a community welcome party, loyalists broke into the monastery through a door that had withstood the worst of the Troubles over 30 years.

"The kitchen storerooms were set on fire. Aidan and I returned home to find the grounds full of policemen."

Truly a baptism of fire. On September 3, the two men rose early, put on their black, flowing habits and left for the Ardoyne Road and the first day of term.

"I thought there would be placards and maybe a bit of shouting but nothing prepared me. Even hardened people who had seen 30 years of the Troubles couldn't believe it. You could hear the missiles bouncing off the side of the plastic barricade. The gardens were terraced and so the protesters could spit down into your hair. They called us everything from being 'impotent' to 'stud of the century'. I had to wash the spit off my hair and face in the sink at the school. I was aghast."

By the third day, the day of the bombing, he says he felt like a sitting duck walking in the middle of the road.

"Aidan usually took the left hand side and I took the right, keeping an eye on things to prevent people shouting back. When the explosion detonated you could hear the screams and I remember a journalist turning and running, almost falling over a child. Children were running towards the protesters in their confusion. Until I saw a TV news clip of the march that day, I didn't even realise what I had done. You can hear me saying, 'Run harder, run faster'. It was me shouting that.

"My initial reaction was to flee but then we saw the wee ones falling and people grabbing them and screaming. Aidan and I were the last two to walk off the road. Underneath my habit, from my knees down I was doing 'Riverdance'. I couldn't get my legs to stop shaking. While we were shepherding the children, I was expecting a second bomb to come over, I thought we were going to die, I genuinely did. You could hear the police dog howling and the injured officer screaming and shouting for the medics."

The aftermath, he says, was almost worse. "We Passionists wear a leather belt which the rosary hangs on, although I didn't wear my rosary during the protest because it was too cumbersome if we had to run or grab a child. A schoolchild came up to me after the bombing and began kissing the belt dozens and dozens of times like a wee woodpecker. Me being physically big, I must have represented safety. I was like the comfort blanket in 'Peanuts'. I remember lifting the wee thing up and her mother seeing where she was. They had become separated. I will never forget it."

The loyalists operated no moratorium on priests, as Father Donegan found out to his cost. After a rally in Belfast, having "decommissioned" his clerical collar yet again, he went to a city centre multi-storey car park and held the door open for a man and his wife.

"She thanked me but he looked at me strangely. I darted up the stairs but encountered them again. The next thing the man hit me a punch in the face and knocked me down the car park stairs. I've done a bit of boxing, but I couldn't have defended myself. If I had got involved in a fight, the headlines would have been 'Holy Cross Priest Involved in Brawl' and children would have disappeared off the agenda. I picked myself up, got into my car and drove off with the guy still shouting on about paedophiles, the 'little bitches' at Holy Cross school and the Garvaghy Road."

There was another day, however, when Father Donegan did lose his self-control. A pipe bomb had landed on the nationalist side of the peace-line at the back of an elderly man's house in Alliance Avenue. The victim was a Protestant who had been quietly living there since the 1950s.

"I went into the house and the old man turned round and said, 'I love everybody'. I just broke down. When I came out, the TV cameras were filming me. Some of the mothers were angry. They didn't want me to be seen on TV like that – but it was printed in the *Irish News* the next day anyhow. What upset me was the thought of this elderly man, living here all his life on the Catholic side of the peace-line, with no problem at all. Just the sadness of having to put up with that at his time of life."

Like Father Troy, Donegan criticises the police operation at the school and, like many nationalists, suspects their allegiances were with the protesters.

"For days on end, the soldiers were in full riot gear, masks and all, so all you could see was their eyes. Then they took the masks off to 'reduce tension' but when you saw the expressions on their faces, it was almost worse. In July, they use these enormous screens to protect Orange marchers. Why couldn't that have been done for the kids? People get hosed off the road in Ardoyne with water cannons. Where were the screens during the protest? How were so many people allowed into the area? If you are trying to encourage people to support an impartial police force then it has to be seen as such. Perception is everything in this area. If loyalists had been arrested, it would at least have been a deterrent, telling people they could not openly flout the law."

He ridicules loyalist claims that the Catholic Church had some kind of territorial master plan to take over more land in North Belfast. "There is no underlying agenda. Father Troy and I were making it up as we went along."

Far from some Machiavellian plan, he says, the two of them would sit up at night and wonder what on earth would happen the following day.

"We were exhausted and both had colds. We lived on this cough medicine at night – it's like poitín mixed with diesel oil – and bacon butties in the morning, trying to keep going. We never missed a day though.

"The whole nonsense was summarised for me one day when a particularly voluble woman in the protest ran up to me and, calling me deliberately, 'Mr Donegan', informed me that I hated Protestants. All I could reply was 'Pet, no harm to you, but I'm half a Protestant myself. My mother's name is West. How can I hate my own family? If I was to stand up at the Holy Cross pulpit one Sunday and say that the Queen was the Anti-Christ and that Protestantism is blasphemy, the biggest ranking Sinn Feiner would run me out of town, it would not be tolerated.'"

On the Protestant side of the community, there were also voices raised against the protest, including that of Archbishop Lord Robin Eames, the Church of Ireland Primate. On September 4 he described it as "disgusting, tragic beyond words".

"We are utterly revolted by those scenes outside the school. There is a wave of revulsion across this province."

Archbishop Eames said the scenes had further damaged the North's image and while he knew there were great complexities, nothing could justify attacks on little children of any denomination. All right thinking people should condemn them, he said.

Eames' statement followed soon after another, issued by someone closer to North Belfast, who had decided to be heard loud and clear. The local Church of Ireland minister, Rev Stewart Heaney, went public on August 30, before school returned. His parish church, Emmanuel, was

located on the main road between Ardoyne and Holy Cross school where
the children walked each day, although he now ministers in the less
troubled Coleraine, County Derry. Heaney, a former fire-fighter based at
the Ardoyne depot, had been worried long before the protest began that
trouble was looming. He says a bad atmosphere had been building up for
some time before the events of June 19.

He was already firm friends with Father Kenneth Brady, then parish
priest of Holy Cross. The minister and priest "were like brothers", says
Heaney, and held joint services in Emmanuel and Holy Cross. One
tangible result was their idea of a "Procession of Witness", whereby one
congregation would walk between the churches to symbolise their
friendship and to foster cross-community contact.

"I used to go into Holy Cross on a regular basis and address the
assembly. They were lovely children and the school is a tribute to Anne
Tanney, for whom I have a high regard."

With sublime irony, Heaney would tell the little girls that when they
walked past his church, they should think "of all of us in there being
their friends".

"I had an ecumenical service in Emmanuel and the Holy Cross
school choir came down and sang there which shows the way things used
to be before all this happened."

Trouble, however, was not far away. "There were growing demands
from loyalists for a wall at the junction between Alliance Avenue and
Ardoyne Road, and Ken and I were against it. We didn't want more
divisions. It's easy to put a wall up, far harder to take it down. Talk of a
wall had spread to the Catholic side of Ardoyne. They didn't want it
either. After a number of meetings, Ken and I went to see the local police
commander and said, very forcibly, that neither of us wanted a wall."

Father Brady had then written a pastoral letter to his congregation
telling them of the two clergymen's joint opposition to the wall.
However, says Heaney, a police officer passed on the letter, with his name
on it, to "some of the extreme elements" in Glenbryn.

"A person from Glenbryn rang me one night and asked me if I
endorsed the letter and, when I said I had, he became very angry. It put
me in extreme danger, in the firing line. I had been shafted by the police
officer. I rang Ken and he and I were furious."

Asked how he knew the police had given his name to the loyalist, Heaney's reply is pretty conclusive. "The chap who rang me to ask me about my name told me who had given him the letter."

Brady then spoke directly to the policeman involved and he was reported to his senior officer. "I don't think anything was ever done about it," says Heaney, "although he should have been kicked out of the job. I felt very vulnerable. Loyalists, some linked to paramilitaries in Glenbryn, looked on me with suspicion. I was living on the front of the Ballysillan Road (strongly loyalist area). It was rough."

Nevertheless, on the eve of the protest, he issued a forthright press statement. In it, he explained that he had no personal "political baggage" and that his interest was purely pastoral.

"After visiting parishioners in the area," it read, "I am clear that there is considerable unease about the situation, particularly about any difficulties created for children travelling along Ardoyne Road to attend school. We all acknowledge that there are many unresolved problems and difficulties in this interface area including damage to property, murder, fear and intimidation." Rev Heaney then advocated a forum to resolve problems.

"This could not happen overnight, so it seems unreasonable to involve the children and insist that they, or their accompanying parents, cannot travel to their school by the normal route until all the problems are finally resolved. Christians cannot sit easily with that position. I want people to consider a return to the status quo prior to June 19, 2001 – children travelling to their school by the normal route of Ardoyne Road, without protest."

Heaney had done his best, but all he could do afterwards was watch in horror as the protest developed. He says he was not forced out of the area, but it seems clear that his opposition to the protest was viewed with disapproval in loyalist quarters. According to loyalist sources in North Belfast, Heaney's statement almost led to the burning down of Emmanuel Church. It was under active UDA consideration. Wiser counsels prevailed, but if nothing else, Heaney's transfer to Coleraine was fortuitous.

Those amongst us who have few dealings with men of the cloth tend to overlook the undoubted fact they have their own rivalries and differences.

There were certainly huge gulfs between their responses to Holy Cross, not just between Catholic and Protestant churchmen, but within both of those main camps as well. Witness this accusation by one Protestant minister (who does not want to be named), commenting on the statement issued by Archbishop Eames on September 4: "He blew it. It was awful, nonsense, posturing. Why attack people without talking to them?"

There are also different views on whether the four main churches should have made a joint statement, as Father Troy would have liked. Another Presbyterian minister, the Rev Norman Hamilton, decided not to make any public statement at all condemning the protest.

"I thought about it very carefully but the history of issuing statements shows they have never stopped anybody doing what they shouldn't. I know people believe that issuing statements is important so the wider world understands where the churches stand, to position ourselves in wider society, but it is a complete myth to think that issuing statements influences anything on the ground.

"If you want influence, you have to find a way of building credible relationships. Haranguing them from afar doesn't do that, it just salves your conscience. I am baffled by this societal demand for condemnation from people who do not go on to take any further responsibility. The fundamental issue here is not condemnation. It is the arrogance of condemning without giving people the dignity of being heard."

The SDLP leader, Mark Durkan, however, is sharply critical of Hamilton's record. "He was quite strident and moralistic and accusatory about relatively unimportant matters such as the date when drawings had to be produced on alterations to the road. He could get very high and mighty but was an absolute moral agnostic when it came to what was being done to the children."

Hamilton's position is also slightly different to that expressed by the Church of Ireland Bishop of Connor, Alan Parker.

"In times of high tension, condemnation tends to runs like water off a duck's back," he says. "Blanket condemnation can harden attitudes and create a siege mentality. But that does not mean that church spokespersons should not condemn the unacceptable. It also needs to be accompanied by attempts to get people off the hook they have impaled themselves upon."

He says members of the Church of Ireland, both ministers and lay people, were involved in behind-the-scenes talks, with some moral qualms. "Effective action to calm the situation took into account the heavy involvement of paramilitaries. These contacts were difficult but necessary."

The President of the Methodist Church in Ireland, the Rev Harold Good, who knows the area well, having served in the Shankill Road during the 60s and 70s when many of his parishioners moved into Glenbryn, says conditions there had worsened in the intervening years. He says he had no equivocation in condemning the protest very publicly, adding that many Glenbryn residents were "horrified at what was happening".

He visited the school more than once, met Anne Tanney and spoke to the children as well as a group of parents to say how distressed he was. The residents he visited, he says, did not want to be associated with the behaviour of the protesters, particularly the older people who had brought up their own children there.

But, he goes on, "I also have to say people were fearful and anxious. There seemed to them to be very real evidence of feeling pushed out. Whether that fear was real or imagined, well-grounded or fictional, it was to them still real. One lady, who had been going to the Ardoyne shops for years to collect her pension, said she felt unsafe. Something had been said to her. The people I met in Glenbryn were frightened.

"There was a firm belief that the situation was being politically orchestrated both ways. There was evidence that many parents were being pressurised to walk up the road. It wasn't always what they wanted to do. All I know is that I would not have walked my child through that protest, whatever right I had. I would not walk my child through that kind of danger, particularly if there was an alternative route. The Presbyterian Moderator and I met with some of the leaders of the protest and did our best to try to persuade them to end it, that it was morally wrong, totally indefensible and counter-productive to what they said they wanted to achieve."

As a result, he says, he took flak from people he was surprised to take flak from.

"They said I didn't understand and that there was another side to it."

Whatever his arguments, however, the Rev Good believes nothing he said or did could have influenced events. "We told them they were going about it in totally the wrong way but I don't think they understood through the fear, hatred, bitterness, anger and recriminations."

He also says he met people in Glenbryn whom he knew to be "activists and not long-time residents" who had recently moved in. "They were people who'd been involved in other ways in this conflict and they brought that with them."

He cautions against blanket criticism of the protesters, saying, "We might all be surprised at what we are capable of if put into a situation where we feel trapped, frightened, fearful and oppressed. It was mob frenzy, a ghastly thing. Sectarianism is alive and well in our community, in the leafy suburbs as well as in the city. Those people were not for listening. It was Northern Ireland at its very worst. All those years of conflict condensed into one small area. It was a drama played out before us all in public, all the years of exclusion and fear and centuries of instilling difference."

The lessons he draws from the protest are that many working-class people, on both sides of the divide, see no benefit from the peace process.

"They are the left behind and feel socially, politically and economically abandoned. As so often happens, in their powerlessness they turn on each other. With our history of exclusion in this province we ignore the lessons of the past to our peril. We must address the grievances of people in areas such as Ardoyne and Glenbryn."

Chapter Fourteen

THE MEDIA

They said things that weren't exactly true. Sometimes they fiddled about a bit to make it suit the people who were watching it.

Amanda Bowes, Holy Cross child

There were very few in-depth reports, with some exceptions. It was just lazy journalism not to ask why we were protesting. To be honest, the reporting destroyed us.

Stuart McCartney, loyalist protester

The loyalist protesters felt portrayed as monsters and unfairly blamed for the children's suffering; meanwhile nationalists felt accused of sacrificing their children's welfare on the altar of republican dogma.

As so often in the Northern conflict, both sides complained about unfair press coverage. That does not mean, however, that the reportage was necessarily objective and truthful. The British press flew in their top colour writers who regaled their readers with lurid descriptions of terrified little girls and thuggish loyalists. They made little effort to dig into what lay behind the protest. There was little focus on the various reasons for demographic change in North Belfast or the shortcomings in unionist street-level leadership in Glenbryn or at Stormont.

The papers and television preferred to concentrate on the spectacle along the Ardoyne Road. It was a photographer's dream, coupling cute kids in red uniforms screaming in terror against a backdrop of urban decay and adult faces deformed with hate. After the drama of the first few days, however, the established British model of covering the Northern Ireland violence then reasserted itself: (i) blame both irrational "tribes"; (ii) hold your hands up in horror; and (iii) commiserate with the British government/police for being the hapless umpires.

Reports (in the British press, in particular), while roundly condemning the tactics of the protesters, were generally sympathetic about their complaints of being "surrounded by oppressive Ardoyne". Many British press reports, while castigating the protesters' tactics, also implicated Sinn Fein because of its perceived failure to make sufficient concessions to unionism in the peace process. Witness this report, carried in *The Scotsman* of September 9, 2001. "Just because Sinn Fein have (*sic*) a masterful understanding of media manipulation and propaganda, it should not blind us to the essential truth of the stalled peace process: namely, that the overwhelming responsibility for that state of affairs lies with the Republican movement. The Battle for Holy Cross Primary has laid a smokescreen across that truth, but in time the smoke of battle will clear and the truth will reappear."

As recently as June 2004, the BBC website summarised the dispute: "It centred on alleged attacks on Protestant Glenbryn homes by the larger nationalist community in Ardoyne." No mention of police statistics telling the opposite story. On the same website, the BBC also said Holy Cross school was the "victim of bad geography". Arguably the school was the victim of bad history, perhaps, or sectarianism, or the UDA, but bad geography?

In defence of journalists, it was difficult, if not impossible, for reporters, parachuted into the maelstrom that was Ardoyne in September 2001, to ascertain whether the grievances were genuine. The protest lasted for three months, however, and (even accepting that September 11 was a massive and understandable alternative focus) the paucity of analysis in the British newspapers is difficult to defend. Media executives stoutly defend their coverage while individual reporters, who covered the dispute on a daily basis, have genuine and honourable concerns about hours of interviews being frequently condensed into 20-second sound bites and pages of notes dumbed down to 500-word stories.

Their audiences in Ardoyne and Glenbryn also have questions. The general complaint in Glenbryn is that they were blamed, unreasonably, for the children's suffering. One angry loyalist is community worker and CRUA member Anne Bill. "People watched the news coverage on their TVs at night and were angry they were being blamed."

Another loyalist, Michael Cosby, said the media did "a lot of damage".

"Interviews were broadcast heavily edited. I can remember getting up out of bed and watching Sky News live from the Ardoyne Road and not being able to believe what they were reporting."

Ronnie Black blames the media for putting the children in the picture. "We were not responsible for what happened to the children, but the media blamed us. All right, there were slanging matches and people shouted angry things, but there was no actual physical violence towards the children. It was unfair, definitely unfair. There wasn't balance. Every report on TV was all to do with the children. We pointed out the protest was against the parents, not the children, but that was never properly reported."

Stuart McCartney digs deeper. "Let's be cynical about all this. An old person getting killed in a car crash is a terrible tragedy, but pictures of five and six-year-old children suffering sell more papers. The press did a great assassination job on the problems we were trying to address – but that's the press for you."

Lollipop lady Amanda Johnson is particularly bitter. "I saw a cameraman ask a British soldier to move slightly so he could get a shot of the children through his legs. Many of the pictures were manufactured. The protest was not as bad as they made out. The propaganda organisers on the republican side knew that would happen, that the coverage would focus on schoolgirls being attacked. That was all you ever heard."

Jim Potts, like many in CRUA, began to turn against the phalanx of reporters who had landed in Glenbryn. "As the weeks unfolded, we began to feel very aggrieved. The interviews we were giving were simply not being carried. As it dragged on, the same people would come back and ask the same questions. We then began declining to speak to them because they had broken their previous assurances.

"There wasn't one single media contact favourable towards us, who we felt comfortable with or openly discuss everything and who would report it. Some of the local Belfast newspapers would carry our point of view, but what were they set against the world's media? We didn't see too many reports taking our side and blaming republicans for not decommissioning and for failing to push the peace process forward. It's only looking back at it that I realise it was an orchestrated propaganda coup for Ardoyne. Catholic parents and children were used as pawns for political and propaganda reasons."

On the nationalist side, while people are also bitter about the coverage, feelings are more complex. One view they share with the protesters is that the global media were more sympathetic towards the parents' case than their domestic cousins in Britain and Ireland.

Parent Judy Haughey initially had high hopes. "I thought if we could only get it across, somebody out there was bound to listen. Some way, somehow, they would listen to our cries and help us. If we had done in our homes what the protesters did publicly to our children in the street, we would have been arrested. I thought if I could get that point across, I would."

Her hopes were soon dashed. "The media saw what was going on, so why did they make up lies to try to balance both sides? Nothing in this world justifies hurling abuse, missiles and bombs at young girls. No matter what your concerns are."

Jeanette McKernan says she viewed the press as a kind of insurance policy against loyalist excesses until the international press corps left Ardoyne after September 11.

"I felt safer when they were there and the whole world could see what was happening. After the loyalists bombed us, there was such an outcry, I thought they wouldn't try it again."

After September 11, it scared her. "There was nobody there for us anymore."

As journalists were sent to cover the protest day after day, the parents got to know some personally. They also have strong views on some of the outside reporters who dropped in for the occasional day's work. Roisin Kennedy says one local reporter in particular was disliked. "She would act all friendly and then slip in a sly question. She tried to make out she was on your side but the answers you gave were never broadcast."

Another journalist, who works for a British breakfast programme, drew hostility from many of the parents. "You remember all of the reporters and all their faces. They were just there to make money," sighs Roisin.

Pat Monaghan does not discriminate against individual journalists. She dislikes them all. "They are bloodhounds. If they can stir things up and keep it going, that's what they'll do."

Tina Gallagher shares that view. "They kept on calling to the house asking if they could follow us up the road. They wanted to film the kids getting ready for school. They're just vultures. Even the day of the bombing, they came straight over and poked their cameras in our faces, with no concern for anybody, they just didn't care."

Like Tina, Sharon Quail has no time for journalists. "We all knew that no matter what we said, something else would get printed. They were all, more or less, trying to say that we were to blame."

Geraldine McGrandles said reporters made her feel like a guinea pig. "We lived on Alliance Avenue and they were rarely away from our door. I gave one or two interviews before I got fed up."

Some programmes, however, came in for praise, such as a local "Spotlight" BBC television discussion which brought the parents and protesters together when they were not in any other dialogue, even privately.

"It was different in that it was at least a serious attempt to get down to the nitty-gritty," says Liz Murphy. "Having that sort of dialogue and debate was fair enough but most of the rest was a mockery."

Lisa Irvine made quite an impact on the "Spotlight" programme, clashing with Stuart McCartney. He asked what Ardoyne was prepared to give to end the protest? The presenter, Noel Thompson, turned to Lisa for a response.

"What can my five-year-old daughter give you?" asked Lisa.

One of the parents' complaints was the media's reticence to ask questions about their claims that UDA exiles from their feud with the UVF had had a significant input.

Many of the parents felt they had a good press at the start, but that it changed as the protest dragged on. The parents' complaints fall into five categories:

- The parents were being equated with the protesters
- They were described as Sinn Fein pawns
- They were accused of attacking Glenbryn
- They were blamed for aggravating the protest by not taking the alternative route
- They were accused of dressing their children up to "look cute" (and even slapping them to make them cry) for the cameras.

Lynda Bowes says the point where the media honeymoon ended came when news broke that some children were taking sedatives. "The doctor who went public may have intended highlighting the damage being done to the children, but it flipped the argument over and became another stick to beat us with. The longer it went on, the worse it got because the initial story was old and, as journalists do, they kept trying to find a new angle. They turned on the parents and asking us why we were doing this to our children."

Tanya Carmichael says it was worse than the media drawing an equivalence between the protesters and the parents. "They insinuated we were more abusive. I am sure they wouldn't like their own children going through the back door of a school."

Then there were the claims that Sinn Fein – or worse, the IRA – was pulling the parents' strings. Lisa Irvine says, "It was as though we were being led a merry dance, but I have no republican connections. My father's a Protestant. I was just a mother taking my child to school. Father Troy wouldn't have walked that road every day if he'd thought it was all a republican ploy."

Martin Monaghan agrees. "It got to a stage when we were being called as bad as the protesters. Outside reporters didn't do any research. They flew in at 6am, did a report and flew out again that evening with no responsibility for the damage left behind. They started to say it was being orchestrated by the IRA and Sinn Fein. It had nothing to do with them. We were parents wanting to take our children to school."

He was also angry that the difficulties faced by Wheatfield parents were equated with those of Holy Cross. "Nobody was preventing them getting to school, only themselves. They made sure their kids were inside their gates before coming onto the road to stop ours."

On the alternative route, Sean Carmichael says the press wrongly portrayed it as though it was just a side entrance. "It wasn't as simple as walking round the side and you were in. One parent, Cathy Quigley, who's in a wheelchair, asked a camera crew to go with her up the long way. They didn't go because it would have killed their story about 'our refusal to walk kids through the back'."

Another recurrent complaint is that the Ardoyne parents were themselves attacking homes in Glenbryn. "It was ridiculous, like we were tucking our kids in at night before going off to throw stones at Glenbryn," says Lisa Irvine.

One family which was particularly badly hit, both by the protest and the attendant violence across the peace-line, were the Lindsays, David and Maura, and their children Amy and Kirsty.

"When cameramen were in our street, filming what was happening, they told us they knew there was nothing coming from our side. They explained that when they got back to their newsroom, they had no say in how they were used."

Maura says it was awful to be under constant attack themselves and watch reports every night claiming they were retaliating. "I can only say what I saw and that I hardly ever saw anybody on our side throwing stones. It doesn't stand to reason. The Glenbryn redevelopment, agreed five years earlier, was underway. Their houses were already empty. What would our ones have been throwing stones at, empty houses? The only time I saw kids throwing stones in their direction, they were picking up the ones that had already been thrown at us. I have to confess I did that myself once. I was angry because there was no police to help us."

Geraldine McGrandles claims to have witnessed one incident stage-managed for a television documentary. "We saw a lorry on the other side of the peace-line, outside a house, with people bringing out furniture and loading it up. After the cameras went, the lorry returned and all the furniture was unpacked right back into the house it had come from."

She also says a family featured in another documentary, who moved out of their home, was immediately re-housed in the next street. "I couldn't move out of my house and do that. We have a massive waiting list. So much for their complaints."

On the parents' side, most pressure from journalists fell on the shoulders of Brendan Mailey, the official spokesman of the Right to Education group. Most believed he rose to the occasion pretty well.

"We didn't have to make much effort at the start. The world came to us. Local press, Irish, British, French, German, Spanish, Italian, Japanese – the lot. At least at the start, they were pretty sympathetic."

Tina Gallagher accuses one Sunday paper in particular of hounding Mailey because of his jail record (he has a murder conviction for killing a police officer). "After that, there were other press reports that 'known

IRA men' were walking amongst the parents."

Mailey's rude awakening came when a reporter from the paper questioned him about his conviction. He says he replied that he regretted what happened, as "I regret every life that is lost", adding that his personal conviction was irrelevant in the context of the crisis.

The newspaper's banner headline the next day read, "Cop killer says policeman's death irrelevant". Mailey phoned the reporter to complain, but his calls were not returned. When he finally managed to contact the reporter, he said he had not called the policeman's death "irrelevant", but had expressed sorrow and regret for all deaths. His meaning, he said, had been quite cynically switched around.

"The guy said something like 'Well, I'll hardly be back near you again'. I invited him straight up to do another interview but he declined."

Mailey, however, believes that however bad the Ardoyne parents came out of it, the loyalists came out worse. "Whoever did publicity for the loyalists should be certified. It wiped loyalism off the face of the earth."

There were also complaints about over-intrusiveness. The school principal, Anne Tanney, says that the press were, on the whole, "responsible". But another teacher at the school remembers one US camera crew who were "really pushing me to talk to them".

"They wouldn't take 'no' for an answer. After that we decided to keep cameras outside the school."

Roisin Kennedy, along with other parents, also became annoyed at camera crews getting too close. "You had to push them out of the way to get moving." Frances Doherty says the camera crews sometimes scared the children. "Flashlights would go off as you were walking through a flock of photographers and, to be honest, they caused accidents. As you tried to get past them, you were falling over them. A parent once fell over a photographer's stepladder where he'd left it in the middle of the road."

On the day of the bombing, that sort of insensitivity caused parents like the normally slow to anger Jim Crawford to lose patience. "I had to tell a photographer to take himself off. He had his camera stuck right into my daughter's face while she was crying."

Elaine Burns says the sheer numbers of reporters upset her daughter, but she found a way around it. "I said they were there to make sure she got to school safely."

Then there were the made-up stories. Some newspapers accused the parents of decorating their children for the cameras.

"What utter rubbish," says Lisa Irvine. "Holy Cross has always been strict about appearance. We all do our best for our children going to school. You would always have their hair neat, a clean uniform and nice socks. That's what wee girls want. They are 'girlie girls'. As if you would drag your child in front of the cameras, screaming, to get her face on TV. It was preposterous."

Jim Crawford says, "It was crap in the papers that the children were being dolled up. Who would even think about hairstyles? It took all of our energy, mentally and physically, to prepare ourselves for walking up that road.

"If," says Lynda Bowes, "you go into Holy Cross school any day of the week, any week of the year, you will see red and white bows. It is what wee girls want."

Tanya Carmichael says, "They all love their big, red ribbons and fancy clips in their hair. They love their style. We were truly so angry."

"You needed all your energy," says Sharon Quail, "to get out of beds in the morning. Parents were wondering what they were going up to face, never mind fancy hairstyles."

And the stories that parents deliberately slapped their children to make them cry in front of the cameras?

"Personally, if I had ever seen a parent smacking their child for a camera I would have smacked the parent. It didn't happen. It was a ridiculous thing to say," says Lynda Bowes.

Kieran McGrandles says, "The loyalists said we were nipping our kids to make them cry. Some of the journalists believed them. It was utter bullshit. What parent would ever do that?"

And what of the reporters themselves? Journalists are notoriously reluctant to speak of their own feelings, but several did explain their personal views. A more general view is impossible to pin down. None wanted to be identified.

The first said, "Of course there were grievances on the Protestant side but anyone with an ounce of sense would have seen that the argument was lost before it even started. At the school I found, as I did throughout the dispute, that it was the calm in the eye of the storm. Mrs Tanney could not have been more helpful and the girls were angelic."

Later, he was interviewing a child and asked about Wheatfield, the Protestant school across the road. One girl replied, memorably, "They are just like us, warm-blooded, except they don't believe in Mary." It was one of those unforgettable lines.

"From then on I was hooked on the story. I ate, slept and drank it, morning, noon and night. Although the pupils seemed amazingly untroubled by what was happening, there were bound to be lasting effects further down the line. I believe the bomb was aimed at the police, but that's not really the point. The screams and cries of the girls will live with me forever."

Although he was not feeling very charitable towards the Glenbryn side, he says, he knew he would have been guilty of dereliction of duty if he had not gone to ask them "what the hell they were doing".

"I had one memorable engagement with a group of women who started telling me they 'felt like the Jews of the situation', but ended up admitting that if one of the girls had been killed or injured they would have felt as bad as losing one of their own. Clearly they were being pushed and pulled about, even if they weren't very good at showing it. In the end, they lost heart, but of course the damage was done, both to themselves and more importantly to the pupils."

Sent to New York to cover the aftermath of September 11, he met a couple whose home had been damaged. "When they realised I was from Belfast, they told me their young daughter had been in tears the night before, watching TV pictures of Holy Cross. We sometimes trot out the clichéd old line about the 'world's press' watching our every move. It's rarely true anymore, but for Holy Cross it certainly was. Sadly it will go into infamy as a by-word for intolerance. I don't believe any story I've ever covered has touched me as much. I know that nobody died, but using children in this way seemed to sum up everything this sad little conflict has become. There were good people in Glenbryn who pursued a grievance in completely the wrong way and allowed loyalist paramilitaries to hijack them for their own ends."

Another Belfast-based journalist says, "On the first morning I was shocked and appalled. It has been a long time since I thought of myself a Protestant, the faith into which I was born. That morning made me totally ashamed. I was stunned at the abuse and the looks on their faces as they made it to the sanctuary of their school complex. It would have brought a shudder to the spine of even the most detached reporter in the world.

"I was even more alarmed to speak to loyalists who claimed 'the wee girls were putting it on'. And their attempts to justify the bomb attack beside the school run. Protestants regularly claimed that our reporting was not balanced and their views not covered. But, after the Shankill bombing, should we have given Sinn Fein the same coverage as the victims? Or given the UDA equal coverage at the time of Greysteel?

"There were almost daily reports from the Glenbryn side. I thought it was fair enough, at the beginning, to probe their case but later on a misjudgement. It turned into one of the most difficult tightrope assignments any of us have ever known. I was not impressed by some reports from the national reporters airlifted into the area. I watched with incredulity reports that never tried to put the protest into context or explain why they had started. I also found it astonishing that it took so long for the loyalist protesters to realise the damage they had done to their own cause. None of us were sad to see the back of it.

"One image, apart from the abuse and the bomb, will live with me forever. I was walking with a group of children. From the right came the cry, 'You are only Fenian bastards, fuck away off'. One parent replied, 'Go and fuck yourself. We are taking our kids to Wheatfield, you stupid bastards!' The protesters evidently couldn't tell the difference between the red of the Holy Cross uniform and the blue of Wheatfield. Who said that some of the protesters weren't bussed in for the occasion?"

As a reporter covering the story on an almost daily basis myself, it would be disingenuous not to say something of my own reaction, professional and personal. I could not prevent myself breaking down in public and I was not the only one. I am not proud or ashamed of that, just puzzled as I have managed to cover many heartbreaking funerals dry-eyed. We all studiously avoided making eye contact.

I reported exactly what I saw and heard, only censoring the grossest of the abuse. I made strenuous efforts to understand and reflect the loyalist side, on grounds of impartiality, believing there was nothing to be lost, but much to be gained by honestly reporting their views. I do not apologise for shining a light on their motives, although it was difficult to find spokesmen for the protesters who were not either hostile or inarticulate.

Reporting the story for a US market (*The Irish Echo* and *The Christian Science Monitor*) forced me to dig deeper into the psyche of the loyalist side. Perhaps we all dug too deep, searching vainly to excuse their actions. The fear and horror on the Ardoyne Road made it as easy for me as others to simply report events, rather than give them context and background.

Broadcasting executives in Belfast believe they did a good job. One senior broadcaster said, "There was a nervousness amongst the higher echelons. We were all concerned about impartiality and independence and what a fine line we had to tread. We asked ourselves if we were focussing too much on the parents and children or on the loyalist residents but generally we were confident we were getting it right. People felt personally horrified at what the parents and children were going through, but they felt we also had to give the other side some time to explain themselves. Personally, I thought the coverage was too ad hoc, that no one had thought it out strategically to give context to events. I also thought we didn't concentrate enough on the human rights angle. It was easy to go into a person's home one day and tell their story and then tell the other side the next day – but to put it into the context of North Belfast and the political background, that should also have been done."

Both the main local broadcasters, BBC and UTV, accept that Holy Cross was a particularly difficult story to cover. UTV, like the BBC, is required by law to be balanced when there are two sides to report.

One UTV source said, "We have to be impartial under Section Three of the Programme Code on matters of major political or industrial controversy. We have to ensure that the two sides have 'due significance'. That doesn't mean we give both sides equal coverage; it's not a mathematical question of giving them each the same time on air, but we have to be even-handed. There is a problem, however. If, for example, there was a story about white racists in England attacking black people, the Independent Television Commission would not expect us to take a neutral stand. But it wouldn't take the same view on the Holy Cross case.

They would expect due impartiality."

Kathleen Carragher, Editor of Radio News for BBC Northern Ireland, says Holy Cross was an exceptionally difficult news story "because you had tiny children being attacked on their way to school".

"The BBC approach is to air both sides and that is what we tried to do. The story didn't just come out of the sky; we knew that there were factors to do with the make-up of Ardoyne and people feeling pushed out and threatened. We showed what was happening to the children, we didn't try to hide or disguise it. We didn't say it was too shocking and that we shouldn't show it.

"But we also had to go in and see how anyone could possibly justify doing that to these small children. It was a question we had to ask. Our main problem was that very often we couldn't get a spokesperson from the Glenbryn side to talk to us in a cogent manner. Holy Cross is a story people will always remember. Both the TV images and the radio. Some sounds, the anger and the hatred, showed how emotional a story it was."

BBC policy – to speak to both sides and reflect that in a report – appears distinct from sending out a reporter to discover the truth. Some might call BBC practice intellectually moribund; others that it allows the viewer to come to their own conclusion.

Not all journalists made heroic efforts to be neutral. Robin Livingstone, the editor of the *Andersonstown News* (a nationalist community paper, circulating in west Belfast), penned the following sarcastic ditty in October 2001:

> BEHOLD THE SONS OF ULSTER
> Tell me son, my father said
> As we spoke upon the Twelfth,
> What have you done for Ulster,
> And how's your mental health?
> Father dear, I cherish the flame
> That's been held in Ulster fair
> By men like Carson and Gusty
> And 'Mad Dog' Johnny Adair.
> I've worn the smock of the UDR,
> The tattoos of the UDA,

From Sandy Row to Drumcree Hill,
From the Shankill to Dolly's Brae.
I've harassed Taigs at roadblocks,
Shot Fenians in their beds,
I've been to jail, done social work,
Got youngsters off their heads.
But my bright and shining moment,
The bravest thing I've done,
Was with the folks of Glenbryn,
When we took on Primary One.
The junior hordes fell on us,
Vile, disgusting creatures,
With Barbie bags and felt-tip pens
And apples for their teachers.
Undismayed, we stood our ground,
Resolve as hard as nails,
Then we opened up with gobs of spit
That soaked their pony-tails.
A volley of 'F' and 'C' words,
We'd die before we'd quit,
And how the schoolgirl cowards squealed
When we covered them with shit.
Chilling threats, balloons of wee,
Bottles, porn and rocks,
Then we really turned on the heat
And pipe bombed their bobby socks.
And when the dust of battle cleared,
We counted up our gains,
The victories that we had won
For Ulster for our pains.
Kids on Valium, broken minds,
An international fuss,
And if we pray to God above,
They'll fail their Eleven Plus.
So father dear, I hope you know
How hard I've hit the Croppy,

Fought the Papist thugs and earned
The right to wear my poppy.
But best of all, you must agree,
As we have this nice Twelfth chat,
The papers and the TV say it's just
North Belfast tit-for-tat.

Prominent journalist Nell McCafferty also didn't mince her words, calling the loyalist protesters an "ugly, illiterate, inarticulate, menacing, rotten mass of lumpen-proletariat".

Liz Murphy says the loyalists came off worse overall. "We had problems, but the loyalists came out badly, although the media constantly tried to even it out by focussing on their grievances. Any right-thinking person watching the coverage and seeing what the protesters did would have to say they came out of it worse."

Some programmes were openly exploitative, notably an attempt to get one person from both sides onto "Big Brother" (a reality TV show where people are locked into a house and their interactions filmed). Only one woman, not directly connected to the Holy Cross story, participated and the experiment was generally regarded in Ardoyne as a waste of time.

US television host, Oprah Winfrey, did a live satellite link-up with parent Elaine Burns and Anne Tanney in Belfast, highlighting the continuing international interest, even after September 11.

There was also the film, "Holy Cross", a joint BBC/RTE production presented to the public as a "drama-documentary" when broadcast and set against the Ardoyne/Glenbryn backdrop. It evoked very different opinions in North Belfast where, roughly speaking, the parents hated it while Glenbryn felt it went some way towards explaining the protest (it also attracted various international awards). The film began life as a BBC Network Current Affairs production, but later it was taken over by BBC Northern Ireland's Drama department. A writer from Lurgan, County Armagh, Terry Cafolla, was drafted in. Using some news footage to give authenticity, the fictional plot is told through the eyes of two dysfunctional families living back-to-back across the peace-line.

The loyalist family is graced by an idle, alcohol-driven male character. The mother, played by Bronagh Gallagher, is a feisty but put-upon single mother living in fear of her Catholic neighbours who, against her own better judgement, finds herself screaming abuse at the children. The nationalist family has another put-upon mother, dominated by a republican husband who insists, against her wishes and for political reasons, that their daughter be taken up to school along the Ardoyne Road. The family breaks up under the strain.

With a handful of stereotypical, near-cartoon characters (UDA thugs, dogmatic IRA men and reasonable, but long-suffering, women) thrown in, the film cannot have greatly informed its audience about what went on in Ardoyne in 2001. Father Troy and other significant figures were written out and, rather than a drama-documentary, it was a feature film based on fictional characters that editorialised in favour of the protesters. As such, it was a lost opportunity to shed light on the motivation of both groups and failed to provide an insightful and incisive commentary on an event of such major political significance.

Writer Paul Donovan, reviewing the film for the *Irish World* (a paper serving the Irish community in Britain) said its "essential flaw" was its lack of context.

"Once again the conflict in Northern Ireland was depicted as being between two squabbling religious groups," he said, accusing the film of ignoring the fall-out from the loyalist feud.

There were glaring misleading claims in the film. Its final shots, showing houses in Glenbryn Park lying empty, failed to explain the cause was not nationalist violence, but a planned redevelopment scheme to provide Protestants with improved housing. It also portrayed parents bickering amongst themselves over the decision by some to take the alternative route. All the available evidence is that each individual family's decision was respected. There is no evidence that any marriage in Ardoyne fell apart as a result of differences over the route, although many were put under severe strain.

The film's producer, then BBC executive, Robert Cooper, said in an interview at the time of its first broadcasting that he wanted to explain why the protesters behaved in the way they had. The protest was shocking, he said, both because of the abuse screamed at the children but also because people had "chosen to take their children through that abuse rather than the back entrance".

"It was," he says, "a story of fear on both sides and about how it must feel to be insecure inside your own home, afraid that something might come through the window or the door at any time. I can only hope we achieved a portrayal that will add to people's understanding and not allow people to consign others as monsters. Whatever they did was informed by some kind of fear."

With that agenda, it is hardly surprising that many parents found their portrayal in the film infuriating and the protesters still refer to it favourably.

Judy Haughey says she was "totally disgusted" and vowed never to speak to any journalist ever again while Father Donegan, a mild man if ever there was one, says it was "simplistic" and sexist in making out that "the men were the ones doing the pushing and the women were being pushed about".

Lynda Bowes said the film was an attempt at a bogus balance. "I am biased obviously but, for a start, why did they choose to show the father character an ex-IRA man? If there had been a large section of the kids up there whose parents were ex-prisoners, then the film would have been representing the way things were. But this is not the case. Ex-prisoners are a small minority. It was untrue, unreal and ridiculous to show a loyalist family lying in bed with nationalist gangs at the door. RUC statistics alone show most violence was carried out by the UDA. The final kick in the teeth was the last scene showing Glenbryn, derelict, as if nationalists were responsible. The run-down of Glenbryn had nothing to do with nationalists. The UDA had ensured the ruination of the area with their sheebeens and drug dens."

Liz Murphy says the film was "total rubbish, pathetic", while Sean Carmichael says it lied in showing rows between different groups of parents over which route to take. "That never ever happened. It was always agreed that it was each parent's right to choose either up the Ardoyne Road, the Crumlin Road or not to send their child to the school at all."

Tina Gallagher had to watch the film twice because she could not believe it the first time. "The message I got from it was that the people in Glenbryn were being petrol-bombed every night. Only the UDA was throwing pipe bombs. Go and ask the RUC who threw the pipe bombs in North Belfast in 2001. Yet the BBC tells us it was tit-for-tat."

Tina has more reason than most for remembering the film. The day after the interview was broadcast, a reporter arrived on her doorstep asking why she thought the UDA had left a bomb at her home the previous night. It was the first Tina knew about it. The police had not called round to warn her, although the coded UDA threat had been passed on to them hours previously.

"The UDA said they were targeting me because I was a spokeswoman for the Holy Cross parents, which I am not. I hadn't made any political statement. I was just airing my own personal disappointment about the film. The Red Hand Defenders (a cover name for the UDA) claimed responsibility, naming me personally."

Friends and neighbours advised her to get her two children out of the house. "It made me very aware of being me, it was so personal. How did they know where I lived? Being aware of yourself is a terrible thing, the thought that someone is watching you. I told Tara that if she saw a package coming through the door, she shouldn't lift it because it might be diseased.

"I had to frighten my own child like that because of an interview I had given about a film that didn't even tell the truth."

Chapter Fifteen

THE WATCHING WORLD

People from other schools across the world also called Holy Cross wrote to us. It was brilliant and reminded us we weren't alone, that people were thinking and praying for us. There wasn't much physically they could do but caring was enough.
Lynda Bowes, parent

We got more support from people in the US than they ever did. People saw we were only standing up for our rights but the people in Ardoyne were turning it around and using it against us.
Anne Bill, CRUA committee member

Holy Cross was one of the relatively few events in the North of Ireland over the last 10 years that attracted significant international press coverage. Foreign television crews flocked to Ardoyne until the September 11 attacks in New York understandably drew them elsewhere.

At the beginning of September 2001, however, the British Army barricade on the Ardoyne Road bristled with satellite transmitters and crackled with the sounds of a dozen languages – Japanese, Spanish, German, Turkish, even Arabic.

The bombing on September 5 brought even more foreign camera crews onto the Ardoyne Road. Holy Cross led the news agenda across the world. Of course, it was, in televisual terms, a highly photogenic story (which helped).

As a result, postal delivery men in North Belfast groaned under tons of extra letters and other gestures of goodwill from around the globe. For the parents, even in their darkest hours, it was all of huge comfort.

Comparisons were also drawn with another infamous school dispute, in the southern states of the USA, when other little girls – black little girls – had faced a similar baying mob. Some found the comparisons unfair because the American parents were demanding the right to integrated education and Holy Cross is a denominational school. That distinction would have been lost on the children.

Sharon McCabe, mother of Gemma, was one parent who says her personal agony was partly assuaged by letters from the US. Sharon, who was seriously traumatised by the dispute, says she will be forever grateful to the hundreds of people who took time to write to someone they would never know. Sometimes, in the dark of night when she can't sleep, she still tiptoes downstairs in the two-bedroom house, leaving her husband, Gerald, five children and grandchild sleeping upstairs. She goes into her tiny kitchen and lifts a box down from on top of one of the cupboards and opens it to read the cards stuffed inside, sent from the United States to her and the other mothers. She still draws reassurance from remembering that people on the other side of the world cared enough about their plight to write and tell them about it.

Other mothers say the same. "American support was fantastic, the volume of cards and letters and messages the kids got," says Lynda Bowes. "So many groups and schools were tuned in to what was going on. Every kid at Holy Cross got hand-written cards addressed to them. There were sack-loads. On just one day, I brought three car-loads of mail up to the school."

Roisin Kennedy says letter writers were also angry about the protest. Her daughter, Niamh, still keeps a big box of the cards. "She wrote letters back and they sent her wee shamrocks and a few dollars of their pocket money."

Judy Haughey says that even when the parents were downhearted, or depressed and angry, the international support buoyed them up. "Sometimes our meetings weren't so good but we stood by each other and grew stronger from it. Every day the kids got wee prayers and words of encouragement; they loved it because it made them feel they were not alone. There were Japanese, Chinese, Spanish and loads of other people sending morale boosters."

Frances Doherty, a slight, shy woman that her friends say has a "heart of gold", remembers the cards had messages like "Our prayers are with you and may God keep you safe" and "You are entitled to go to school" and "All we can do is pray to God that this won't keep on."

"On September 11," says Frances, "most people were stunned. There was silence because all our minds and hearts were on those people in America. I thought to myself, maybe a little good will come out of something so bad and it would bring the protesters to their senses. These were innocent people, in their thousands, who were blown up, but the loyalists still went ahead with the protest. Not only that, they were shouting abuse about the Americans, yelling, 'Sure they are only IRA-supporting bastards and they deserved what they got'. They were really sick individuals. I don't think I heard a word spoken by any parent walking up that day, not even to each other. We were in total shock and disgust. For once we were not thinking of ourselves – we were thinking about the Americans and how they were coping."

The parents also used the international support as best they could to bring the protest to an end. A delegation of parents went to the US and met congressmen. They also went to Westminster. Parent Pat Monaghan believed it was their only leverage to get the British government to act. "But," she says, "it is pathetic when you have to go outside your own country to get help."

One American teacher got more than she bargained for when she wrote a letter of support to the Belfast-published *Irish News*. Diane Curran, from Charleston, South Carolina, wrote saying her pupils had been stunned by the violence and were praying for all sides. Within days, she received an anonymous reply. The envelope was scrawled with comments like "The night cometh" and drawings of the flames of hell. It was at the time of the anthrax scare in the US and looked very threatening, but she opened it to find pages of anti-Catholic rhetoric. The letter was addressed "Dear misguided and totally unscriptural Roman Catholic", and went on to say she was praying in vain because the Holy Cross parents and children, as Catholics, were "already lost". The letter's anonymous author advised the Holy Cross children to take the alternative route. Catholics, he (or she) said, were determined to outbreed Protestants.

Responding, Curran, a theology teacher with ancestors from County Tyrone, said she believed the letter "was a gift, in a strange way" because it gave her an insight into the deep pain and anguish of people in

Northern Ireland. Americans, she said, had been insulated from the pain of other countries but September 11 had changed all that. "We have had our comeuppance. We have to realise that we are part of a world community."

A delegation of New York firemen visited Ardoyne and were photographed with the schoolchildren. They said they would never forget the letters sent to their stricken city from Ardoyne after September 11. It was heartening, said the firemen, that in the midst of Holy Cross's own agony, the children and their parents had taken time and energy to write to New Yorkers.

New York Senator Hillary Rodham Clinton wrote to Anne Tanney saying she prayed for the children every day. The letter is carefully preserved in one of Anne Tanney's many files. More than just letters of support arrived from the US, though.

"Among the many gifts I received," says Anne Tanney, "was a rag doll. I gave her to a little girl who was having nightmares and was unable to sleep in her own bed. She called the doll Rosie and took her to bed every night. I suggested she could tell Rosie all her troubles and this gave us the idea of buying all the children rag dolls. We used some of the money sent to us from abroad and gave them to the children at Halloween. They were delighted. We used some of the rest of the money to buy cuddly dogs for the boys in the Holy Cross pre-school group who were suffering too."

An anonymous, but most welcome gift from the USA was delivered to Anne Tanney soon after the protest began. It was a book about the struggle for integrated schooling in the US and the true story of six-year-old Ruby Bridges, the first black child at the all-white William Frantz school, New Orleans, in 1960. It was tailor-made for Mrs Tanney's determination to persuade her small charges that their tormentors were more in need of prayer than condemnation. "It was beautifully illustrated, about little Ruby walking to school with everybody shouting at her, yet she still prays for them."

Mrs Tanney was concerned about one small girl in particular who had, while travelling past the loyalists by bus, given them a two-fingered salute. She asked this child to read the Ruby Bridges book again: "It's so important that our children don't grow up in fear and hatred."

She also decreed that the Ruby Bridges prayer be said twice a day at school, at morning and afternoon assembly:

> Please God try to forgive those people.
> Because even if they say those bad things,
> They don't know what they're doing.
> So You could forgive them,
> Just like You did those folks a long time ago
> When they said terrible things about You.

Further comparisons with the battle in the United States over integrated education were again inevitable in late 2001 when Minnie Jean Brown-Trickey – one of the "Little Rock Nine", sent to school in September 1957 through a baying mob of 1,000 white racists in Arkansas – visited Holy Cross. The protest was on the point of suspension. The parents were still unsure if it was truly ending and were at a low ebb. The timing made her visit particularly welcome. Anne Tanney says the parents found her talk both inspirational and shocking at the same time because she was able to remember her feelings from so long ago and how awful it had been, not only walking to school, but also when she was in class.

"The children's questions were very instructive. Had she had been afraid to go to the shops in the evening? Minnie Jean said she had been, because her face had been on television and people could recognise her. She reassured them that everything would be OK in the end and that she had lots of white friends now and was even married to a white man."

Two parents, in particular, were entranced with Minnie Jean. Liz Murphy says, "It was like swapping roles. She was sorry and hurt for us and we were so sorry and hurt for her. She was the nicest woman I have ever met, she was so real, so honest and so sympathetic because she'd been through the same herself. Somebody, at last, was feeling what we were feeling."

Another mother, Lynda Bowes, says Minnie Jean's visit was lovely because she had "kept her head proudly up and walked past her abusers into school".

"Time was going by and there seemed no end in sight, but I left our meeting feeling great. At that stage, there were not too many people supporting us but Minnie Jean told us we were right and that meant a hell of a lot to us. At least our children were safe once they were in school – her teachers had not wanted her there at all."

Lynda says Minnie Jean also confided to the parents that she had never told her own parents about half the abuse she had endured. "She told us that our children also wouldn't be telling us everything they were going through. They would want to protect us. We felt we were not alone and that people were fighting like us all over the world for their rights. Until that day, I had never seen what was happening to us as of any historic or international importance. Her visit lifted us onto a whole different plane."

After Minnie Jean's visit, the Belfast artist Danny Devenney painted a mural drawing direct comparisons between Arkansas, Alabama and Ardoyne. Depicting, in part, Philomena Flood's daughter, Eirinn, it still survives and can be seen at the Ardoyne shops. It must be said, however, that comparisons with Alabama and Arkansas offended the protesters and some others deeply. They argued that black people in the US were struggling against discrimination while Catholics in the North are not. Protestants, they said, are not in any sense a dominant community. Holy Cross, whatever the rights and wrongs, said the protesters, was a particular school at a particular time and it was wrong to draw comparisons.

One of them, Anne Bill, puts it like this. "We thought the comparisons with Alabama were utter crap. One of our supporters, whose wife was coloured, made the point that the US fight was about integration, so Holy Cross was totally opposite. Our people were angered by the Alabama stuff because it showed that the parents were out to get us any way they could. They would use any tool they could to whack us with."

Ian Paisley, the DUP leader, also opposed the US comparison. Speaking during the September debate at Stormont, in characteristically robust style, he accused Sinn Fein of trivialising the horror of the segregation and degradation of African-Americans by comparing it to "a squalid local turf war".

Another morale-boosting visit came when the South African civil rights and anti-apartheid campaigner, Archbishop Desmond Tutu visited the school – apparently against the advice of the political establishment at Stormont.

Anne Tanney was delighted to find out Tutu's favourite prayer was also her own. "We always said the prayer of St Francis in school, 'Lord make me an instrument of thy peace'. We all prayed together."

Little Niamh Murphy takes a somewhat more down to earth view. "He was lovely because he shook hands with all the children." Her mother, Liz, said it was immensely comforting and reassuring, psychologically, to see him make the effort of visiting the school.

At a press conference in Belfast, Bishop Tutu spoke of his deep distress for the children who should not be used as "pawns and hostages". Offering to intercede, he said, "People around the world are appalled. How can people have got themselves to such a stage?"

EPILOGUE

When the politicians, civil servants and press went away, the communities were left barely acknowledging each other's existence. The peace-line has been just rebuilt by mutual consent. That epitomises where it has left us.

Rev Norman Hamilton

People seem to think that you should be over it, but you can't be over it. You will never be over it. You can't treat people in that way and expect them to forgive and forget. There are wonderful people in Ardoyne who can forgive but I can't. This wasn't just something accidental. It was prolonged, it was personal and it was pathetic.

Lynda Bowes, Holy Cross parent

It has turned me into a terribly different person. I would fight Goliath now if I thought somebody was wronging me. The only winners were the kids for being so brave.

Roisin Kennedy, Holy Cross parent

Glenbryn in mid 2004 is desolate: a wasteland of smashed bricks and windows, its houses flattened. But it has a future: bigger, semi-detached homes with garages and gardens are being built in their place.

On the main peace-line separating it from Ardoyne a slogan gloats "Eddie One Ball" – an unpleasant reference to the under-car booby-trap bomb that seriously injured Ardoyne republican, Eddie Copeland, before the loyalist ceasefire. It did not, however, deprive Mr Copeland of a testicle, as implied by the misplaced glee of the graffiti artiste.

In the ruins of the derelict houses, pictures still hang drunkenly on walls. Blocked-up windows carry posters demanding loyalist segregation at Maghaberry jail, just as loyalists outside demand segregation in their everyday lives. Seagulls roost on chimney pots. Young men in baseball caps drive beaten-up cars up and down the empty streets but new homes are beginning to spring up from the bottom of the old roads. Because of the larger size of the new homes, fewer than half the number of Glenbryn's former households can be accommodated in the new scheme. Across the peace-line, teeming Ardoyne continues to crumble.

On the horizon from Glenbryn, looking across Belfast Lough, you can see the gleaming white homes of the rich on the north County Down "Gold Coast".

There has been much violence in the North: shootings, bombings, arson attacks, pickets, stand-offs, boycotts and protests. Holy Cross was unique in that those involved consciously knew children would suffer. There doesn't seem much point, however, in finger-pointing as a response. It is, of course, important to log and detail what happened, how each side felt, and suffered, and how they reacted, if only to set the record straight; but without drawing lessons and learning, it would be a backward-looking exercise.

What truly motivated the protesters? Legitimate grievances or UDA opportunism? Why did they continue long after any rational person knew it was a lost cause?

Why did the parents and children doggedly continue to demand their right to walk up Ardoyne Road? Were they politically manipulated or motivated by a passionate determination to vindicate their human rights?

Did the police genuinely do their best, or was it a botched and ineffective job, despite all their past experience at crowd control and quelling protests? Did the British government turn a blind eye and leave the "natives" to fight it out amongst themselves? Was there a failure at leadership level at Stormont and were the unionist parties content to tolerate the protest if the alternative was to tell their supporters some hard political realities?

How do the protagonists themselves, three years on, see their own roles in events in North Belfast? Have they any regrets? Did they learn anything? Can we see any glimmer of hope in the blackness that descended on to Ardoyne Road? How, above all, did something so totally execrable drag on for a full three months?

There is a mix of bitterness and optimism in the loyalist camp.

Lollipop lady Amanda Johnston tends to the former. "The nationalists don't like it because the media attention has died down. I see them some days, walking up again, hoping to get intimidated. All the lovely children that were crying on the television, you see them go by on the buses giving me the two fingers, their parents giving me dirty looks. I just wave at them. They'd love to get it started again."

There is a depression in the air, says loyalist community worker Anne Bill. "For years the Glenbryn people felt like they were the scum of the earth. Then they were told they were, around the world. Now they feel it even more. There are people sitting in their houses in Glenbryn asking themselves what on earth it was all about, what was the point of it all? In the end, we were ignored."

Loyalist Ronnie Black has no regrets. "It was worth it because it made people sit up and see what this community was going through. We were deprived, run down, nobody wanted to help. It was worth it because it changed our lives."

Jim Potts has no doubts either. "In the face of it all, all the attacks on us – the media, the police, the government – the people of this community stood firm for their beliefs."

Stuart McCartney's views are more complex. Asked if he would do it all again, he pauses for a long while before answering. "I wouldn't have bothered. I would have helped the community any way I could with support and advice but not the protest. I think human beings being what they are, it was always going to end up the way it did. The community had been provoked too much. I don't say this glibly, but it hurts me that we couldn't fix it. And it hurts me that many people, the normal Joe who reads the papers, will look on me as a bigot, which I never was. It kills me that some people still don't realise what I was trying to do."

Jim McClean, the "man up the ladder", ended up spending nine months in Maghaberry jail on three counts of riotous assembly, unrelated to Holy Cross. He spent part of it in a double cell, sharing with a Catholic post office robber.

"I'm still in contact with him. I've nothing against him or other Catholics although I still don't like Sinn Fein or the IRA. But now I just don't care any more. It doesn't matter what I feel, it's not going to change anything."

Released in August 2003, he moved out of Glenbryn and lives with his family on the edge of the city in a bleak and totally segregated loyalist estate.

David Trimble's adviser, David McNarry, says the loyalists are right to feel cheated and betrayed. "In the end they got nothing. Both communities were damaged. The problem hasn't gone away and is likely to erupt again at any time but at least the Protestant community learned you don't protest when there are children involved."

Ronnie Black says both communities have learned. "People have moved on, they don't want to see their streets ruined, their kids arrested, their cars damaged. Both sides are saying, let's stop this, you can't go through life rioting on the Ardoyne Road every night, it has to stop somewhere."

The Rev Norman Hamilton says that the Protestant "Upper Ardoyne Community Partnership", which he chairs, was one good thing that came out of the dispute. "I am not trying to say that it makes a bad thing good, but it did lead to the community getting its act together."

Another lesson, he says, is that the political elite need to find better ways of understanding and engaging with the electorate in urban areas. "That's reflected in the current change of electoral preferences," he says, in an apparent reference to the DUP's electoral successes.

Anne Bill sees some positive results also. "It was brilliant to see the community standing together for the first time. If it happened again I would be there but I would do it differently, although I don't know how."

UUP Assembly member, Fred Cobain, says the fact that both communities want to avoid a repeat is a good sign. "We need to work with people in Ardoyne and build a relationship with them. It was a sorry tale but not a huge waste because out of it came an understanding in Glenbryn that they have to live alongside Catholics. There has to be some understanding between the two. I always make sure that Gerry Kelly and the rest of them in Ardoyne know exactly what we are doing. If it's possible to work on a cross-community basis, we do it. Small steps but you have to keep on taking them."

Perhaps understandably, the parents are not as sanguine. Ardoyne Focus Group member Mickey Liggett says the loyalists broke every law in Europe and got away with it but all they really did was humiliate themselves. "If any of them who were involved don't see now that they were wrong, it's very sad. I feel sorry for them, because they have a terrible legacy to live with."

Parent David Lindsay, whose family lost their home because of the protest, says the only winners were in Glenbryn. "They got this money on the backs of our kids. What kind of a message is that sending out? Most of the kids will be traumatised for the rest of their lives. It will never leave them. What a brave achievement for the Glenbryn protesters."

Tanya Carmichael does not believe there were any winners, although it irks her that the Glenbryn people believe they benefited financially. When the protesters shouted at her on the road that they had won extra funding, she says, "I sat down and cried. No matter what they did, the British government bent over backwards for them."

One definite negative in the overall fall-out on the nationalist side is that some of those who had been to the fore in cross-community work no longer have the heart.

A case in point is Pat Monaghan. "I will never go back to it – not because I don't believe in the future, but I can never get over what they put those children through and will never ever trust them again. I would have stood in the middle of the road crying, 'Please make peace'. I thought it was absolutely fantastic that my kids were mixing with Protestants and one day we would all live in peace and happiness. Somewhere in the back of my mind I still have that hope.

"On a one-to-one basis I don't have a problem, but I've been in a couple of situations where Holy Cross came up and I have had to leave the room. If I was to say what I really felt, there would be problems. It is a scar that has never healed. I would have always told my son not to use sectarian language, words like 'Orangies' and 'Huns'. Now when he comes in from school, he might say he saw 'lots of Huns today' and I will just reply, 'Did you?' That is not right, I know that, but things are still so raw inside me. It will be raw inside me until somebody says, 'We are sorry, we were wrong'."

Frances Doherty's kids have also changed. "Before, they never even thought of religion, they didn't know about it. These days they would say things like 'Orange this and that'. They might say Protestants are bad

'Orange bastards'. I have to tell them off but it's all down to what happened."

Patricia McAuley agrees. "I was raised to call the police 'Peelers' because I was born during the Troubles. My children were raised to be tolerant and to respect everybody and call them 'police' and 'officer', but they are now very bitter towards the police and the Glenbryn residents."

Martin and Pat Monaghan both say the link with Wheatfield has suffered. "The two schools had a good relationship going. It was two schools working together to educate their children about difference. That has stopped," says Martin. "I think the parents in Glenbryn don't want their children mixing with 'dirty Fenians'."

His wife Pat adds, "If that's the case, it's mutual. To be honest, never ever again will my child put her foot inside Wheatfield."

Chris McDonald, who lost his job and home due to the protest, is understandably despairing about the future. "Ardoyne has a totally different atmosphere. My own outlook on life is also completely changed. We were always dead easy-going. I believed there was always hope at the end of the rainbow."

He and his wife decided, after much agonising, to take their daughter, Nicole, out of Holy Cross. "We had moved from that end of Ardoyne, so why put the child through it? But we felt we were letting everybody down, we felt terrible, really demoralised. Our Nicole broke her heart."

The day after they made the decision, the couple bought a bouquet of flowers for Mrs Tanney and apologised. "We were there from the very first day but we just couldn't cope with it," says Chris. "I didn't want my family to suffer at the hands of the loyalists anymore."

Nicole was so badly affected she would not sleep or be left in the house on her own. She would not even go upstairs on her own. Three years later, Nicole McDonald cannot go to the bathroom on her own, although she is now 14. She attends a secondary school in West Belfast, right across town from her home. "We didn't want to take a chance. You just don't know what could happen. It's terrible," says her father.

Brian Barrington, Mark Durkan's adviser, says the protest shows how far the North has yet to travel before becoming a normal society. "It shocked everybody, it was very depressing. The fact that paramilitary activity has declined doesn't mean sectarianism has declined. It was a very strong warning. I think there was a huge sense of shame about it within everyone."

For many of those involved, Holy Cross was a personal watershed, and not just for parents and protesters. Donal Flanagan of the CCMS is, like many, haunted by the thought that he might have done more.

"It was one of those life-changing events in the history of Northern Ireland because it brought to a head all that is really bad in our society, altogether in one event."

The Rev Norman Hamilton says it was certainly a watershed in his Christian ministry. "It was at every level one of the biggest events of my life, theologically, family, church, community, philosophy. It was draining. Sometimes the days were very routine, others were horrible, without hope. At other times I thought I could see some light. There was every conceivable emotion."

And what of the long-term future of Holy Cross school itself, with numbers falling gradually, year on year. Donal Flanagan says there is demographic decline in the area but CCMS policy is based around the concept of at least one school per parish.

"We are conscious that Holy Cross as a building is not acceptable to the people of the immediate area. We are sensitive to that. If we ever get round to looking at options or amalgamating it with another school, if there were two sites available, obviously that would be a factor. We are not into making political points; we are in the business of making school provision but it would be very dangerous to make policy based on a matchstick. We don't want the future to be determined by arsonists."

The future of Holy Cross, says Flanagan, "is not under consideration", and if it ever is, the protest would not influence decision making either way.

Although most people believe a resumed protest is unthinkable, loyalists still don't rule it out. Stuart McCartney says he does not, personally, believe it will happen – but then contradicts himself by adding, "It could easily erupt again because all we have to show for it are a few ramps."

Jim Potts says that if the community came under the same type of pressure, they would not think twice about blocking the Ardoyne Road again. "We have always seen the school as an intrusion. This is about territory, not about the kids going to school."

Most of the children now take a bus to school every day, although some still walk up. Tina Gallagher does not even like her child getting the bus in case it is attacked.

"I prefer the girls take a taxi, although the school bus goes up and down and it's free. It seems like a time bomb to me, waiting to go off. I will never let my kids walk that road again. I don't trust those people up there."

Judy Haughey's youngest daughter, Mary-Jo, who was too small to go to Holy Cross during the dispute, is now a pupil. "She goes to school on the bus in the morning but in the afternoon I walk up and collect her. It's too hard getting the buggy on the bus. It can still be very scary at times. You would see fellas standing at the corner who you can identify as protesters. I remember walking by 'Spiderman' one day and I was petrified. There wasn't another sinner on the road." Another day, she says, a bald man in a car gave her "the finger" and she fears a lurking possibility of it starting again. She feels the hate is still there.

Jeanette McKernan thinks about it every single day of her life. On her way to a recent meeting at the school, she says, she shook from head to toe until she was inside the gates. "A teacher asked me if I was alright, that's how bad I was. It was the first time since the protest that I walked up the road on my own. There was nobody about but it was still a bad experience."

Something similarly nasty happened to the hapless Rev Stewart Heaney on the Ardoyne Road after the protest ended. He was driving from church one evening after a riot on the Ardoyne/Alliance interface.

"There were some Catholic people there, obviously hurt. There was blood. Heads were split open. I stopped the car and said to one lady that I was from the Glenbryn community and I just wanted to say how sorry I was about it all and that not everybody supported the protest."

For the first time ever, someone from Ardoyne told the poor man, who had risked so much to speak out publicly against the protest, to "fuck off". He was hurt because he thought that most nationalists knew by then what he had done.

"It is just a pity that some people in Ardoyne still don't know that there were an awful lot of people, particularly mothers and fathers in

Glenbryn, who wanted to express their sympathy and sorrow to them," he says, sadly.

However critical the Rev Heaney is of the protesters, a Protestant academic, who "crossed over" by marrying a Catholic, and therefore wishes to remain anonymous, is harder on his co-religionists. "Holy Cross was simply about the fact that some loyalists don't want Taigs about the place, with any power or influence. They don't want Protestants to like Taigs, they are to be kept down and put in their place. Even though the people in Glenbryn were living in squalor and worked for a pittance of a wage, they were happy because the Taigs were one step behind. The big problem comes when republicans get one step ahead. I don't think anyone can understand, unless they come from that community, the power of the concept of betrayal. If loyalist voices had been raised to condemn the protesters, they would have come under attack themselves.

"Unionists want simple messages. You can't deliver that if you complicate it by telling them they are causing children a great deal of distress. If you criticise sectarianism you are seen to be weak. It is always about 'What the IRA did to us'. Never about what loyalist paramilitaries and the unionist establishment did to Catholics for decades."

Former Assistant Chief Constable Alan McQuillan speaks of a less harsh lesson he hopes loyalists have learned. "I think Holy Cross did an immense amount of harm to the peace process. It was a catalyst that kept the violence going at interfaces across the north of the city for the best part of 12 months. We are not good at learning lessons as a community but loyalism should have learnt that if it wants to achieve things, it needs to organise itself and find a political channel."

If housing was an underlying cause of the protest, what does the future hold for North Belfast's changing demographics? Neil Jarman of the Institute for Conflict Research says Protestants are engaged in self-delusion if they believe building nicer houses will being people flooding back.

"It will be interesting to see if people do move back into Glenbryn, or if in five years time they are knocking the new houses down and building another scheme."

Housing and the immutability of the peace-lines, despite

demographic changes, will not be tackled, he says, while the loyalist paramilitaries are in a position of strength. Areas like Torrens, now denuded of its Protestant inhabitants would quickly fill up with nationalists if the peace-line could be moved. Similarly, the Protestant Tiger Bay area would "fill with Catholics in no time at all".

Dr Peter Shirlow says the peace-lines will not move, however, in the short to medium term because of the Protestant fixation with borders. "The words that define Orangeism are 'deliverance' and 'maintenance'. You maintain your boundaries, you maintain your culture, you maintain your identity, and then you are delivered."

That means, he says, that the peace-lines will remain, artificially boosting house prices in nationalist areas by between 20% and 40% because of the discrepancy between supply and demand. Any consequent concerns about human rights and equality, says Shirlow, are confined to the nationalist community.

"Protestants don't care where Catholics live, so long as none of 'their' territory is conceded. I would not like to be the first Catholic who moves into Torrens, for example. There is a force and a threat within loyalism that dictates housing policy in North Belfast, although we are all supposed to be living in a liberal democracy."

Echoing the words of Jim Potts, Shirlow says Holy Cross was, at least in part, a territorial dispute. "A rational debate would centre on the question of available land, housing need and accommodating the two. Housing has been turned from a social justice issue into a sectarian issue. There will be no change. It has all been reinforced by the Holy Cross dispute."

Everything Shirlow and Jarman say is endorsed by Fred Cobain of the UUP who says the peace-lines will not move. "No. It's not going to happen. What Catholic is going to live in the middle of Glenbryn? It is just nonsense but even talking about it helps to undermine Protestant confidence."

So how are Catholics to be housed in North Belfast? "They are not," says Cobain, "They are just going to have to move out, like the Prods."

That, of course, is not how it looks in Ardoyne. Veteran community worker Elaine Burns rages against what she sees as discrimination. "A lot of people moved out of Glenbryn. There is massive demand for Catholic housing. Land is land. It's not green or orange. Housing provision should be based on need. They can live behind their walls but if it's a dying community the peace-line should come down to provide houses for those that need them."

Mickey Liggett, the great proponent of a "shared North Belfast" and opponent of more peace-lines, has not given up. "The protest has focused attention on the waste land in Glenbryn. Nationalists will be looking there to expand. Will Protestants even want to move back into Glenbryn? It hasn't a very good reputation. Who would want to bring up children in it? The Housing Executive has to challenge the assumption that land is either Protestant or Catholic. It has to happen. Torrens and other former Protestant areas are ghost towns. Ardoyne is bursting."

Sinn Fein's Gerry Kelly similarly does not accept that Catholics will have to leave North Belfast to be properly housed and says there is room for everyone. "All you have to do is look at the vast spaces of land on the Protestant side of the interface walls. The unreasonable loyalist demand to hold on to every scrap of what they call their 'territory', even though no one wants to live on it, deprives hundreds of Catholics of their right to a home."

While housing remains an unresolved issue, nationalists have other burning questions arising from Holy Cross. Where is there an explanation for why the protest dragged on for so long, given that virtually everyone accepts nothing similar would be tolerated in the Republic or Britain? Martin Morgan, the local SDLP councillor and former Lord Mayor of Belfast, draws some grim conclusions. "I don't believe the British government took it seriously or cared enough. They didn't intervene. The children were expendable. Look at other episodes in our history – the use of plastic bullets, torture in police stations, shoot-to-kill. None of it would have been acceptable in Britain. People here were always treated differently. One in five people in the Troubles were murdered in North Belfast, most of them Catholics. What were the British doing? Nothing. They take the path of least resistance. A dead nationalist; sure no one will remember his name in a week's time."

Father Aidan Troy agrees, in part. "In a simple phrase, there wasn't the political will to stop it. It was better to tolerate the protest than to confront it head on. Ending it would have led to mass arrests. It would have meant an angering of the loyalist community that might have had repercussions, not only in North Belfast but much further afield. I remember talking to government officials and statutory bodies in the early days. They were talking about a strategy six months down the road. My reaction was that I was more concerned about the next six hours."

Father Gary Donegan has also tried to answer the same question. "There was a great fear that the Executive could collapse. Keeping the First Minister and Deputy First Minister in office seemed London's top priority. Everything else went by the wayside, which meant turning a blind eye to what was happening at Holy Cross. Can you imagine it in Brixton or Glasgow or Toxteth or Dublin? I can't get over why every school, every trade union, didn't come out on the second day. The day the bomb went off, the third day, was three days too many. They will come out on strike for a small wage rise, but not for the most innocent and vulnerable people in their own society."

Like Martin Morgan, and many others, Father Donegan believes that North Belfast is different, and Ardoyne very different. "It was as if the children were going to be scarred anyway, merely because they were born here, so what's a little more pain? The Irish nation took an antiseptic approach. The peace process came first. If a child had been seriously hurt, or even killed, God forbid, priorities might have changed. But otherwise, the protest was tolerated."

Parent Lisa Irvine asks, "How could anyone sleep in their beds at night, knowing that little children had to face that every morning, especially if there was the slightest chance of talking them round. Why would you not do it? What could be the reason for doing nothing?"

Fred Cobain, ever the realist, says the answer probably lies in the years of violence, from which the North was emerging. "If there had been 35 years of violence in Birmingham, with 30,000 people dead, maybe Holy Cross could have happened there. This is a totally different environment than across the water. If there hadn't been any violence here then, yes, the protest would have lasted a day or two and pressure brought to bear to end it. But Belfast is difficult. There were paramilitaries involved, people from outside the area."

Searching for light in the murk of Holy Cross is an onerous task. Alan McQuillan says that at least the police learnt lessons about managing

large-scale operations. He hopes the politicians learned too, but has
doubts because he sees no evidence of it.

Fellow senior police officer Roger Maxwell is similarly pessimistic. "It
was a huge, unmitigated disaster. I don't think any good came out of it
whatsoever. Look at the loyalists; it might take five or ten years, but that
community is wrecked. What will be the long-term effect on those
children? I don't know. A lot of police officers are also badly affected,
physically and mentally."

The police take comfort from the fact that at least no one was killed
on Ardoyne Road during the protest. Alan McQuillan, however,
concedes that the dispute ran like a poison through North Belfast that
year. Arguably, then, six people died who might be alive today, if not for
the Holy Cross protest. They include:

Gavin Brett (18), shot dead on July 29, 2001: a Protestant, killed
    when loyalists opened fire on youths standing at the entrance to a
    GAA club in Glengormley, on the outskirts of North Belfast.

Thomas McDonald (16), a Protestant run down by a car on
    September 4, 2001 after he threw a half-brick at a Catholic
    woman driver in North Belfast. She was later found guilty of
    manslaughter.

Glen Branagh (16), a Protestant who blew himself up with his own
    bomb on November 11, 2001, in North Belfast. He was a
    member of the Ulster Young Militants, the UDA's youth wing.

Daniel McColgan (20), a Catholic postal worker shot dead by the
    UDA on January 12, 2002. He was killed as he arrived for work
    in Rathcoole, North Belfast.

Stephen McCullough (39), a Protestant found dead at the bottom of
    a cliff in North Belfast on January 16, 2002. Loyalist sources
    claimed he had offered police information about McColgan's
    murder.

Gerard Lawlor (19), a Catholic shot dead on July 21, 2002, in North
    Belfast. He was killed walking home from a night out locally.

The book *Lost Lives* recalls: "Sectarian tensions had been at an even higher level than normal in North Belfast for more than a year as a result of repeated clashes at Holy Cross primary school."

The Holy Cross protest was, undoubtedly, the result of the continuing failure of politicians in the North to deliver what the electorate expected and wanted from the peace process. Holy Cross is yet another example of many showing the continuing weakness and fault-lines in the Irish peace process. An uneasy peace now prevails on the Ardoyne/Glenbryn interface, but it is imposed from outside rather than negotiated from within and therefore unstable and liable to fissures.

Neil Jarman of the Institute for Conflict Research says the Holy Cross phenomenon is not explicable by a single cause alone. "There are multiple layers which you need to unravel. At the party leadership level, you had both sides taking pleasure in each other's various difficulties, rather than admit that all of us are in this together. There was no reciprocity about each other's political needs or a genuine attempt to understand each other's difficulties. There was no willingness to engage politically, either locally or at leadership level."

Did the UDA foment the protest? Undoubtedly it was influential and fostered a sense of paranoia in Glenbryn, prolonging the agony, but arguably it would have started even without its baleful influence. As Dr Peter Shirlow argues, people tend to credit the UDA with a far greater organisational ability than it deserves.

Chief Superintendent Roger Maxwell agrees. "The UDA has no strategy. It is a loose collection of criminal gangs," he says.

Did the unionist leadership fail its people? The results are there for all to see. The DUP, by adopting its usual populist approach, came out on the winning side within unionism, as evidenced by subsequent election results. The UUP continues to decline, as does the economic status of Protestant communities in Belfast. One can only hope that those loyalists who are struggling along the peace-lines to find areas of co-operation with nationalists are rewarded with electoral success, but the signs are not good.

There are questions too for nationalists. At a time of great need, neither their own political parties nor the Irish government were effective in persuading London to act swiftly to bring the protest to an end. They were, as usual, themselves alone. Nationalists in Ardoyne were forced to face the unpalatable reality that many loyalists bear them an implacable hatred and show no desire whatsoever to share North Belfast, as so devoutly wished by Mickey Liggett and other republicans.

Can sectarianism be defeated by merely hoping it will go away? Does confronting it head-on only escalate problems? The record shows that trying to appease sectarianism by ignoring it or refraining from giving it a name is ineffective. Had, for example, Gerry Adams, David Trimble and the leaders of the four main Christian denominations walked the Ardoyne Road one afternoon early on, in joint and unequivocal condemnation of the protest, would it have ended earlier? It is difficult to see why not but such a powerful statement would never have been possible in the atmosphere of hostility and mutual suspicion pertaining at Stormont.

The questions for others who failed to come to the aid of the children of Ardoyne are similarly tough. Why were the children forced to suffer for so long? Did governments decide that the fragile peace process might have faltered terminally had the police and civic society confronted the loyalists head-on? Did the British government fear that unionist support for the peace process, always a delicate flower, would wither and die if the protesters had been forced off the streets? Tony Blair, for all his vaunted determination to improve the lives of children, particularly working-class children, and his commitment to fundamental Christian values, did not make any noticeable impact, although he made the usual condemnatory banalities.

Was David Trimble's leadership of unionism regarded as so important that the children were left to the wolves in a futile bid to protect him from the DUP? Or is that conclusion unfair to the British government? Some of the Holy Cross parents believe their children were, in effect, held to ransom to preserve the peace process. If so, what kind of a peace process is it?

Did it last for so long because the outside world regarded the children as somehow guilty by association for being born into what is perceived as a "republican community"? Were the children deemed to have brought their agony on themselves merely by being born in Ardoyne? Were their feelings viewed elsewhere as being of lesser value than the feelings of black, Muslim or Jewish kids? Or children born to middle-